Charles Alden John Farrar

Farrar's Illustrated Guide Book to Moosehead Lake and Vicinity

The Wilds of Northern Maine, and the Head-Waters of the Kennebec, Penobscot,

and St. John rivers

Charles Alden John Farrar

Farrar's illustrated Guide Book to Moosehead Lake and Vicinity
The Wilds of Northern Maine, and the Head-Waters of the Kennebec, Penobscot, and St. John rivers

ISBN/EAN: 9783337236526

Printed in Europe, USA, Canada, Australia, Japan

Cover: Foto ©Lupo / pixelio.de

More available books at **www.hansebooks.com**

FARRAR'S
Illustrated Guide Book

TO

MOOSEHEAD LAKE

AND VICINITY,

THE

WILDS OF NORTHERN MAINE,

AND THE HEAD-WATERS OF THE

KENNEBEC, PENOBSCOT, AND ST. JOHN RIVERS,

WITH

A New and Correct Map of the Lake Region,

Drawn and Printed Expressly for this Book.

ALSO CONTAINS THE

GAME AND FISH LAWS OF MAINE

(As revised by the last Legislature),

RAILROAD, STEAMBOAT, AND STAGE ROUTES,

Time Tables, Table of Fares, List of Hotels, Prices of Board, and other valuable Information for the Sportsman, Tourist, or Pleasure-Seeker.

By CHARLES A. J. FARRAR,

Author of "Richardson and Rangeley Lakes," Illustrated, "Camp Life in the Wilderness," etc.

BOSTON:
LEE AND SHEPARD.
NEW YORK: THE AMERICAN NEWS COMPANY.
1884.

The illustrations in this book have been engraved from original drawings, and stereoscopic views made at the places represented, by the best artists in their respective lines of business that could be procured.

PREFACE.

IN presenting the seventh edition of MOOSEHEAD LAKE AND THE NORTH MAINE WILDERNESS to the public, the author would gratefully acknowledge the kind reception of the other six editions.

The encomiums from private individuals and the press have encouraged him to give the work more careful attention this year than ever, and the present edition is an improvement over former ones in many ways.

As this is the only guide to Moosehead Lake published it will be kept up to its present high standard of excellence.

The author has endeavored to make this volume pleasant and interesting, as well as reliable and instructive, and to impart information without the dry paragraphing common to most guide-books.

By means of our little book thousands have become acquainted with the Moosehead Lake Region in the last eight years that had never heard of or visited it before; and we hope that through its influence thousands more may visit this beautiful summer resort where everything combines towards one's pleasure and health.

The completion of the Bangor and Piscataquis Railroad to the shores of the lake has made the disagreeable stage ride a thing of the past, and passengers can now make the trip the entire distance by rail.

PREFACE.

The Mount Kineo House, Phœnix-like, has arisen from its ashes, and in place of the old structure stands to-day a new and larger building, capable of accommodating four hundred people, and fitted with every modern improvement that the ingenuity of man or the expenditure of money could provide.

It is the desire of the author in this volume not only to give a correct description of the country to which he invites the attention of the traveling public, but also to thoroughly post them up in all the details of route, expense, hotels, and other little matters that one so anxiously inquires about, when contemplating a first visit to a strange place.

While he is not egotistical enough to declare that he has wholly succeeded in his wishes, he is certain that for any person making a first trip to MOOSEHEAD LAKE the book will prove invaluable, and that it will even be read with interest by the older *habitués* of this noted locality.

This seventh edition has been rewritten and carefully revised. Thirty pages of new reading-matter have been added, also several illustrations. It is the author's intention to have the book keep pace with and faithfully chronicle all changes and improvements in the entire Moosehead Lake Region.

With the promise that any mistakes, omissions, or errors, that occur in the **pres**ent volume will be carefully corrected in the edition of 1885, he calls the attention of his readers to the more interesting parts of the book.

CHARLES A. J. FARRAR.

ROCKVIEW, JAMAICA PLAIN, May 1, 1884.

CONTENTS.

CHAPTER	PAGE
I. — The Lakes of Northern Maine	9
II. — Rail and Steamboat Routes from Boston and Portland to the Lake Region	16
III. — From Milo to Brownville and Katahdin Iron Works. The Gulf and its surroundings	35
IV. — Monson and vicinity	47
V. — Greenville and its attractions	53
VI. — Up the Lake. From Greenville to Mount Kineo . .	63
VII. — Kineo. Its Legends, Hotel, Sights, Fishing, etc. . .	71
VIII. — Two Routes from Boston to Moosehead Lake, via the Forks of the Kennebec and Moose Rivers . . .	97
IX. — From Kineo to the Head of the Lake	117
X. — Camping-Out	124
XI. — The Head of the Lake and its surroundings. Where to Go. — What to See. — Fishing, Hunting, etc. . .	132
XII. — Tours beyond Moosehead. Down the West Branch .	140
XIII. — The Ascent of Mount Katahdin. Four Different Accounts	156
XIV. — Down the West Branch (concluded)	189
XV. — Tours beyond Moosehead. Down the East Branch of the Penobscot. Up the Penobscot	192
XVI. — Tours beyond Moosehead. Down the St. John . .	200
XVII. — Game Laws of Maine	204
XVIII. — Game-Fish Laws of Maine	207
XIX. — List of Hotels, etc.	217
XX. — Table of Fares	221

LIST OF ILLUSTRATIONS.

	PAGE
Moosehead. Frontispiece	2
At Anchor at Moose Brook, Moosehead Lake	10
Cedar Beach, north of Mt. Kineo	20
Fort Point House	29
Moosehead Lake, from Indian Hill	30
Billings' Falls, West Branch Pleasant River, Me.	36
Lake House, Greenville, Me.	40
Face in the Rock and Jaws of the Gulf, West Branch Pleasant River, Me.	43
Lake Hebron Hotel, Monson, Maine	50
The new Mount Kineo House, Moosehead Lake	68
View from Kineo House Piazza, looking west	74
Socatean Falls	82
View from Mount Kineo	86
Mount Kineo from North Bay	96
Hotel Heselton, Skowhegan, Me.	102
The Forks of the Kennebec	108
Long Pond Outlet, Moose River	114
Rapids at Outlet of Brasseau Lake	118
Ox-Railroad Train leaving the Station	120
Camp at Head of Lake	130
Landing the Canoes	138
Inspection of a Day's Fishing	158
The Camper-Out	188
Lake Hebron, looking west	216
Map of Moosehead Lake	220
Moosehead	223

CHAPTER I.

The Lakes of Northern Maine.

PROBABLY there is not another State in this country that can boast of more Lakes, Ponds, Rivers, and Streams than Maine, whose large territory contains many beautiful sheets of water, surrounded by grand mountain peaks and wild forests, making the whole northern half of the State a vast park, ornamented only by the hands of nature, and free from the trammels of art.

Here it is still possible to see the largest wild animal to be found east of the Rocky Mountains, the noble moose, in his native freedom, as he wanders about in quest of food, unconscious of exciting admiration. In these vast woods, reaching to Canada and beyond, may also be found the beautiful deer and the fleet caribou, bears, wolves, foxes, and numerous smaller animals.

While the forest is well supplied with game, the waters of this New England Paradise teem with fish of various species, the trout being the best for eating, and furnishing the visitor to these wilds, piscatorially inclined, the finest sport.

It is not to be wondered at, then, with the attractions Northern Maine presents, both in beautiful and romantic scenery, pure air and water, game and fish, that, as the rivers and lakes are freed from their icy bonds, thousands of people should annually turn their eyes in this direction; and the fact that travel to the lakes of Maine has largely increased in the last five years is indisputable evidence that people who have visited these romantic sheets of water have returned home satisfied with their sojourn in the wilderness.

How a person can fritter away two or three months of pleasant weather at fashionable summer resorts, surrounded by false glitter and senseless show, when the lakes and forests and mountains of the Pine-Tree State are smilingly beckoning them to explore their hidden mysteries, is something hard to understand. But many do not know that this vast wilderness, with its forests primeval, with its lofty mountains, many of whose summits have been untrodden by the foot of man, its mirrored ponds and lakes, its picturesque

AT ANCHOR AT MOOSE STREAM.

streams, broken by rapids and falls, its healthy and bracing atmosphere, redolent with the resinous perfumes of the pine and fir, is within two days' travel of the great metropolis of New England. And yet such is the fact.

Of all these crystal bodies of water,

Moosehead Lake

is the largest and best known. It is on the outskirts of a far-reaching wilderness, almost beyond the pale of civilization, the little town of Greenville at its lower end being the one connecting link between isolation and the outer world. It lies in Somerset and Piscataquis counties. It is thirty-six miles long, from a mile to fourteen miles in width, and has three hundred miles of shore; it is the unfailing reservoir that supplies the beautiful and picturesque Kennebec, and renders accessible its powerful rival, the wild and turbulent Penobscot.

Islands, varying in size from the solitary and barren rock to those containing thousands of acres, well wooded and watered, deck its bosom, and add to the attractiveness of its features. It is surrounded by mountains, some of which descend to its shore and are laved by its waters, while others are some distance away, mantled in a rich blue haze that gives them a peculiar charm in the eye of the beholder.

Its borders, winding and irregular, are broken up into little coves, bays, points, and peninsulas, and are indented by the mouths of streams that empty into it or flow from it. They are covered by dense forests, wherein the light and graceful foliage of the birch and poplar intermingles with the dark and sombre covering of the fir and spruce.

A sheet of water fair to look upon, and capable of affording unbounded pleasure to those who would woo nature in her sublime solitudes.

Brassau Lake

lies about four miles west of Moosehead, Moose River forming the connecting link between the two sheets of water. It is about six miles long and two wide, and contains several small rocky islets. It is a shallow lake for its size and its shores are fringed with rough boulders. Near the outlet is a large hay farm.

Long Pond

is an attractive sheet of water, about twelve miles long and two wide, a little south-west of Brassau Lake with which it is connected by Moose River. It furnishes excellent fishing.

Lobster Lake

lies east of the upper end of Moosehead, and is connected by a small stream with the west branch of the Penobscot, into which river its waters empty. It is about five miles long and three wide. Its shores are remarkably pretty, being divided into alternate beaches and headlands. It contains a number of peculiar-shaped islands.

Ragged Lake

is a small, irregular-shaped body of water, lying between Lobster Lake and Caribou Lake, being connected with the latter by Ragged Stream.

Caribou Lake

is a very pretty sheet of water, lying south-west of Chesuncook, and connected with it by a short stream, navigable for canoes. It is about six miles long and two wide. Its shores were formerly a favorite resort for caribou.

Chesuncook Lake,

a large and handsome body of water, lies north-east of Moosehead, some twenty miles distant. It is reached by crossing the North-east Carry, then descending the West Branch of the Penobscot in a canoe. The lake is about eighteen miles long, and from a half mile to two miles wide. At the head of this lake is a small settlement, with a public house.

Chamberlain Lake

lies some ten miles north of Chesuncook, and is about the same size of its neighbor. It forms an important link in the trip down the St. John River. The Chamberlain Farm lies on its eastern shore, and here one can secure entertainment when needed.

Caucomgomoc Lake

is a romantic sheet of water lying a little north-west from Chesuncook, and about fourteen miles from it. It is about seven miles long and three wide in its broadest part, and offers some of the best fishing to be obtained in the Moosehead Lake region. From the head of Caucomgomoc to the Woboostoock Stream there is a carry of about nine miles. From Caucomgomoc Lake to Round Pond is about two miles, and a carry from the pond of about four miles will take you to Allaguash Lake, from whence you can reach Chamberlain Lake by water.

Allaguash Lake

lies a little north of west of Chamberlain Lake, and connects with it. It is a lovely piece of water, five miles long and three miles wide at the northern end.

Eagle Lake,

although smaller than some of the others, is one of the most beautiful and picturesque lakes of Northern Maine. It is connected with Chamberlain Lake by a canal, and lies north of it. The entire length of the lake is about ten miles, and it varies in width from half a mile to about three miles. There are quite a number of islands in it. Several small streams, navigable for a short distance with canoes or light boats, empty into it. For many years it was the haunt of a noted hermit, Donald McDonald, who, on account of his slovenly habits and appearance, was more commonly called "Dirty Donald." He was a character in his way, and some of the old guides tell stories of him that have to be swallowed with a due amount of allowance for that "stretch of imagination" that is common to all backwoods story-tellers.

Churchill Lake,

about five miles long by three wide, lies a little north-east of Eagle Lake. The Allaguash River gives an outlet to its waters, as also to those of Eagle Lake.

Ripogenus Lake

is a lovely body of water, oval-shaped, surrounded by forest and hill, and overlooking Mount Katahdin, which towers up beyond it twenty miles to the eastward. It is about two miles long, and a mile across in its widest part. There is excellent fishing at the mouth of Ripogenus Stream, which empties into the lake from the north, also at the mouth of Frost Brook, and in pools below the lake.

Harrington Lake,

about four miles long and two wide, lies north of Ripogenus, and is connected with the latter lake by Ripogenus Stream.

Pamedumcook Lake

is one of the largest bulges in the Penobscot River. It is very irregular in shape; it varies in width from half a mile to about six miles, and is twelve miles long. NORTH TWIN LAKE and SOUTH TWIN LAKE lie below it, and are connected with it. RAINBOW LAKE and NAHMAKANTA LAKE also empty into Pamedumcook, through Nahmakanta Stream, which enters the lake at the western end.

Milinokett Lake

lies a short distance east of Pamedumcook, and is about six miles long by four wide. There are several islands in the eastern part of it. About its shores are several clearings, some of which are quite large.

Sourdnahunk Lake

is between three and four miles long and about two miles wide in its broadest part. It lies north-east of Harrington Lake, and its waters empty into the west branch of the Penobscot, through Sourdnahunk Stream. There is excellent fishing at and near the mouth of this stream, and pleasant camping-grounds in the vicinity.

The Roach Ponds,

of which there are three, empty into Moosehead Lake, at Spencer Bay. Roach River forms the connecting link. The largest of these ponds is about six miles long and three wide.

Spencer Pond

is a small sheet of water lying north of Spencer Bay. It is about a mile long and is nearly circular in shape. It is connected with the lake by a small stream about a mile and a half long. In the fall it is a favorite resort for gunners.

The Wilson Ponds

lie east of the southerly end of Moosehead, and from three to six miles from the hotels at Greenville. There is a carriage-road two miles of the way, the rest of the distance being done by foot.

The ponds furnish excellent fishing, and the scenery in the vicinity is very fine.

Indian Pond

is a bulge in the Kennebec River, commencing five miles below the lake, at a point where the two outlets unite. It is some four miles long and a mile and a half wide. It furnishes good fishing at some seasons of the year.

Sebec Lake,

a large body of water lying south-east of Moosehead, is reached from the stations of South Sebec, Dover, or Foxcroft, on the Bangor and Piscataquis Railroad. It furnishes excellent sport early in the spring, being well stocked with land-locked salmon. It is just coming into the notice of sportsmen; a steamer plies upon it in summer, making tri-weekly trips.

Ship Pond,

whose waters empty into Sebec Lake, also furnishes trout and land-locked salmon. The pond is about five miles distant from the north-western corner of the lake.

The Monson Ponds.

In the town of Monson are a large number of small ponds, and within a radius of seventeen miles are thirty-two ponds whose waters teem with trout, perch, pickerel, and other fish. Their shores also offer excellent hunting in the fall. Among those most resorted to for trout fishing are Hebron, Monson, Spectacle, Twin Doughty, Bunker, Bog Stream, Bell, McLaren, North, Moors, Bear, South Senior, South Junior, Meadow, Meadow Stream, No. 18, Grindstone, Buttermilk, Benson, Greenwood, Long, Hedgehog, Big Indian, Little Indian, Herring, and Greenleaf.

CHAPTER II.

Rail and Steamboat Routes

FROM

BOSTON AND PORTLAND TO THE LAKE REGION.

PEOPLE from the West wishing to visit MOOSEHEAD LAKE should travel by Grand Trunk Railroad to Danville Junction, where connection is made with the Maine Central Railroad, or to Portland, connecting there with the steamer for Bangor, and then pursue their journey by routes hereafter mentioned. Parties from Philadelphia and New York have choice of several pleasant routes to Boston, either by Sound or rail. Reaching Boston, the most direct route is by night train to Bangor, as by it one saves an entire day. The Pullman train leaves the EASTERN RAILROAD DEPOT, Causeway, foot of Friend Street, at 7.00 P.M., and passengers go directly through without change of cars, over the Eastern and Maine Central Railroads, arriving in Bangor about six o'clock the next morning, in time to take breakfast at the saloon in the depot, or, what is preferable, at one of the hotels in the city, the Bangor House and Penobscot Exchange being the best. Baggage is checked from Boston to Greenville. The Pullman car fare for a double berth between Boston and Bangor is $2.00.

An evening train also leaves the BOSTON AND MAINE RAILROAD DEPOT at 7.00 P.M., reaching Portland in time to connect with the Pullman night train on the Main Central. Change cars at the TRANSFER STATION in Portland.

The Maine Central train, which hauls the Bangor and Piscataquis cars as far as Oldtown, leaves the Maine Central Depot about 7.20 A.M., and crosses the city to the Exchange-street Depot, from whence it starts at 7.30 A.M. Take a seat in one of the Moosehead Lake cars, and you will not have to change at Oldtown.

If you prefer to leave Boston in the morning you can take the cars at the BOSTON AND MAINE RAILROAD STATION, Haymarket Square, head of Washington street, at 9.00 A.M., and be whirled rapidly along over a first-class road, arriving in Portland at 12.30, in time for all Eastern connections. Dinner can be procured at the Transfer Station, just outside the city, where connection is made with all trains on the Maine Central Railroad.

A splendid parlor-car accompanies this train, and passengers can take advantage of all its conveniences, for an additional charge of sixty cents. Leaving Boston, the train crosses the salt water, for a mile or more, over substantial bridges, passing through a part of Charlestown, in sight of the Old State Prison, Bunker Hill Monument, and other buildings of note. At SOMERVILLE, one and three quarters miles from Boston, we stop a moment, and then dash onward, by Wellington, Edgeworth, Malden, Oak Grove, Wyoming, Melrose, Stoneham, Greenwood, and Wakefield, slacking up at READING, twelve miles from Boston. The scenery between Somerville and Reading is quite attractive, and there are many beautiful suburban homes along this part of the line.

Again in motion, we pass Reading Highlands and Wilmington, slacking up a moment at Wilmington Junction, where we cross the Salem and Lowell Railroad. The next station is LOWELL JUNCTION, where you change cars for LOWELL, one of the great manufacturing cities of Massachusetts. Leaving here, we pass Ballardvale, making our next stop at ANDOVER, a large and smart town, where considerable manufacturing business is done; it is the home of one of the best Theological Seminaries in the State.

Three miles further on we stop at SOUTH LAWRENCE, twenty-six miles from Boston, one of the smartest manufacturing cities in the State, containing the largest cotton-mills in this country. People going to North Lawrence, Manchester, and Concord change cars here. Leaving this city of spindles, we continue on our way east, and soon reach the Merrimack River, which we follow down to North Andover and Bradford (change cars here for Newburyport), where is located the Bradford Female Seminary; and then, crossing the river, over a fine bridge, eight hundred and fifty feet in length, reach the city of HAVERHILL, thirty-three miles from Boston. A large manufacturing business is done here, principally in the boot and shoe line; the city is a wealthy one, and has many fine public buildings and private residences.

A short distance from Haverhill we cross the New Hampshire State line, and run through a pleasant farming country, passing the stations of Atkinson and Plaistow, and put on the brakes at NEWTON JUNCTION, forty-one miles from Boston. A short branch road runs from here to Merrimack, an enterprising town, noted for its large carriage-manufacturing business.

A very short stop suffices here, and we rattle on to East Kingston and EXETER, an important manufacturing town fifty miles from Boston, where is a first-class dining-room. Ten minutes are allowed here for refreshments, and then we move forward to South Newmarket, where the extensive works of the Swamscot Machine Co. are located, and SOUTH NEWMARKET JUNCTION, fifty-six miles from Boston, where the Portsmouth Railroad crosses the Boston and Maine. Manchester, Concord, and Portsmouth passengers change cars here.

The conductor calls "All aboard!" and we move forward, stopping at Newmarket, Durham, and Madbury, arriving at DOVER, a large manufacturing town, fifty-eight miles from Boston, where connection is made with the Dover and Winnipiseogee Railroads, for Alton Bay, on Lake Winnipiseogee. A large travel goes over this branch in summer, *en route* for Wolfboro', Centre Harbor, and the White Mountains.

Leaving Dover, a few moments ride brings us to ROLLINGSFORD, where passengers for Great Falls, noted for its cotton manufactures, change cars. We reach SALMON FALLS next, another cotton manufacturing town, seventy-one miles from Boston, where we stop a moment. South Berwick station is next passed, and then we stop at NORTH BERWICK, seventy-eight miles from Boston, where we cross the Eastern Railroad. Continuing on we pass the stations of Wells Beach and Kennebunk, and come to a stop at BIDDEFORD, ninety-nine miles from Boston. From here a ride of a mile brings us to SACO, on the other side of the river. These are two of the smartest places in Maine, and are both noted for their manufactures, the most important of which is cotton cloth.

OLD ORCHARD BEACH, one hundred and four miles from Boston, is our next stopping-place. This is one of the greatest summer resorts in New England, and is annually visited by large numbers of strangers. By taking a seat on the right-hand side of the car you will have a fine view of the beach and the restless sea. From here the road runs for some way in sight of the ocean, and we skirt the beach, watching the gulls hovering over the water, and the white-winged vessels in the distance, some so far away that only the sails are visible. Pine Point and SCARBORO' BEACH stations are next reached, the latter one hundred and nine miles from Boston. From the depot to Scarboro' Beach is about two miles, and teams run in summer between the railroad and the hotels. A few minutes' ride from here brings us to Portland, there being only one station, Lygonia, between.

Parties for Moosehead Lake leave the train at the BOSTON AND MAINE TRANSFER STATION, a short distance from the Portland depot; we arrive here at 12.55 P.M., one hundred and fifteen miles from Boston; time, four hours. You have ample time here for dinner.

Or, you may take the cars at the EASTERN RAILROAD DEPOT, on Causeway street, opposite Friend street, the train starting at 9.00 A.M. A Pullman palace car accompanies the train, running through to Bangor, and a seat will cost you $1.00 additional to the regular price of a ticket. On a long ride, the extra cost of riding in a Pullman is more than compensated for by the advantages it offers. Leaving the Boston station, you pass Charlestown and Somerville, stopping at CHELSEA, four miles from Boston. Leaving here you notice the United States Marine Hospital, a fine-looking building, and the hotel on Powder Horn Hill, a place patronized by city people during the hot days of summer. The

CEDAR BEACH, NORTH OF MOUNT KINEO.

country along here is very pleasant, and one sees many things worthy of note. The train rushes by Revere and Oak Island, across the salt meadows, giving one good views of Chelsea Beach, Nahant, Egg Rock Light, and the ocean beyond. With a warning whistle we dash by the West Lynn station, and our snorting steed in a moment or two more comes to a halt in LYNN, eleven miles from Boston, a populous and thriving shoe town, and one of the smartest cities in the State.

Again our iron horse starts, and the train rolls along through a comparatively level country, dotted here and there with romantic cottages and villas, the summer homes of wealth and refinement. We pass through SWAMPSCOTT, which is fast becoming popular as a sea-shore resort, and catch a glimpse of its pretty depot; but make no stop until we reach SALEM, sixteen miles from Boston, one of the oldest settled cities of the Bay State. A branch road extends from here to Peabody, Danvers, and Lawrence. Passing through the tunnel we next stop at BEVERLY, eighteen miles from Boston. From this place a branch road runs to Gloucester, largely engaged in the fish business, and Rockport, a well-known resort for summer boarders. Leaving Beverly we whisk along by the stations of North Beverly and Wenham. From the latter place a short branch extends to Essex. At IPSWICH, the next station on the main line, twenty-eight miles from Boston, we stop ten minutes for refreshments. The inner man satisfied, on we dash, passing through Rowley, and come to a halt at NEWBURYPORT, on the Merrimack River, thirty-seven miles from Boston. This is a very pleasant old city, and at different times a great deal of ship-building has been done here. A short branch road runs from Newburyport to Salisbury and Amesbury, — the home of the famous Quaker poet, Whittier. On the move again, we pass the stations of Seabrook and Hampton Falls, stopping a few moments at HAMPTON, the next station, forty-six miles from Boston, and the point at which passengers bound for HAMPTON BEACH leave the train. Moving eastward again, we go through North Hampton and Greenland, coming to a five minutes' stop at PORTSMOUTH, one of the largest cities of New Hampshire, pleasantly located on the banks of the Piscataqua River. This is one of the oldest places in New England; it is fifty-six miles from Boston, and has one of the best hotels in the country, the ROCKINGHAM HOUSE, of which

Thompson is the proprietor. Portsmouth presents a lively appearance, during the season of summer travel, as all visitors to the ISLES OF SHOALS leave the cars here, and take steamer to the islands, eight miles from the city. Branch roads run from here to Dover and Concord. Having made a change here in locomotives, we make a fresh start and are soon crossing the river, the boundary line between Maine and New Hampshire, over a bridge seven hundred feet in length, obtaining a good view of the United States Navy Yard in Kittery, Maine. A momentary halt is made at the Kittery depot, and then we sweep on by Elliot, and "brake up" at CONWAY JUNCTION, sixty-seven miles from Boston, where passengers bound for North Conway and the White Mountains change cars. From here we steam along to South Berwick Junction, North Berwick, where we cross the track of the Boston and Maine Railroad, Wells, a farming town of some importance, and halt at KENNEBUNK, eighty-five miles from Boston. Here is a good eating-saloon, and we have the customary ten minutes for refreshments. Our next two stops are at BIDDEFORD and SACO, situated on each side of the Saco River, the latter being ninety-five miles from Boston. Bidding adieu to these thriving cities, we pass West Scarboro', and then stop at the SCARBORO' (Oak Hill) station, to leave passengers bound to SCARBORO' BEACH. We are now but a short distance from Portland, the next station being CAPE ELIZABETH. We make our last stop here, and then run across the bridge into Portland, which we reach at 12.55 P.M., the distance being one hundred and eight miles, and the time three and three quarter hours. Here we have sufficient time to partake of a good dinner at a first-class dining saloon in the depot.

After dinner the train makes a new start, this time over the MAINE CENTRAL RAILROAD, first-class in every respect. Between Portland and Waterville one has a choice of two routes. Taking the first or Upper Route, the train leaving at 1.25 P.M., makes the first stop at the BOSTON AND MAINE TRANSFER STATION, then sweeping to the eastward, passes the stations of Woodford's and Westbrook (connection made here with the Portland and Rochester Railroad), two of the most pleasant suburbs of Portland. We are now riding through a farming country that furnishes occasional choice bits of landscape, and we note the names of the stations, Falmouth, Cumberland, Walnut Hill, Gray, and New Gloucester,

MOOSEHEAD LAKE AND VICINITY.

as we pass them in regular order. Next comes DANVILLE JUNCTION, twenty-nine miles from Portland, where we cross the Grand Trunk Railroad. There is a first-class dining-room here kept by Mr. Clark. Leaving the Junction, we soon reach the flourishing cities of AUBURN and LEWISTON, two of the largest manufacturing cities in the State, situated respectively on the west and east sides of the Androscoggin River, that furnishes the vast water-power for the busy mills. The train crosses the rushing stream, over a fine iron bridge, giving one an excellent view of the falls. Lewiston is well laid out; it has some very good streets, a fine park, and many nice buildings. Among the latter is a first-class hotel, the DE WITT HOUSE, handsomely furnished, and containing all modern improvements. The house is centrally located, and stands in the handsomest part of the town, near the City Hall. Mr. Frank A. Hale, the pleasant and gentlemanly landlord, is also proprietor of the Lake Auburn Mineral Spring Hotel, situated at a popular summer resort five miles from Lewiston. Under his charge the DE WITT has regained all of its old-time prestige, and is not to be surpassed in comfort or convenience by any house in the State.

Once more on the wing, a run of seven miles brings us to Greene, and three more to LEEDS JUNCTION, forty-six miles from Portland, where connection is made with the Brunswick and Farmington trains. From Leeds the road winds through several pleasant farming towns,—Monmouth, Winthrop, and Readfield, — and we notice several beautiful sheets of water along the line, on the right-hand side of the cars. This chain of ponds extends to West Waterville, and materially adds to the beauty of the ride in summer. They are known locally as the Winthrop and Belgrade Ponds. Passing Belgrade, North Belgrade, and Oakland (from here the Somerset Railroad runs to North Anson), we make our next long stop at WATERVILLE, eighty-four miles from Portland. This thriving town is charmingly located on the Kennebec River, and is noted as being the seat of one of the best colleges in New England. The railroad depot is directly opposite the college grounds and buildings. Quite an amount of manufacturing is also done here.

Or you may leave Portland on the 1.30 train over the Maine Central Railroad, passing the stations of Woodford's, Westbrook,

Falmouth, Cumberland, and Yarmouth, stopping a few moments at YARMOUTH JUNCTION, sixteen miles from Portland, where we cross the Grand Trunk Railroad. The principal business in these towns is farming and ship-building. Leaving the Junction, we next stop at FREEPORT, twenty-one miles from Portland, a handsome, lively farming town, containing a thickly settled village, where considerable business is done. Continuing on we pass Oak Hill, and slack up next at BRUNSWICK, the seat of Bowdoin College. This place is twenty-nine miles from Portland, on the Androscoggin River, and is quite a railroad centre, roads diverging from it to Bath, Lewiston, and Leeds Junction. They are all operated by the Maine Central, whose aggregate line is 355 miles. There is a dining-saloon in the depot at Brunswick, and all trains stop here from ten to twenty-five minutes, giving ample time for refreshments. Crossing the river, we find ourselves at Topsham, and hurrying on pass Bowdoinham and Harward's, coming to a full stop at RICHMOND, forty-five miles from Portland, and one of the prettiest places on the Kennebec River. Again in motion, we pass the Camp Ground and South Gardiner, slacking up at GARDINER, fifty-six miles from Portland. During the summer months the steamer "Star of the East" runs from this place to Boston. Our route still lies eastward, and we soon reach HALLOWELL, sixty miles from Portland, an important point on the river. Two miles beyond, the train rolls into AUGUSTA, the capital of the State, and the head of tide-water on the Kennebec. It is sixty-two miles from Portland. It is a lovely ride between Brunswick and Augusta in summer, the road following the Kennebec River, which is in sight nearly the entire distance. The right-hand side of the train is the pleasantest until you reach Augusta, and there you should change, if possible, to a seat on the left of the car. There is a large amount of lumbering and ship-building carried on in the towns along the Kennebec between Bowdoinham and State capital. Ice-cutting on the river is also an important industry in winter, and thousands of tons are annually shipped each summer from Richmond, Gardiner, Hallowell, and Augusta, to different parts of the United States and to foreign countries. Augusta has also a large manufacturing business, and contains several mills of various kinds. A large dam extends across the river just above the city. There is a sluice-way on one side through which the logs are run during the driving season.

Leaving Augusta, we cross the river over a splendid iron bridge, one thousand feet in length, and continue on up the Kennebec, which is now on our left. We pass in succession the stations of Riverside, Vassalboro', Winslow, and cross the river again just before reaching Waterville, over another iron bridge, eight hundred feet long, reaching the depot at WATERVILLE, eighty-one miles from Portland, six minutes behind the other train. A branch runs from here to Skowhegan, nineteen miles distant. The ride from Augusta to Waterville is as pleasant as any part of the route, and while crossing the bridge at Waterville one has a nice view of the falls. We soon leave Waterville, the two trains having been united, the cars now being hauled by one locomotive, and in charge of one conductor. You have choice between Portland and Waterville of either of the above-described routes. Our experience would suggest that in going to the lake you take one route, and in returning the other, thus giving greater variety to your journey. The best hotel in Waterville is the "Elmwood."

Steaming along once more, we pass Benton, Clinton (Kendall's Mills are in sight from here on the opposite side of the river), BURNHAM, ninety-five miles from Portland, from whence a branch runs to BELFAST, an important seaport town, thirty-four miles from the main line, Pittsfield, a smart and thriving place, Detroit, and NEWPORT, one hundred and nine miles from Portland. From here a branch fourteen miles long extends to DEXTER, a busy, populous town. As you leave the station at Newport, you will notice on the left a large fine sheet of water, known as Newport Pond; this remains in sight for some minutes. The next station is East Newport, then Etna, Carmel, and HERMON POND, one hundred and twenty-six miles from Portland. There are several mills at this latter place, and a beautiful pond, from which the station is named. Moving onward once more, we pass Hermon Centre, and are soon in sight of the Penobscot River, which runs on our right, following it to BANGOR, arriving at 7.00 P.M., one hundred and thirty-six miles from Portland, where we stop over night. You have a number of hotels to choose from, the two best being the BANGOR HOUSE and PENOBSCOT EXCHANGE, both first-class houses. Bangor is one of the finest cities in Maine, and a large amount of business is done here, the principal industries being lumbering, manufacturing, and ship-building. Steamers run from Bangor to Mount Desert, Portland, and Boston; a branch of the Maine Central Railroad runs to Bucksport, while the main line stretches away eastward with its connections to St. John, N.B.

BAR HARBOR, MOUNT DESERT, is only forty-eight miles from Bangor, and is reached by rail or boat. The completion of the Shore Line Railroad to Hancock offers a pleasant and speedy way of reaching Mt. Desert. Leaving Bangor the road passes through the towns of Brewer, Ellsworth, and Hancock, to Hancock Ferry, opposite Sullivan. Here passengers change from the cars to a fast and comfortable steamer, making the run between Hancock Ferry and Bar Harbor in from a half to three-quarters of an hour. During the summer season there will be three trains daily each way between Bangor and Bar Harbor. The first will leave Bangor after the arrival of the night Pullman train from Boston, at 7.00 A.M., enabling passengers to reach Bar Harbor about nine o'clock. The second train will leave Bangor about 2.00 P.M., enabling passengers to reach Bar Harbor at five o'clock. The third train will leave Bangor at 5.00 P.M., or on arrival of the 9.00 A.M. train from Boston, and, making only one stop (Ellsworth), will enable passengers to reach Bar Harbor at 7.30, in good time for supper.

Returning, leave Bar Harbor about five o'clock in the morning, reaching Bangor in season to connect with morning train for Boston, due at 5.00 P.M. Second, leave Bar Harbor about 11.30 A.M., reaching Bangor in time to connect with the "Flying Yankee Express" for Boston, due at 10.00 P.M. Third, leave Bar Harbor at 5.00 P.M., arriving at Bangor, and making connection with the night Pullman train, due in Boston the following morning at six o'clock.

Of MOUNT DESERT, Browning has written —

> An island full of hills and dells,
> All rumpled and uneven,
> With green recesses, sudden swells,
> And odorous valleys, driven
> So deep and straight that always there
> The wind is cradled in soft air.

The ride from Bangor to Mount Desert, by either rail or boat, is very pleasant, and the scenery about Bar Harbor is enchanting. Of the mountain and stream, island, cave, and lake, with the river, bay, and headland, which answer to names suggestive of tender memories, and whose "melody yet lingers like the last vibration of the red man's requiem," a volume might be written.

Four miles from Bar Harbor, southerly, at Schooner Head, are Spouting Horn and Devil's Oven; the one a cleft in the crag, through which, during an easterly gale, the sea spouts with terrible force, and the other a huge cavern, which should be visited at low water. Miss Barnes beautifully pictures it in her monograph of Mt. Desert. "Here," she says, "the sunlight reflected from the blue waves shone on the dark vault above us as through broad chancel window down cathedral nave; and sitting there one morning, with wind and wave and echo for organ roll, we sang Old Hundred."

The fine steamers of the BANGOR AND BAR HARBOR STEAMBOAT COMPANY, "Cimbria," "Queen City," and "Florence," run four times per week each way between Bangor and Bar Harbor during the season of summer travel. The steamers of this line are new and commodious, and running as they do, inside nearly all the way, rough water is very seldom experienced. The boats leave Bangor at 8.00 A.M., after the arrival of all morning trains, and arrive at Bar Harbor at 4.00 P.M. This trip introduces one to the beautiful scenery of Penobscot River and Bay, and is well worth taking. The sail down the Penobscot and along the Eastern Coast is delightful, touching the quaint old seaside town, Castine; thence across to Islesboro', which is fast becoming a watering-place for summer tourists; then back across the bay by bold Cape Rosier, and into the quiet, river-like Egge Moggin Reach, where sea-sickness is unknown, the steamer glides along so smoothly. Passing Deer Isle and Sedgwick, the course across Blue Hill Bay, with old Blue Hill itself looming up in the distance, guarding, as it were, the entrance of the bay and all its surroundings, while just ahead the Bass Harbor Lighthouse opens up and Mount Desert hills begin to uncover themselves. From this point to Southwest and Bar Harbor one cannot conceive of more beautiful, grand, and varied scenery.

Boston to Bangor via Boston and Bangor Steamship Company's Steamers.

Embark on one of the fine steamers "Penobscot," "Cambridge," or "Katahdin," leaving Lincoln's wharf, Boston, daily, except Sunday, during the summer season, at 5.30 P.M., giving a beautiful sail down Boston Harbor and along the eastern coast of Massachusetts before darkness veils the scene. Forts Independence, Winthrop, and Warren, Rainsford Island, Deer Island, Long Island, Nix's Mate, and Boston Light, each excite interest in the minds of the passengers as they are successively passed. Minot's Ledge Light, the bold and ragged bluffs of Nahant, Egg Rock Light, Norman's Woe, Thatcher's Island Light, are all to be seen from the steamer. After passing Cape Ann the course is more to the eastward, and Monhegan Island, off the coast of Maine, is reached about daylight. Passing this you notice next Whitehead Point, then Dix Island, with its extensive granite quarries, Owl's Head, an old landmark, and other objects of interest. At Rockland the boat stops for the first time, and here connections are made with the Knox & Lincoln Railroad for Bath, and all stations on the route; also with the fine steamer "Mount Desert" every morning, except Monday, for North Haven, Deer Isle, Green's Landing, Swan's Island, South-west Harbor, and Bar Harbor; the new steamer "Rockland" connects at Bar Harbor with steamer "Mt. Desert," and makes two trips daily to Lamoine, Gouldsboro, Hancock, and Sullivan; also connects with steamer "Lewiston," at Rockland, every Wednesday and Saturday for Castine, Millbridge, Jonesport, Sedgwick, and Machias. Stages also leave Rockland and Camden for the surrounding towns, and small steamers and packets for adjacent islands. Pursuing her way up the western shore of the beautiful Penobscot Bay, the boat touches next at Camden, noted for its fine scenery and beautiful surroundings, and excellent fishing. The third stop is at Northport, the celebrated camp-ground, that is fast attaining a popularity as a summer resort. The next landing is at Belfast, where connections are made with the Belfast & Moosehead Lake Railroad for Burnham and intermediate towns, and with steamers for Castine and adjacent islands. Again the steamer ties up, this time at Searsport. Once more under way, Fort Point, a charming

MOOSEHEAD LAKE, FROM INDIAN HILL.

sort, leaving as above during the season of summer travel, and connecting the next morning at Rockland with steamers for Bangor. By this route you reach Bangor about eleven o'clock the next morning, and can spend a few hours in rambling about the city, and take dinner at a good hotel, then leave on the afternoon train for Greenville, arriving at Moosehead Lake early in the evening, and the Mount Kineo House the next morning.

The train leaves the Exchange-street depot at 7.30 A.M., and as the road runs close beside the Penobscot River, you are favored with many charming landscape views. A short distance from the depot you pass the dam on the river, built for the purpose of furnishing the city with an unfailing supply of pure water; it also furnishes the power to run the immense pumps located in the Bangor Water Works; these buildings are situated on the side of the river just above the dam. As the train sweeps along, you see enormous piles of lumber manufactured at the mills that line the left bank of the river. The first stop is made at Veazie, and we then pass the stations of Basin Mills, Orono, Webster, and Great Works, arriving at OLDTOWN, where, in the centre of the river, on an island, is an Indian village, which has been there for years. Oldtown is a smart and thriving place, and has large lumbering interests. Leaving Oldtown at 8.20, we commence our journey on the Bangor and Piscataquis, and shortly lose sight of the Penobscot. Our route lies to the west and north, up the valley of the Piscataquis River, and we pass the stations of Pea Cove, Alton, South LaGrange, LaGrange, Orneville, and MILO. There is a project under consideration of changing the route of the road between here and Oldtown, and building it to Bangor in a different direction, following down the valley of the Kenduskeag to the city.

The proposed new route would take the road through a more populous and better freighting country than that in which it now runs, and would also shorten the distance between Bangor and Milo some twelve miles.

The train for Moosehead Lake is made up in the Maine Central Depot, and leaves there at 7.20 A.M., crossing the city to Exchange street. The Bangor & Piscataquis cars are attached to the Maine Central train, and, to avoid an unnecessary change at Oldtown, be sure and take seats in the Moosehead Lake cars.

Between Bangor and Oldtown the entire train runs over the Maine Central Railroad; at the latter place the Bangor and Piscataquis train is detached and switched to the left of the depot, and is hauled from there to the lake by its own engine. The view from the right of the car is the most pleasant between Bangor and Milo, while the remainder of the distance to the lake the left-hand side of the car is preferable.

Connection is made at MILO with the Bangor and Katahdin Iron Works Railway for Brownsville, and the Katahdin Iron Works. At the latter place teams and guides can be engaged for a trip to the "Gulf," a picturesque rocky canon on the West Branch of Pleasant River.

Leaving Milo (in this vicinity you obtain the best view from the road of Mt. Katahdin) a ride of twelve or fifteen minutes brings us to the station of South Sebec. Here the sportsman or tourist bound for SEBEC LAKE leaves the cars, and takes stage for the hotel, five miles distant; fare, twenty-five cents. One can obtain guides, canoes, and campers' outfits at Sebec Village, which clusters around the lower end of the lake.

The landlocked salmon in Sebec Lake furnish excellent sport in the spring, soon after the ice goes out. They run from a pound to five pounds in weight, and are as gamy as a black bass. During July and August, pickerel and white-perch are taken readily. The entire length of the lake is twelve miles. The eastern half is very narrow, from one to two hundred rods wide. The western half is nearly three miles wide from north to south. The Lake House is located at the western end of the lake, near the mouth of Wilson Stream. It has accommodations for about thirty guests, and canoes, boats, or camping outfits, can be obtained of the proprietor. A steamer plies upon the lake during the season of summer travel.

Passing on we stop for a moment at East Dover, and from there a short ride brings us to DOVER and FOXCROFT, two smart and enterprising towns. They are situated opposite each other on the south and north banks of the Piscataquis River, and, as the railroad runs near the boundary line of the towns, one depot answers for both places. A few summer visitors are attracted to both of these places, each year, by the beauty of the scenery in the vicinity, and their proximity to Sebec Lake, which is only six miles distant. From Foxcroft to Blethen Landing on the lake is a distance of about five miles; fare by regular conveyance, fifty cents. The steamer touches at Blethen Landing each way, on her trips up and down the lake.

Again the train starts, and we pass the stations of Low's Bridge, Sangerville, Guilford, Abbot Village, arriving at MONSON JUNCTION, in the town of Abbot, where connection is made with the MONSON RAILROAD, two-foot gauge, for Monson, six miles distant. This is a pleasant and wide-awake little village, situated in the midst of a mountainous forest country that stretches beyond it for many miles. It has a good hotel, two churches, several stores, post-office, academy, and the dwelling-houses are well built. There are several large slate quarries adjacent to the village which furnish work for a number of men the entire year. In Chapter IV. we speak more particularly of Monson and its surroundings.

Leaving Abbot the scenery grows wilder and more picturesque, and the hills develop into mountains. Russell Mountain, one of the highest in this vicinity, will be noticed on the left-hand side of the road as you approach the Blanchard station, and the view of the valley is charming. A ride of little more than twenty minutes brings us to BLANCHARD, for several years the terminus of the road. Between here and the lake the road is mostly through the woods. The train makes one stop at Shirley, and reaches West Cove, in Greenville, at the foot of Moosehead Lake, at noon. If you wish, you can change directly to the steamer, and take dinner at Mount Kineo; or you can avail yourself of the conveyances in waiting, and be driven to one of the hotels at the East Cove, a distance of a mile and a quarter, and, stopping over night, proceed up the lake the next morning.

It is expected that a hotel will be built at the West Cove before another summer, a movement being already started in that direction.

At Greenville (East Cove) you have choice of two excellent hotels, the EVELETH HOUSE, or the LAKE HOUSE, both of which run free carriages to the trains.

During the season of summer travel it is expected that the railroad company will run two trains a day each way between Bangor and Moosehead Lake. Probably the afternoon train will leave Bangor on the arrival of the "Flying Yankee Express" from Boston; if so, passengers will be able to leave Boston at nine in the morning and reach the lake the same evening between eight and nine o'clock, proceeding onward by boat the next morning.

Having now given all the different routes by which MOOSEHEAD LAKE and MOUNT KINEO may be reached, we will retrace our steps and devote a chapter to the country in the vicinity of the KATAHDIN IRON WORKS, and also one to MONSON, and the facilities it offers to the sportsman and tourist.

CHAPTER III.

From Milo to Brownville and Katahdin Iron Works. — Fishing Resorts in the Vicinity. — The Gulf and its Surroundings.

CHANGING cars at MILO you proceed by the Bangor & Katahdin Iron Works Railway to the KATAHDIN IRON WORKS, via Brownville, a distance of about nineteen miles. In leaving Milo station the road descries a circle, and then runs north and north-west through Brownville and Williamsburgh to the station at the Iron Works. At BROWNVILLE, five miles distant from Milo station, we make a brief stop. Brownville is celebrated for the fine quality of slate manufactured in the town, and it contains several of the largest quarries in New England, furnishing employment for a large number of men. A mile or two from the village a branch road runs north-east to SCHOODIC LAKE, four miles distant from the main thoroughfare. There is good trout-fishing at this lake, but you will need a boat or canoe. A logging road leaves the Schoodic Lake road near Norton's and continues on to SOUTH TWIN LAKE, passing near the EBEEME PONDS and JO MARY LAKES. Teams and guides can be procured at Brownville for a trip to the ponds and lakes above spoken of. With good luck you can get through to Jo Mary Lakes in a day. The Ebeeme Ponds are about a half a mile apart, and are connected by the East Branch of Pleasant River, navigable part of the distance. In this whole vicinity there is good hunting and fishing, and picturesque scenery.

Between Brownville and the Iron Works the railroad runs mostly through a dense forest; occasional pretty glimpses of the Pleasant River are caught, however, from time to time, from the right-hand side of the cars. In November, 1883, a tornado swept along the line of this road, doing a great deal of damage to the timber, and its effects are still seen. The road ends at the Furnace, the depot being located but a few rods from the hotel. A telegraph line runs from Bangor to the Iron Works.

At the time of the hurricane the most of the Iron Company's

BILLINGS' FALLS, WEST BRANCH PLEASANT RIVER, ME.

buildings were burned to the ground; but they will probably be rebuilt. The village is small, there being but one store, and the hotel, the Iron Company's buildings, and the Railroad Company's buildings, with a few small houses inhabited by the workmen, are about all there is of the settlement. The time from Bangor to the Iron Works is three hours and a half, and there are two trains each way daily, excepting Sundays. The fare from Bangor to the Iron Works is $2.50, and from Milo to the Iron Works $1.00.

As you leave the cars you will notice the appearance of iron everywhere. On the road, in the streams, around the buildings, and away beyond, you can see the Iron Mountain where the ore is mined.

The Katahdin Iron Company, at their works, turn out the best car-wheel iron in this country, the furnaces being all fed with charcoal. When the furnaces are in full blast, about seventy-five men find employment here, and some four thousand tons of iron are manufactured each year, which finds a ready market. The Iron Mountain, where the ore is obtained, is but a short distance from the hotel, and is well worth a visit. In digging for the ore many curious specimens of former vegetable matter are unearthed, such as leaves, ferns, grasses, limbs of trees, etc., that in the course of years, and through some chemical process of nature, have all been turned to iron, but still retain their former shape, and the delicate veins in the ferns and leaves are as perfect as they were before the change, and there is no doubt but what this wonderful transformation is still going on.

The Silver Lake Hotel has been recently enlarged and improved and offers to the sportsman or pleasure-seeker comfortable quarters at reasonable prices. An energetic and capable manager has been engaged to run the house the present season, and, under his efficient rule, the hotel will, without doubt, continue its long career of prosperity.

This hotel is fast attaining a popularity as a summer resort for invalids, who visit it for the purpose of drinking the celebrated waters of the mineral springs, of which there are several in the vicinity. These iron and sulphur spring waters have been found to contain unusual tonic properties, and as a cleanser and purifier of the blood they are unequalled. They are also found invaluable for all kinds of weakness and female complaints, and thousands who have visited the hotel from a distance have been greatly benefited, and many entirely cured, from drinking the waters.

As will be seen from a glance at our map, there are quite a number of ponds within a radius of ten miles from the village, all of which furnish good trout fishing. Houston Pond, three miles distant, is the largest, and Long Pond and B Ponds are the next in size. The first is about eight miles distant from the hotel, the second, ten. East and West Chairback Ponds, and Spruce Mountain Pond, distant in order named from the village, six, seven, and eight miles, are often resorted to by fishermen.

If you have the time to spare you will find that you can pass several days here very pleasantly, as the Ore Mountain, the Mineral Springs, and the Blast Furnace, where the celebrated Katahdin Car Wheel iron is manufactured, are all worth visiting, while Silver Lake and the dozen or more trout streams in the immediate vicinity of the hotel furnish excellent chances for boating and fishing. There are good carriage-roads in the neighborhood, and, if you wish to drive, teams may be procured from the hotel. Pedestrian excursions can be made to the summits of Chairback and Horseback Mountains, from both of which good views of the surrounding country can be obtained. The distance from the hotel to the top of either mountain is about four miles.

The country is wild and unsettled, and in the fall one can obtain excellent partridge-shooting, beside having a chance at larger game, as deer, caribou, and the common black bear, are to be found, with the aid of a skilful guide, without much trouble. The following amusing incident was an actual occurrence:—

One day, several years ago, while Billings, the guide, and a gentleman from Bangor were driving in the vicinity of the Iron Works, they were surprised by seeing a large black bear come out of the woods on their right and cross the road a few rods in front of them. Their rifles lay in the bottom of the wagon, but the bear crossed so quick they did not try to use them. The first bear had scarcely reached the woods on the left of the road, when out stalked a second from the right hand. He shuffled across the road so fast that the colonel had scarcely time to say, "There's another bear, Billings," before the animal was out of sight. As he disappeared, both men made a dive for their rifles, and while they were getting them ready to use, out from the same piece of woods came a third bear, which stalked solemnly across the road, stopping in the middle of it to take a good look at the team. This was too much for Billings, who jumped up on his feet, exclaiming, "My God, colonel, the woods are full of bears!" and, cocking his rifle, let drive at Bruin over the head of the horse. The bear was not hit, however; but they stopped the horse and took to the woods, but did not get another glimpse at those "bears." About a week after this incident, Billings set a couple of iron traps in the vicinity, but was not successful in catching a bear, and he concluded that the three he had seen were looking for a good place in which to den during the winter, and had kept on traveling for some distance.

Before visiting the Gulf you will have to procure a guide, and we know of none better than T. W. Billings, Brownville, Me.

The GULF is located on the north-west branch of Pleasant River, in the eastern township of the Bowdoin College Grant, and is a rocky cañon in the mountains, three miles long. From the Iron Works hotel to the head of the Gulf is ten miles, of which the first three can be done in a team, and the balance on foot. The road runs for three miles through a rough clearing, and then enters the forest. In summer the path is dry, and the streams so low that they can be easily forded. The trail is an old tote road, hard to follow in some places where it is nearly overgrown, in other parts comparatively easy. Arrived at the upper end of the GULF, you will notice the dam, seven hundred feet long, situated at the head of a rocky gorge, where the cañon really commences. Six hundred thousand feet of lumber were used in building this dam. Directly below is a series of beautiful falls and cascades, and on the right side of the river is a cave fifty feet deep. The banks of the stream at this place are about fifty feet high, and are composed of slate ledges, whose tops are covered with several varieties of moss, and a thick growth of spruce, fir, and pine. A short distance below, the ledges that confine the stream increase to a hundred feet in height. The banks are curved nearly to a half-circle, giving one the idea of an amphitheatre. In the centre of this half-circle a heavy volume of water makes a jump of thirty feet through a natural cut in the rock, and pours with a roar of thunder into the abyss below. BILLINGS' FALLS are one of the most considerable falls in the GULF. Just to the left of where the water pours over

the rock, is a strong eddy, where the bubbles of foam gather and grow until they form grotesque shapes, reminding one of white beaver hats, cream-lemon pies, or innumerable ice-creams that float continually in circles. Never for a moment still, the eye soon wearies in following them on their ceaseless rounds. The water below the fall is black and deep. From out this dark pool the stream dances onward in the form of flashing rapids, between the same precipitous and rocky banks, until it makes another heavy fall of about seventy feet, but not perpendicular. This is known as RANKIN'S FALLS. Below it is another deep pool and still water for some distance. Along here the cañon narrows, forming another amphitheatre, and the walls that encircle it rise to a height of two hundred feet from the water. In many places the sides of the gorge are a solid mass of smooth rock, without a crevice for bushes or weeds to effect a lodgment. At irregular intervals the tops of these massive walls overhang the stream, so that a stone dropped straight down would strike the centre of the river. Occasionally there are clefts in the wall from which water of more or less volume emerges, forming silvery cascades that fall a distance of fifty or sixty feet.

As you follow the stream down, the walking varies considerably. Where there is only moss and bushes it is easy getting ahead; but sometimes the trees are so thick you can scarcely force your way through them. To offset this, you find, once in a while, a bare ledge in your pathway that overhangs the cañon. From some of these ledges you obtain a glimpse of the stream for two hundred rods above and below you, the water shimmering in the sunlight like brilliants.

The immense piles of slate that uprise from either side of the river sometimes appear in regular layers, as if piled up by the hand of man. Again they are very irregular in shape and appearance, forming queer joints and angles. These are ofttimes scarred and worn by the frost and rain, and in some places huge masses of the rock have succumbed to the wear and tear of time and the elements, and fallen into the yawning gulf below, to fret and madden the stream whose sanctity they have invaded. The highest point from the water to the top of the banks is from three to four hundred feet.

The stream varies in width from four or five rods to a few feet, and through these rocky gates the waters pour with relentless fury, making a noise that drowns all others. Continuing on, we pass a half-mile of still water and rapids, that culminate in a fall of fifteen feet, below which the stream boils and foams like a witch's caldron. On top of the right-hand bank in this vicinity are to be found some very pretty specimens of crystallized quartz.

As we follow the GULF down, it presents the same characteristics the entire distance. An open-mouthed chasm, with huge boulders at the bottom, the banks in some places receding, in others overhanging; the continual roar of the water follows you, sounding, as it ascends from the cavernous depths below, like a funeral dirge; in some spots the sunshine enters, lighting up the dark recesses of the gorge, and casting a silver gleam over the hurrying waters, as they rush on their long and circuitous journey toward the sea.

Sometimes a feeling of utter ruin, of chaos, as if the eternal hills were crumbling into dust, possesses you, and prompts you almost into seeking safety in flight. At others, awe and solemn wonder hold you spellbound, and you scarcely dare to move or breathe. Perched upon some jutting crag, hundreds of feet above the mad waters that mock you with their angry laughter, you involuntarily shrink back from the edge of the precipice, and cast a frightened glance around, as if feeling the presence of some undefined, mysterious thing, who, out of mere wantonness, would hurl you over into the boiling surge.

One needs days, and even weeks, here to get a complete idea of the awe, the grandeur, the solemnity, the wildness, the romance, and the picturesque beauty of the scenes.

A mile and a half below the dam are the "Jaws of the Gulf." Here the rocky sides almost meet, there being only six feet below and twenty above between the walled banks. Several deer have jumped the GULF at this point, and a rustic bridge, that would furnish a splendid view in either direction, might easily be thrown across.

The "Face in the Rock" is near this place, and shows one of the singular freaks that nature sometimes takes in stamping the human features on a solid rock.

A short distance below here a deer was found last summer at the bottom of the GULF, with nearly every bone in his body broken. He had fallen over the cliff above.

FACE IN THE ROCK AND JAWS OF THE GULF, WEST BRANCH PLEASANT RIVER, ME.

All through the cañon trees struggle for an existence from the bottom clear to the highest peak, sometimes growing on a little crag that scarcely furnishes a foothold. Every year the place grows wilder. Each spring pieces of rock, worn away by the continual dripping and flow of the water, go tumbling into the stream below.

In some places there are fissures in the cliffs, thirty feet deep and from one to three feet wide, suggestive of terrible land-slides. On each side of the river there are a number of ravines that run back from one to five hundred feet from the stream. By these one can easily descend to the bed of the river. The water is very high in the spring, but at any time in the year there is a large amount at the falls. There are trout in the stream, and it furnishes good fishing in the early part of the season; and slate enough along the bank to run a quarry from now to the end of time.

Some years ago logs were driven down this stream, but they jammed so badly that the lumbermen soon had enough of it. In several cases men were lowered from the top of the banks two and three hundred feet, by a rope tied around their body, to cut away logs in a jam. The bare thought of it fills one with horror. The river in some parts is straight for a few rods, but generally it winds in easy curves, descending with each curve.

It appears in some places as if the mountain had been split in two by some great upheaval of nature. And again one might suppose that this fearful cañon had been worn out of the solid rock by the action of the tireless water which for countless ages has poured over it.

About two miles and a quarter from the head of the gorge, the river makes two sharp turns, one to the west, the other to the east, giving the stream here the shape of an elongated letter S; at the first bend of the river, a prominent cliff, called LOOKOUT CLIFF, gives one the best view up the river to be obtained anywhere on the stream. The river has a fall here of about one hundred feet in several small falls. The ledges that form the "Lookout" are wedge-shape, with the sharp end resting in the stream. They preserve this shape from top to bottom; "wonderful" and "sublime" are but tame expressions for the beauty of the scenery; you should go up one side of the river and down the other to see the GULF to the best advantage. A good guide is absolutely necessary, unless you know something of the country. June or September is the best time to visit the GULF, as the flies are very thick in the vicinity through July and part of August. If you would get an idea of it, visit it yourself, for no pen can do it justice. There is a continual fall in the river from the time it leaves the dam until it emerges from the cañon, furnishing a charming succession of rapids, pools, cascades, stretches of dead water, and falls, the entire distance. After the river makes the two sharp turns near the foot of the cañon, the banks on either side rapidly decrease in height, and there is nothing of especial interest until you get half a mile below, where you reach what are called the LOWER ARCHES; here there is another fall.

It is to be regretted that there are no hotel accommodations in the immediate vicinity of the GULF, for such a charming and romantic locality should be visited by all who can spare the time and money for the trip. Such a show piece as the GULF offers a strong inducement to some enterprising individual to engage in a hotel speculation, which could hardly help being remunerative when you take into account the excellent fishing and hunting only a short distance away, as well as the beautiful scenery. A carriage road has been built from the IRON WORKS through to the GULF, and ladies who wish to make the trip can now ride. From the GULF across to Greenville is only fifteen miles, and by crossing the ponds that lie between in a boat, one has only six miles to walk. A spotted line from the head of the GULF to the UPPER WILSON POND will probably be run next winter.

CHAPTER IV.

Monson and Vicinity.—A Pleasant Summer Resort for the Tourist and Fisherman.

THE town of Monson is situated in the north-western part of Piscataquis County, fourteen miles south of Moosehead Lake, ten miles west of Sebec Lake, and six miles north of the Bangor & Piscataquis Railroad. The Monson (narrow-gauge) Railroad runs from Monson Junction to the village, a distance of six miles, and two miles beyond to the slate quarries. The town is over nine hundred feet above the level of the sea, and three-quarters of its area is yet an unbroken wilderness.

Monson is about thirteen hours' ride from Boston by rail, and by the present existing railroad arrangements, during the summer season the traveler can leave Boston at 9.00 in the morning, and reach Monson by 8.00 the same evening, or, by leaving Boston on the night Pullman train, at 7.00 o'clock, reach Monson at 11.00 o'clock the next morning. From Portland the route is *via* Maine Central, Bangor, & Piscataquis, and Monson Railroads.

Through the energy and enterprise of wealthy capitalists from Lowell, Mass., to whom the town owes nearly all of its present prosperity, the village is graced by one of the best hotels in the State, a new and commodious structure, eligibly located on high land, overlooking a beautiful sheet of water known as Lake Hebron, from which the hotel takes its name. The house is comfortably and handsomely furnished, and contains accommodations, with the annex, for seventy-five guests. The building is surrounded by broad verandas on the ground floor and second story, offering a fine chance for a promenade, while the views from the piazzas are pleasant and varied. The parlor, office, wash-room, water-closets, dining-room, kitchen, pantry, etc., are on the lower floor, while the two upper stories are divided into sleeping-rooms, all of which are pleasant. Every floor in the house is supplied with running water from the Sherman Hill Springs, famous for their rare medicinal and healing qualities. There is a large and well appointed bath-room on the second floor, a luxury seldom found in a country hotel. The dining-room will accommodate fifty people at once. The terms are from $2.00 to $2.50 per day, and Mr. Elisha Taft, who leases the house, possesses all the necessary qualifications to make it a success. Mr. Taft's long hotel experience, covering a period of years, during which he was proprietor of some of the largest and best-managed hotels in New England, have well-fitted him to make the stay of his guests pleasant and agreeable.

A good livery is connected with the house, and teams may be procured for a drive at any time at reasonable prices.

There are two trains daily, excepting Sunday, each way between Bangor and Monson, and a team from the hotel meets each train during the season of summer travel. There are several well-stocked stores in the village, where tourists or sportsmen can find most of the articles needed for a camping-out trip.

There are four slate quarries owned by Lowell capitalists, known as the Hebron Pond, the Kineo, the Pine Tree, and the Monson Pond, beside two others, owned by different parties.

The slate was first discovered in 1870. It has now become an important industry of the place and the State. About three hundred men are employed steadily at the four Lowell quarries, and the monthly pay-roll amounts to over eleven thousand dollars.

The slate is quarried in huge blocks by the aid of steam drills and blasting powder, and is hoisted out of the pits by immense derricks operated by steam, deposited on dump-cars, and run on a railroad track to the buildings where it is manufactured. The large blocks are separated into convenient size for handling by steam augurs and hand wedges, and then the expert workmen, with chisel and mallet, split the stone into thin sheets, as easily as a boy can kindling-wood with a sharp hatchet. The edges are squared by a revolving cutter turned by steam, and the size of the slate regulated by a slotted gauge on which it rests. Twenty-eight different sizes are made, the largest being twenty-four by fourteen inches, and the smallest nine by seven inches. It is sold by the square, or one hundred square feet, and there are from ninety-three to six hundred pieces in a square. The price at the quarries is about four dollars per square.

Branches from the Monson Railroad penetrate every quarry, and the slate is loaded on the cars direct from the storehouses, but has to be transhipped at Monson Junction to the cars of the Bangor & Piscataquis Railroad, by which it is distributed to the different markets. Eight hundred car-loads of slate are manufactured yearly. George S. Cushing, Esq., Lowell, Mass., is the treasurer and general manager of the slate quarries and the railroad company.

LAKE HEBRON, near the hotel, is one of the most beautiful and picturesque sheets of water in northern Maine. It is three miles long and about a mile wide, and is skirted by magnificent forests and mountains. Its waters abound with the spotted brook-trout and "lakers," the latter being caught in deep water.

MONSON POND is about the same size of Lake Hebron, although differently shaped, and contains both brook and lake trout. It is a little more than a mile from the hotel. Boats can be procured at the pond.

DOUGHTY PONDS. These ponds are about three miles and a half from the LAKE HEBRON HOTEL. You can drive with a team to the Doughty farm-house on the top of Doughty Hill, the highest point of land in Monson, and from here walk a distance of half a mile to the first pond, in the midst of a dense forest. It is a beautiful sheet of water, covering about thirty acres. Crossing the first pond it is a distance of about an eighth of a mile to the other pond, — also surrounded by woods, and the larger of the two. The camp is by the side of Cold Brook, which runs from a large spring, and empties into the farther pond. It is a delightful spot for a sportsman's camp, — good water within a few feet of the door, and an abundance of firewood close at hand. The only fish in these ponds are beautifully spotted trout, resembling the common brook-trout in outward appearance, with red meat. They weigh from a quarter of a pound to one and a half pounds, averaging, perhaps, three-quarters of a pound in weight. They will rise to a fly, and many handsome strings of these trout from both ponds have been taken in this way.

Besides the lake and ponds already mentioned there are within the town many others, each well-stocked with trout, distant from two to four miles from the LAKE HEBRON HOTEL, called as follows: —

Spectacle East, Spectacle West, Bunker North, Bunker South, Tibbets, McLarign North, McLarign South, Bell, Lillie, Ward,

Strout, Doe, Duck. Goodale, Eighteen, Squaghquign, Jacobs, Thatcher, Curtis, Bog, and Juniper.

The next most important chain of lakes and ponds in the vicinity of Monson is in the town of Elliottsville.

LAKE ONAWAY, otherwise known as Ship Pond, is located in the township of Elliottsville, eight miles from Monson, and is the best known and most famous of any in this entire region. It is a handsome sheet of water about four miles long, and two wide, surrounded by the towering Boar, Rochelle, Benson, Houston, Barren, and Greenwood Mountains, all within a dense forest, extending many miles in every direction farther than the eye can reach. Its waters abound in "lakers," spotted brook-trout, and land-locked salmon. Other ponds in and around the township of Elliottsville, which contains forty-six square miles, are Big Greenwood, South Greenwood, Bear, Round, Long, South, Barren Mountain, Twin Benson, Sluegundy, Rochelle, Summit, and Buttermilk.

An old highway, scraggy, moss-grown, and hoary, leads through several miles of the township. Where there was in the days of yore a thriving settlement are now seen only a few scattering houses, its melancholy appearance suggesting thoughts of a deserted village.

Shirley, on the west, which is a portion of the immense wilderness reaching through to the forks of the Kennebec, contains some forty-eight square miles. For a distance of twenty miles in a westerly direction, and at the north as far as the Canada line, this vast forest has no human habitants except the hardy lumbermen in winter, and the sportsmen in summer.

Among these wilds in Shirley, Moxie, Square Town, and Squaw Mount Town, within a radius of eighteen miles from the LAKE HEBRON HOTEL, are a large number of attractive and charming ponds, whose waters teem with the spotted brook-trout, the most beautiful of fresh-water fish. The most inviting of these are Moxie, Knight's, Trout, Frying Pan, Potter, Riddle, Big Indian, Little Indian, Coffee House, Carter, Bog, Marble.

In Willimantic, five miles distant, is Grindstone Pond. The following ponds are also within a few miles of the hotel: North Guilford Pond, in Guilford; Greenlief, Foss, Wheatstone, Thorn, and Piper Ponds, in and around Abbott, on the south. The last named is the only one in all of the above-mentioned ponds that contains pickerel. In Piper Pond, however, there is an abundance of this, with some, favorite fish. In Blanchard, on the west, are Russell Mountain, Thorn, and Mud Ponds, besides several others.

Lake Onaway.

This lake is of an irregular, odd, and curious shape, having many quaint coves and bays, skirted and fringed with a growth of light and graceful white birch, and dotted with picturesque islands. It is in the midst of a vast and unbroken wilderness, and is surrounded by several mountains, some of which rear their majestic heads more than a thousand feet above its crystal surface, and a succession of rounded forest-clad hills, huge and broken bluffs, and fragmentary boulders encircle its shores. Its original name is *Onaway*. This information, and the authority for this name, came from the late Lewis Annance, who was for many years a well-known and exceptionally intelligent Indian, who spent many of his years around Moosehead Lake. The route to the lake is by team, eight and one-half miles over an old but pretty road, leading through Elliottsville to Wilson Stream. From this point there are two ways of reaching the lake. The shortest is to ride to the shore of Greenwood Pond, and there embark in a boat or canoe, and sail across the pond, a distance of about one mile, and then walk across the carry, three-quarters of a mile, to your place of destination. The other route from Wilson Stream is to follow a rough, wild, and winding road around the west side of Boar Mountain to Long Pond Outlet, which empties into ONAWAY, and which you reach from this point without any walk or carry. Your journey down this lovely stream will be pleasant and enjoyable.

You will find at the lake two primitive hotels, where sportsmen and fishermen are well cared for. One is kept by a Bangor boy, Mr. E. H. Gerrish, and is located on the north shore in a large cove, at a place called Haynes' Beach. The other is run by Mr. Henry Lane, and is located on the south shore. Each have a good supply of boats and canoes for their patrons. A few weeks spent at this forest retreat, fishing, gunning, or rowing, will do you good, and every night you can listen to the plaintive notes of the whip-poor-will, the gruff hoot of the owl, or the shrill cry of the loon. If these odd sounds do not lull you to sleep they will, at least, afford you food for thought while awake.

The Indian name of this lake, "Onaway," has a traditional history, handed down from past generations of red men, and runs as follows: —

Many years ago, before the smokes of the pale-face settlers had begun to arise in northern Maine, and when the red man inhabited this entire region unmolested, there was among the Penobscot Indians a brave warrior and honored chief named Wawhook. He was respected by his tribe for his valor, courage, and great wisdom.

He had a daughter, — a lovely Indian maiden, beloved by her people, and by all neighboring tribes who knew her, — named Onaway, which, in the Indian vocabulary, means "awake." When the daughter of the great chief had lived about twenty summers, the Chesuncook Indians, from the far North, became hostile to Wawhook's tribe, and war was waged between them.

To break down this invincible and irrepressible leader, to curb his turbulent spirit and seek revenge for his many daring deeds, was the ambition of his enemies, and, in a council of the hostile tribe, it was decided to capture the beautiful maiden, who was besides the Great Spirit, the only being that the great Wawhook ever worshipped. Young, cunning, and brave warriors were selected to perform this hazardous feat. After many weary days of travel and exposure on the part of her captors, Onaway was snatched from her father's wigwam, and, bound and tied, was carried north to be held as a ransom and means of gaining unfair terms of peace with Wawhook, as it was well understood that he would make almost any sacrifice to secure his daughter's liberty.

While travelling north with their victim these warriors camped for the night on the shores of this lake, near the mouth of a stream now called "Sluegundy." The maiden's night vigils, while the warriors slept, were attended by the Great Spirit, who came and unbound the rude fetters which held her, and, directing her footsteps by the light from a big torch which illuminated the heavens, she was enabled to find her way back to her own tribe, and was thus miraculously saved.

For many generations after, whenever any of the Indians belonging to the tribe from which these warriors came, tarried around this lake, a pall of darkness shrouded everything, and hideous and unearthly warwhoops and sounds were heard everywhere, so that it was impossible for them to repose in the vicinity; while, on the other hand, any who belonged to the maiden's tribe could remain there in peace; but there would always appear to them such a wonderful light from the Great Spirit, casting such a radiance over every object, that it kept them continually awake. However absurd this legend may seem to the prosaic reader of to-day, the appropriateness of the name *Onaway*, or "awake," will be fully realized by any person how pays it a visit, when, be he ever so dull, he will awake to the beauty and grandeur of all around him.

This vicinity is rapidly becoming popular, not only with the disciples of Izaak Walton, but also with those admirers of nature, who love a quiet resting-place afar from the busy haunts of man.

Before closing this chapter I will acquaint my readers with the fact that the Piscataquis Game and Fish Protective Society is located at Monson, and has done, and is still doing, a good work in stocking the ponds in the vicinity with trout and salmon, and severely discouraging all who would hunt or fish during the close seasons, or take game and fish by any other than lawful means.

J. F. Sprague, Esq., of Monson, who is one of the officials of the above society, and a smart and enterprising lawyer, has done a great deal to forward the society's noble work; and to him we are indebted for much of the information contained in this chapter. Sportsmen or fishermen visiting Monson should call upon Mr. Sprague, as they will find him a gentleman whose acquaintance they will like to cultivate.

CHAPTER V.

Greenville and its Attractions.

This little town nestles cosily at the foot of the lake, which is here very narrow, and is thickly studded with rocky islands covered with fir and spruce trees, presenting from the street near the post-office the appearance of a beautiful archipelago.

The people live mostly by farming in the summer, and lumbering in the winter. There is considerable trade in GREENVILLE from furnishing supplies for the lumbermen, many of whom congregate here every fall on their way to the numerous logging camps around and beyond the lake.

The LAKE HOUSE, the larger of the two hotels, has accommodations for about one hundred people. The house, as one will see in our engraving, stands at the very edge of the water, and from its piazza one can see all that is going on at the lower end of the lake. All of the rooms are well furnished and pleasant, and some of them are larger than one usually finds in a country hotel. Charlie Sawyer is a young man, and attends to the business of the house; but the senior proprietor, Ivory Littlefield, or "Uncle Ivory," as he is universally called by those who know him best, is one of the oldest guides in the region, and is always ready to tell a story or take a tramp, and is considered good authority upon all matters appertaining to hunting and fishing.

The EVELETH HOUSE is located on a little hill, a short distance from the steamboat landing. It is directly opposite the post-office, and stands out prominently among the other buildings, and furnishes accommodations for about fifty people. The proprietor of this house, Mr. Amos H. Walker, is a young man, and a general favorite with his guests. Mr. Walker and others interested in the lake travel are making arrangements to build a new hotel at West Cove, near the railroad station. A public house is very much needed there, but it is uncertain at this writing whether the building will be erected in time for use the present season or not.

Besides the hotels there are a large number of stores, shops, etc., that give quite an air of business to the village. The largest of these are the establishments of John H. Eveleth & Co., D. T. Sanders, and M. G. Shaw & Sons. There are at present seven steamers on the lake, the "Gov. Coburn," "Wm. Parker," "Twilight," "Day Dream," "Fairy of the Lake," "Rebecca," "Ripple," and "Kineo," built during the spring of 1881, by the management of the Mt. Kineo House. The first three steamers are owned by the Gov. Coburn Steamboat Company, and are used for towing, and the general passenger and freight business of the lake. The towing amounts annually to a large sum, and pays better than passenger and freight traffic. A new boiler was put into the "Parker" during the spring of 1881, and other improvements were made in her. The "Day Dream" and "Kineo" are the popular excursion boats of the Mount Kineo House, and are owned and run by the proprietors of the hotel, who find plenty of work for them in the summer season, conveying fishing parties and excursionists to different parts of the lake. The "Fairy of the Lake" and the "Rebecca" are owned by J. H. Eveleth, who uses them for towing and the general business of the lake. During the spring of 1880 the "Fairy" was thoroughly rebuilt and lengthened out twenty feet. Mr. Eveleth's new steamer is a fine propeller, seventy-five feet long and twenty feet beam. She has a very powerful engine and large steel boiler, is splendidly fitted up, and is one of the most comfortable and fastest boats on the lake. Her model and moulds were made by Charles Harrington, of Bath, and her machinery was built by James H. Paine, of Boston. The other new boat was built in Dover, taken by rail to Blanchard, and then hauled up to the lake. She is fifty-four feet long, and a beautiful model. Her cabin and other joiner work is alternate black walnut and pine, making a very handsome finish. Her engine was also built by Paine. She is owned jointly by Mr. Charles Sawyer, of the Lake House, and Capt. Samuel Cole, who commands her. She may be hired by excursion parties for trips to any part of the lake for any length of time desired, the price per day depending on the length of the trip. The guides are about equally divided into Yankees, Indians, and half-breeds, and can generally be engaged through the hotel proprietors, who know them all. They are well posted on all the country north of Moosehead, and can take you in any direction you may wish to go.

Those who stop at Greenville, at the foot of Moosehead Lake, have choice of a variety of excursions, either by water or land, which enables them to pass the time very pleasantly. They have, on the water, a choice of canoes, row-boats, or sail-boats, or one can hire either of the small steamers plying upon the lake.

To West Cove and back, a distance of four miles, is an easy paddle in a canoe, and shows one some pretty scenery.

To Moose Island and back, a distance of seven miles, is a nice sail in a row-boat, and introduces one to some charming views. The way lies among the little islands that cluster about the mouth of East Cove, and in full sight of Sandy Bay and the McFarland Place.

Squaw Brook is six miles from Greenville, and furnishes some excellent fishing, as does also Fitzgerald Pond, which lies a mile back from the lake, under the shadow of the mountain. With a canoe or light boat one can get up the stream connecting the pond with the lake. With a sail-boat and a good breeze this is a nice trip. Squaw Mountain, or "Big Squaw," as it is sometimes called to distinguish it from "Little Squaw," a lesser mountain which lies south of it, is a grand old peak that rises to a height of over four thousand feet, furnishing, from its summit, a panoramic view for miles in every direction. It is usually ascended by visiting Squaw Brook, which is navigable for a canoe for a mile from the lake, and then the rest of the distance is done on foot. There is some talk of cutting out a foot or bridle-path to the top, and if that is done, one can go up with much less fatigue than at present.

Sandy Bay, an excellent fishing ground, is just above the McFarland Place, on the eastern side of the lake. The distance from Greenville there and back is seven miles, and makes a nice excursion in a row or sail boat.

A trip to Beaver Creek, seven miles from Greenville, will enable one to pass an enjoyable day. Start early, and take a picnic dinner on shore.

The Kennebec Dam, at the outlet, is one of the greatest fishing resorts on Moosehead Lake, and is twelve miles from Greenville. One should visit it by either sail-boat or steamer. There is a hotel near the dam, where one can procure dinner, or stop over night, if they wish.

Deer Island is ten miles from Greenville, and is easily reached by steamer. There is a house and farm upon it near the steamboat wharf, and one can procure meals and lodgings at the house, if they wish to spend the night there. There are some pretty walks on the island.

Roach River, a splendid place for fly-fishing, is twenty miles distant from Greenville. It is reached by boat to Lilly Bay, twelve miles, and then by road, eight miles. Good accommodations may be found in the vicinity at the Roach-river Farm at reasonable prices.

There are a number of pleasant drives in the vicinity of Greenville, all over good roads.

A ride to the top of Indian Hill, three-quarters of a mile from the hotels, about an hour before sunset, will enable visitors to overlook the lake at the pleasantest time in the day; and the beautiful landscape spread out before them, bathed in the departing rays of sunlight, will well repay them for the time spent. The many mountains in the vicinity also appear to the best advantage at this time, robed as they are in violet and purple.

Whitcomb Stream is a small brook, a mile from the hotels, on the lake road, that furnishes good fishing during spring and early summer. It is a pleasant walk to it.

Gerrish Pond, a small piece of water, two miles distant from the hotels, offers good fishing in summer. It is within easy walking or riding distance, over a good road, from which one can catch occasional glimpses of the lake.

Eagle Stream is two and a half miles from Greenville by road. It is one of the best trout-brooks in the vicinity of the hotels, and large strings of small trout are taken from it each season. Flowing, for the most part, through an open meadow, it affords excellent chances for casting a fly, as well as bait-fishing.

The Wilson Ponds, near Greenville, are a great fishing resort in summer, and attract large numbers of sportsmen to their beautiful shores. In July and August, when the fishing on the lake is dull, one can always obtain a good string of trout from either of these ponds. The larger sheet of water is three miles distant from the hotels, two of which are over an excellent carriage-road. The last mile crosses a farm, then descends through a pleasant woodland path to the lower pond.

Parties who ride usually leave their team at the farm, or send it back to the hotel. In the clearing on the back side of the farm- on a knoll overlooking the pond and the hills beyond, is a pretty little cottage, erected some four or five years ago by G. G. Gren- nell, Esq., of New York. He has shown excellent taste and a love of nature in selecting his location, and the attractions in the vicinity are sufficient to hold him captive here the entire summer.

The pond lies in a deep basin, surrounded by high mountains. Its shores are very irregular, and add to its attractive appearance. Its waters abound with trout, all of which are caught in deep water with bait. There are quite a large number of boats on the pond that may be hired for from fifty to seventy-five cents per day. At the boat-landing is a rude camp, offering a shelter to those who wish to spend a night at the pond.

A sail of two and a half miles across the lower pond, and then a walk of less than quarter of a mile, brings us to the Upper Wil- son, like its sister, enclosed by mountains. Persons should take two days to visit this pond, camping out one night, if they wish to make an enjoyable trip of it. There are boats on the upper pond belonging to the hotels.

A visit to the McFarlane Place, a large farm under excellent cultivation, gives one a pleasant ride over a very good road, that furnishes fine views of the lake for part of the distance. It is three miles and a half distant from the hotels, on the eastern shore of the lake. From the hill above the house one overlooks the lake for many miles, land and water being mingled in such confusion that one can scarcely tell where the first begins or the latter ends.

During the spring of 1879 a large house was erected on the McFarlane Place, to be used as a private club-house. It will accommodate from fifteen to twenty people, and will be well filled each summer by Mr. McFarlane's friends.

Wilson Stream, a good trout-brook, is three miles from the hotel in Greenville. The greater part of the distance lies over a good carriage-road, the last half-mile through a field, where one is obliged to walk. A short distance below the dam commences a series of rapids, cascades, and falls, that terminate in one perpen- dicular fall of about fifty feet, known as Hell-Gate Falls. A short distance above, the stream makes a sharp angle curving to the left, and sliding over an immense slate-ledge slippery with dark-green moss, flows for about forty feet in the shape of a cascade; beyond this it turns abruptly to the right, and without any sign of hesitation takes the final leap into the boiling caldron beneath. The width of the fall is about fifteen feet.

The banks of the stream for some distance above and below Hell-Gate are thickly wooded, and very precipitous. In a few places perpendicular ledges of a respectable height overhang the water. The romantic appearance of this place, its seclusiveness, its delightful shade, its beautiful ferns and mosses, the musical echo of the restless waters, all combine to make it a favorite haunt of the pleasure-seeker, and as a suitable spot for a picnic it cannot be surpassed.

Coffee-House Stream is about six miles from the hotels, as the Wilson, approached in the same manner, — part of the distance by team, and the remainder on foot. It furnishes excellent fishing, the smaller brook-trout being very plenty in its waters. A day is needed to make a trip to either of these brooks.

The ride round the Square, so called, gives one a drive of six miles, and presents fine scenery all the way. Leaving the hotels the route lies over the east road for two miles, then, turning to the left again, follows the road about three miles. At this point we make another turn to the left, near the Gerrish Pond, striking the home road, running nearly parallel with the lake.

From the hotels to West Cove is a distance by road of a little over a mile. It is a pleasant walk or ride over there, and near the further farm-house one obtains a glimpse of the lake, and a fine view of one of the Spencer Mountains. West Cove Brook empties into the lake here, and near the foot of it is an old dam.

The birch canoe is one of the most popular means of conveyance used on Moosehead Lake, and Theodore Winthrop has paid the following tribute to these graceful water craft: —

"Moosehead also provides vessels far dearer to the heart of the adventurous than anything driven by steam. Here, mayhap, will an untraveled traveler make his first acquaintance with the birch-bark canoe, and learn to call it by the affectionate diminutive 'Birch.' Earlier in life there was no love lost between him and whatever bore that name. Even now, if the untraveled one's first acquaintance be not distinguished by an unlucky ducking, so much the worse. The ducking must come. Caution must be learned by catastrophe. No one can ever know how unstable a thing is a birch canoe, unless he has felt it slide away from under his misplaced feet. Novices should take nude practice in empty birches, lest they spill themselves and the load of full ones, — a wondrous easy thing to do.

"A birch canoe is the right thing in the right place. Maine's rivers are violently impulsive and spasmodic in their running. Sometimes you have a foamy rapid, sometimes a broad shoal, sometimes a barricade of boulders with gleams of white water springing through or leaping over its rocks. Your boat for voyaging here must be stout enough to buffet the rapid, light enough to skim the shallow, agile enough to vault over, or lithe enough to skip through the barricade. Besides, sometimes the barricade becomes a compact wall, — a baffler, unless boat and boatman can circumvent it, — unless the nautical carriage can itself be carried around the obstacle, — can be picked up, shouldered, and made off with.

"A birch meets all these demands. It lies, light as a leaf, on whirlpooling surfaces. A tip of the paddle can turn it into the eddy beside the breaker. A check of the setting-pole can hold it steadfast on the brink of wreck. Where there is water enough to varnish the paddles, there it will glide. A birch thirty feet long, big enough for a trio and their traps, weighs only seventy-five pounds. When the rapid passes into a cataract, when the wall of rock across the stream is impregnable in front, it can be taken in the flank by an amphibious birch. The navigator lifts his canoe out of water and bonnets himself with it. He wears it on head and shoulders, around the impassable spot. Below the rough water, he gets into his elongated chapeau and floats away. Without such vessel, agile, elastic, imponderable, and transmutable, Androscoggin, Kennebec, and Penobscot would be no thoroughfares for human beings. Musquash might dabble, chips might drift, logs might turn somersets along their lonely current; but never voyager, gentle or bold, could speed through brilliant perils, gladdening the wilderness with shout and song.

"Maine's rivers must have birch canoes; Maine's woods, therefore, of course, provide birches. The white-birch, paper-birch, canoe-birch, grows large in moist spots near the stream where it is needed. Seen by the flicker of a camp-fire at night, they surround the instrusive traveler like ghosts of giant sentinels. Once, Indian tribes, with names that 'nobody can speak and nobody can spell,' roamed these forests. A stouter second growth of humanity has ousted them, save a few seedy ones, who gad about the land, and centre at Oldtown, their village near Bangor. These aborigines are the birch-builders. They detect by the river-side the tree barked with material for canoes. They strip it, and fashion an artistic vessel which civilization cannot better. Launched in the frail lightness of this, and speeding over foamy waters between forest solitudes, one discovers, as if he were the first to know it, the truest poetry of pioneer life."

The prices of birch canoes run from fifteen to forty dollars, according to size and style of finish. They are manufactured at Greenville during the winter, and at Mount Kineo during the summer months, and may be obtained at either of those places as well as at Oldtown. For rough work, however, we think a canvas canoe is preferable, as it will last longer and stand more abuse, and the difference between them in speed is very little. The first cost of a canvas, however, is more than that of a birch.

Distances from Greenville to Various Places.

Mile Island, 1 mile by water.

Ledge Island, 2 miles by water.

Moose Island, 3½ miles by water.

Squaw Brook, 6 miles by water, then to top of Squaw Mountain, 3 miles.

West Cove, by road, 1¼ miles, by water, 2 miles.

McFarland Place, 3½ miles by road, 3 miles by water.

Sandy Bay, 3½ miles by water. First-rate fishing-ground.

Grinnell's Place, by road, 2 miles.

Lower Wilson Pond, by road, 3 miles.

Upper Wilson Pond, 5½ miles by land and water. About five minutes' walk between the two ponds, both of which are well stocked with trout, and furnish excellent fishing in the summer season.

Gerrish Pond, by road, 2 miles. Good fishing here.

Wilson Stream, 3½ miles by road.

Eagle Stream, 2½ miles by road.

Hell-Gate Falls, on Wilson Stream, 6 miles. Ride 3 miles, walk the rest.

Coffee-house Stream, 6 miles. Ride 3 miles, walk the remainder.

Spencer Bay, 16 miles by water.

Lily Bay, 12 miles by water.

Deer Island, 10 miles by water.

Outlet, Kennebec Dam, 12 miles by water.

Beaver Creek, 7 miles by water.

Roach River, 20 miles; 12 by water, 8 by road. Furnishes some of the best fly-fishing in the lake region.

Whitcomb Stream, 1 mile by road. Excellent brook-fishing here.

Fitzgerald Pond, 7 miles by water.

Indian Hill, ¾ mile by road.

The "Gulf," 15 miles, across the Wilson Ponds and through the woods.

A telegraph line now runs from Bangor to the Mount Kineo House *via* Greenville, and there is an office at the latter place.

CHAPTER VI.

Up the Lake.— From Greenville to Mount Kineo.

At three o'clock, P.M. we leave Greenville on the fine new steamer "Governor Coburn," in charge of Capt. Thomas Robinson, an old resident of Greenville, and a courteous and efficient officer. As the steamer leaves the wharf, the lake in all its beauty stretches for miles before us, dotted with islands of all shapes and sizes. Half a mile from the wharf we notice a little indentation of the shore on our left, called Centre Cove. Threading our way among the cluster of smaller islands that lie at the entrance of East Cove we pass, on our left, Mile Island, a small, rocky islet, surmounted by a beacon, giving its location when under water in the spring. A delightful panorama of mountain scenery unrolls itself as we proceed. Squaw Mountain looms up grandly to the west, while in the far north one of the Spencer Twins, over four thousand feet above the sea level, displays its blue peak.

Passing Ledge Island on the right, the last of the smaller ones, two miles distant from Greenville, we notice Hosford's Point just ahead on our left, strongly resembling an island. Nearly opposite of this point, on the eastern shore, we catch a glimpse of the McFarland Place, three miles from Greenville, the private residence of a New York gentleman of wealth and refinement. We look off to the east into Sandy Bay, and then notice Moose Island, which lies to the left of our course on the western side of the lake. It is five miles from Greenville, has a large farm upon it, and is owned by John Cusac, who is by turns guide, farmer, and lumberman. The island is nearly two miles long, and contains about four hundred acres; all the land except what John has cleared up for his farm being thickly wooded. We next get a look at Squaw Bay, which lies off to the left of us.

A short distance farther on Burnt Jacket lifts up his sugar-loaf head, behind Goodrich's clearing on our right, while beyond we discern the narrows leading to Lily Bay. The steamers run through the narrows to Lily Bay, when the water is sufficiently high. At low water, generally after the first of September, they have to go around the upper end of Sugar Island, making ten or fifteen miles difference in their route. The lake at this point attains considerable width. Still farther east the Lily Bay range of mountains stretch away, their summits beautified by the flitting shadows of the clouds that move above them.

Deer and Sugar Islands claim our attention next, the first on our left, and the second on our right hand. These are the two largest islands in the lake, and both are thickly wooded, and still contain good timber.

Deer Island has about three thousand acres, and is owned by Aaron Capen. He tills a large farm upon it, and keeps a hotel — the Deer Island House — where summer boarders are accommodated. The island is about ten miles from Greenville, and offers a pleasant stopping-place in summer, the steamer landing here when desired.

Sugar Island is about seven miles from Greenville, and comprises some five thousand acres of land all in a wild state. The island is about five miles long, and belongs to Shaw Brothers, of Greenville, who purchased it a few years since, for seventeen thousand dollars.

Birch Island is a small island lying to the left of Sugar Island, and is eight miles from Greenville. It is a pretty spot, and is one of the few smaller islands that has retained its original growth beyond reach of the rise of water occasioned by the building of a dam at the outlet. Passing between Deer and Sugar Islands, we find the steamer in the broadest part of the lake, and Mount Kineo, which has hitherto been concealed from our gaze by the large wooded islands, bursts upon our view, and, from its peculiar shape, is immediately recognized by all on board. The hotel stands upon a point of the peninsula, a short distance from the base of this frowning pile of rock, and, being painted white, and so far away, it reminds one of a sea-gull nestling on the bosom of the lake.

Four miles west of us the Outlet House is just discernible. It stands on the lake shore near the Kennebec dam. The steamer runs in here when desired to leave or call for passengers. An extra fare is charged, as the place is some distance from the regular course of the boat. The hotel is kept by Henry I. Wilson, an old resident of the lake.

From the outlet across to the eastern shore of Spencer Bay is fourteen miles, — the broadest part of the lake.

Leaving Deer and Sugar Islands behind us, we obtain a fine view of the twin peaks of the Spencer Mountains, fifteen miles or more away. At the base of the most northerly is Spencer Pond, noted for its excellent fishing and duck-shooting. Its great distance from both Greenville and Kineo makes it a long trip to take, and only the more adventurous and those with plenty of time at their disposal visit the spot. Forty miles eastward, the seamed and scarred side of old Katahdin, the monarch of Maine, lifts its hoary head nearly six thousand feet above the sea.

We have now arrived at Hog Back and Sand Bar Islands, which are within five miles of the Mount Kineo House. Passing to the right of these, we notice on the western shore of the lake, Ed. Masterman's farm, and, a little way above it, John Masterman's place. Ed. is a son of John, who is an old trapper and hunter. Sand Bar Island is an island only in the spring when the lake is high. Then the steamer can cross the bar between the island and the main land, there being five or six feet of water over it. In the fall the bar is about a foot out of water, and Sand Bar becomes a peninsula instead of an island.

Just beyond the elder Masterman's place is the Lamb farm, and between this and the West Outlet is Dutton's clearing.

Spider Island is a small island, with three pines on it, near Hog Back.

After passing Sand Bar farm, we notice the West Outlet, the smaller of the two. By a strange freak of nature the lake has two outlets, which unite at Indian Pond, several miles below the lake.

Roach River, the outlet of a number of ponds of the same name, empties into Spencer Bay, about five miles from the narrows. It cannot be seen from the steamer's course.

Mount Kineo, the monarch of the lake, now confronts us, a bold promontory, whose precipitous sides rise eight hundred feet above the water, and awes us with its solemn grandeur.

A group of islands, known as the Moody Islands, attract our notice, as we pass them on our right. Sloop Island, a mass of rock, with a dead pine tree upon it, lies in close proximity.

The lake has now narrowed considerably, and, leaving the

islands behind us, we soon pass the Gull Rocks on our right, and enter the little cove, and run alongside the wharf, but a few rods from the hotel. Here our baggage is taken to the house by the well-known donkey-cart, "Kineo House Express," which is one of the institutions of Kineo, and we walk up to the house and enter into hospitable precinct, where we are cordially greeted by the polite and attentive host.

At Mount Kineo you do not enter the conventional country hotel, but a first-class house in every respect, that is second to none in the State. It accommodates, with the annex, between four and five hundred guests, and is under the management of Mr. O. A. Dennen, who devotes all his time to it, and with the happiest results, for everybody who has stopped here has always a good word to say for the hotel, and its jolly, good-natured manager. Some men are born with a peculiar genius for filling certain positions in life. Dennen found his vocation in hotel-keeping, and at Mount Kineo is the right man in the right place. The demands upon his time and patience, during the busy season, would frighten an ordinary man. But through all the hurry, and rush, and bustle, incidental to taking care of five hundred people away from home (many of the camping-out parties in the vicinity take their meals at the hotel), with innumerable wants and fancies, and with appetites like sharks, he preserves his smiling demeanor, and has a pleasant word for all. An excellent table and pleasant rooms are two of the leading features at the Mount Kineo House. The dining-room will seat about three hundred people. The house is heated by steam, lighted by gas, and has a steam elevator, and all modern conveniences.

The stains of travel removed from our person, we enter the pleasant dining-room, where the cravings of hunger soon fade away before the well-supplied tables, and having partaken of both an abundant and satisfactory supper we take a stroll about the hotel, scan the guests, enjoy the sunset and scenery while the light lasts, and finally retire to a pleasant room and comfortable bed, and secure a good night's rest.

A writer in the August (1875) number of "Harper's Magazine," who has visited Mount Kineo, says:—

"The great question on the morning after arrival is what to do. People have heard of Moosehead as a watering-place, and have come in order to be able to say that they have exhausted the pleasures of the lake. They don't fish or shoot; they can play billiards anywhere, and they pace up and down the piazzas after breakfast, anxiously studying the possibilities of enjoyment. The attempts of the average American at personal pleasure have often been dwelt upon. He makes hard work of it, and returns to his routine intensely satisfied with what God has given him. Here the variety is limited. There is no stable. You can walk, you can run, you can row, you can fish, you can climb the mountain, you can lie down and go to sleep, you can take a steamer and ride up and down the lake; but your real pleasure must come from yourself. Thus the prospect is not bright to the man or woman who has come to be entertained; you just have to take care of yourself, and make the best of it. At such a place women are like a flock of sheep, — one does what the others do, — and unattached women are in a miserable plight. The lone female is here lonely indeed. She can't fish, because it is not the respectable thing to do. Being paddled about in a canoe by a guide hasn't any romance, and the same may be said of mountain-climbing or anything else; but when young men bring their sisters, husbands their wives, and papas their daughters, it is a different thing, and the parties which are made up for a day's excursion in canoes to different points on the lake are charming and delightful. Bright women are interesting anywhere; and when people are thrown so much upon their own resources for enjoyment as they are here, their presence in these rambles into the forest, or in the recounting of the day's adventures at the hotel in the evening, makes the hours pass merrily by.

"The guests at Mount Kineo are generally agreeable and well-educated people, those whom it is a pleasure to know, and when you have stayed long enough to get acquainted, nothing can be more entertaining than the social enjoyments which mingle with the out-door sports. Your fishermen may be silent all day while casting his fly, but not so when he has laid his day's sport triumphantly upon the piazza, the envy of unlucky fishermen, and eaten his supper. The walks in the twilight upon the piazzas, the groups of friends clustered here and there, the peals of laughter from the adjoining rooms, the universal stir and movement of the place, the free intercourse of the guides with the sportsman,

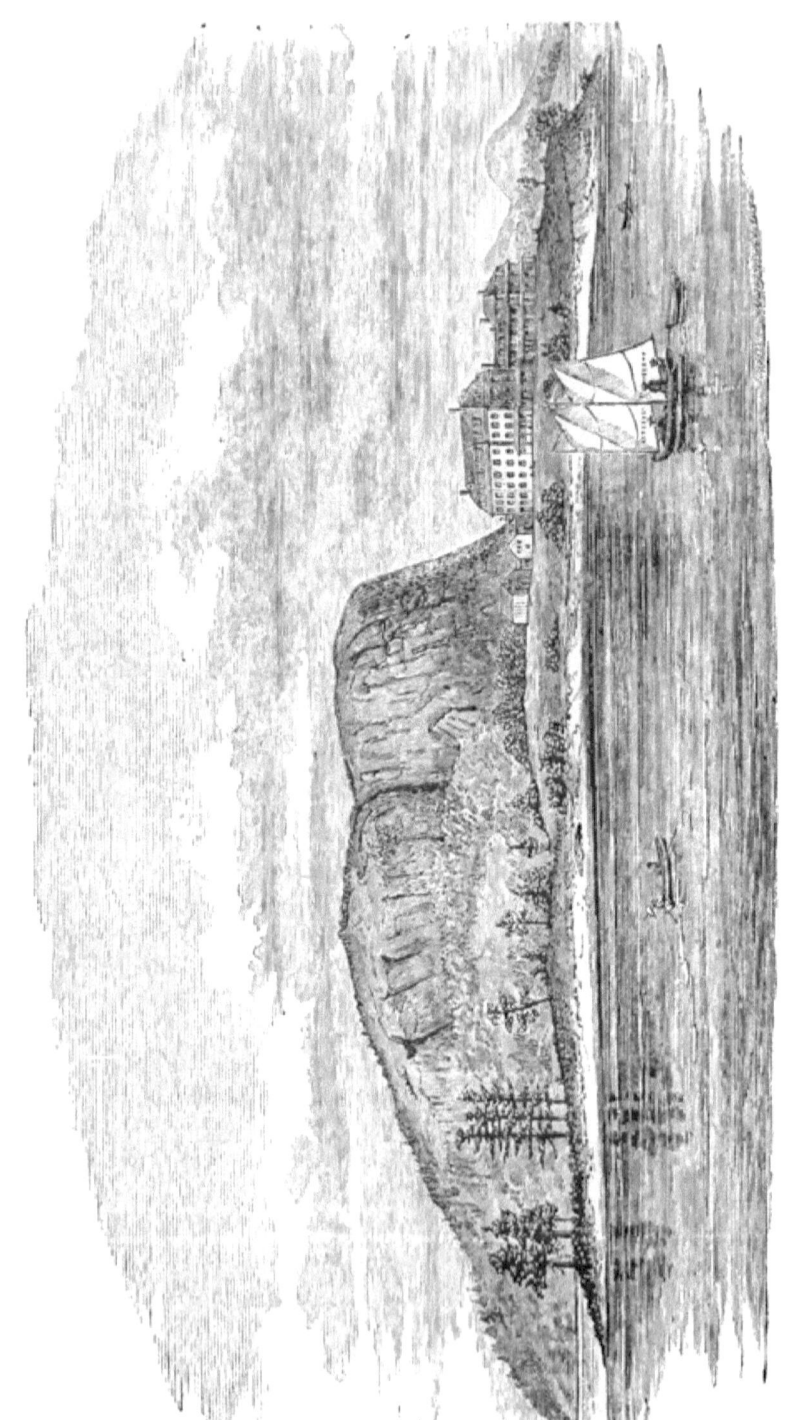

Mount Kineo, Moosehead Lake.

the admitted privilege of anybody speaking to anybody if he chooses to, the chattering at every available point, make a joyous life whose like can hardly elsewhere be found. It looked dismal at first to interest one's self in this lonely spot of the creation, with mountains and forests as your companions; but each day it is less so. The place grows upon you; the common feeling is, 'It is unlike any place I've been in before.' You eat more and more heartily as the days go on, and grow healthier and jollier; and the great world goes on without you, and you don't care if it does. It is impossible to bring your cares up here into the wilderness. Old men find that they can be young again, and young men have the spice and fun of recreation without dissipation. And so it happens that the people who have the capacity of enjoying themselves in close intercourse with nature come to Moosehead again and again, and those who have to be entertained come but once. The company is choice and of the best. In fact, the persons who love the woods, who are patient to fish and hunt, who feel that they are in their element when they are out-of-doors, who take to the woods as ducks take to water, are generally delightful company. They have something in reserve to talk about; you can't read them through like a newspaper at a sitting; they come direct from the original stock of mankind. It would have been to build a fool's castle to erect a hotel in the centre of Moosehead Lake for any other class of people.

"There is a great difference in sportsmen. Your city-bred man comes with any number of flies, with patent rod, with all the latest improvements. He dresses in corduroy and flannel, twines his extra flies around his hat-band, and tucks his trowsers into his huge boot-legs with the significant air of knowing what he is about. Quite another man is the genuine fisherman, whether from the city or living at the lake. He indulges in no superfluities, don't talk, goes straight for game. He has the best guides, the best canoes, the best fishing-ground. Generous as he may be in all things else, he is always selfish in fishing. He cannot endure a rival. Most of the guides understand all that can be known about fishing. It is one of the strong points in their profession. They invest but little in novelties. They are not confined to the fly. A stick, a hook, a worm, make their equipment, and you can always count on their success. Many a minister, apostolic with his rod if not in his commission, and many a lawyer, have the same tact in catching trout. They know how to do it. They can no more impart the skill to others than you can make the divining-rod work with unfitting hands. The birch skiffs shoot out from the Kineo pier at 9, A.M. or earlier, often wives and daughters accompanying the fishermen, and go to the famous fishing-pools, returning at night with the brilliantly spotted game, which is served for breakfast the next morning. The guides have wonderful skill in handling these birches in quick water and amidst heavy seas. They are Yankees, Indians, and half-breeds, intelligent, thoroughly wide-awake and interesting in all that relates to backwoods life, and capable of story-telling to any extent. The 'Day-Dream' takes parties to all points on the lake for fishing or pleasure, — to the Outlet, to Lily Bay, to the Socatean Stream, to the North-east or North-west Carry, to Spencer Stream, and to the North Bay, the east side of Kineo Cliff. Guides and fishermen rapidly assimilate in appearance as the days go on, till you can hardly tell the bronzed faces one from the other, and are forced to confess the truth of the saying that dress makes the man, — certainly makes the distinction which we too often ascribe to birth and fortune."

CHAPTER VII.

Kineo, its Legend, Hotel, Sights, Fishing, etc.

MOUNT KINEO itself is the chief centre of attraction at Moosehead Lake, and will doubtless always remain so. It is composed almost entirely of hornblende, presenting the largest mass of that material known to geologists, and is acknowledged by all who have visited it to be a great natural curiosity. It is doubtless rich in legendary romance; could one only unearth its history in bygone times, when the red man was the king of the forest and proud possessor of this vast domain.

Several years ago the following legend appeared in print, and we give it for the pleasure of our readers, although we have been unable to learn its authorship.

The Legend of Mount Kineo.

As one sails over the calm bosom of Moosehead Lake, and casts a glance towards Mount Kineo, it awakens a desire to gather what there is of legendary lore connected with this wonderful spot; and when one has climbed to the summit of this steep bluff, and gazes over the enchanting scenery before him, diversified by mountain, lake, and stream, the desire is heightened many fold, — a desire to know something of the beings who in days gone by had chased the moose and deer over these mountains and through these forests; who had paddled over these waters, and caught from them their supply of fish. Feeling thus, we gathered, from one and another, the main facts connected with the old Indian tale known as the legend of Kineo.

Some two centuries since, when all the north of Maine was one great forest, and before the "pale-face" had hardly thought of exploring it, there belonged to the tribe of Indians inhabiting this region an old chief named Mackæ. Reserved, morose, and repulsive, he abstained from mingling more than was necessary with other members of the tribes, and seldom engaged in any of their many expeditions except when matters of a decidedly hostile nature required it. He had taken to wife a squaw of marked beauty, and one whose nature was the very opposite of his own. While Maquaso, the wife, cheerfully cooked his fish and game, and performed those many menial duties which devolved upon the wife of a chief, he sat upon a pile of skins in his wigwam's corner without even a smile brightening his countenance.

Kinneho, their only son, was the centre of attraction for Maquaso. From the time of his birth she had watched over him with that instinctive affection common to the women of her race. With her own hands she had taught him the use of the bow and arrow, and had prepared him for the chase and the war-path. As the years passed, she saw her labors rewarded in this direction; for among all the braves of the tribe there was none swifter to lead in the chase, none more daring in battle, or more certain of achieving success over the savage foe. Among the warriors he was the leader, and their courage was wont to fail them in battle if Kinneho were not there. His foes feared him, and they dared not make expeditions in small companies, lest Kinneho should surprise and slay them in a hand-to-hand contest.

But a feeling of terrible sadness took possession of the proud spirit of Maquaso, when, in watching her idol, she found that he had inherited much of the sullen nature of his father.

While at home from the chase and the war-path he spent his time in solitary wanderings about the little Indian village, caring little for the scenes around him, and doing nothing in return for those favors which his mother was constantly bestowing upon him. This produced a feeling of alienation between mother and son.

The wigwam became a prison to Maquaso, life a burden. She was too proud to own her grief, but it was nevertheless apparent to all observers. One morning they found, by the side of a smouldering fire, a few articles of clothing which they knew to have been the possessions of Maquaso, but she herself was nowhere to be found.

Strong suspicion rested upon Kinneho. His weeping and lamentations were in vain, and the earnestness with which he prosecuted the search was not sufficient to prove to the tribe that Kinneho had not been the murderer of his mother.

About this time hostilities broke out between the Indians along the Piscataquis and those dwelling on the Androscoggin. A council of the leading men of the tribe was called. Kinneho met with them. Hitherto he had been the foremost to advise, and his advice had been most frequently acted upon. Now he was held in such disgrace that he was not permitted to speak, nor was he permitted to become one of the war-party which was then organized. He left the council, made a few hasty preparations, took his arrows and tomahawk, and silently stalked forth into the forest.

Hardly two moons had passed before the two tribes met in active warfare. The tribe of which Kinneho was a member sorely missed his able council, his wonderful daring, his bloody action. In the enemy's country it had suffered many surprises, and many times had been sadly repulsed. In a bloody encounter, which was likely to determine the result of the war, Kinneho's friends were greatly surprised to see him come suddenly upon the field of battle. With an unearthly yell he dashed upon the foe; one after another they fell before him, and shortly the enemy were driven from the field. Cheer after cheer for Kinneho rent the air. Gladly would they have borne him from the field in triumph, but he, without speaking a word to his old companions, silently left the field, and betook himself to the forest.

Nothing further was heard of Kinneho until it became noised abroad among the Piscataquis Indians that he had erected his wigwam on the summit of the mountain in Moosehead Lake, which still bears his name. Of savage disposition, and of mighty power in a hand-to-hand contest, the Indians gave him a wide berth. As they looked towards the ragged crag by night and saw the blaze of his camp-fire, or saw the smoke wreathing upwards by day, a sort of mystic awe took possession of their minds, and they shrank from nearing his solitary abode. Superstitious traditions still lingered in the minds of the tribe in regard to the mountain, and so Kinneho was left to himself as if he had been superhuman.

To the south of Kineo is Squaw Mountain. While Kinneho had looked towards it by night, his eagle eye had discovered upon its side a bright light. Evening after evening it appeared, and burned until far into the night. Finally he decided to make an excursion

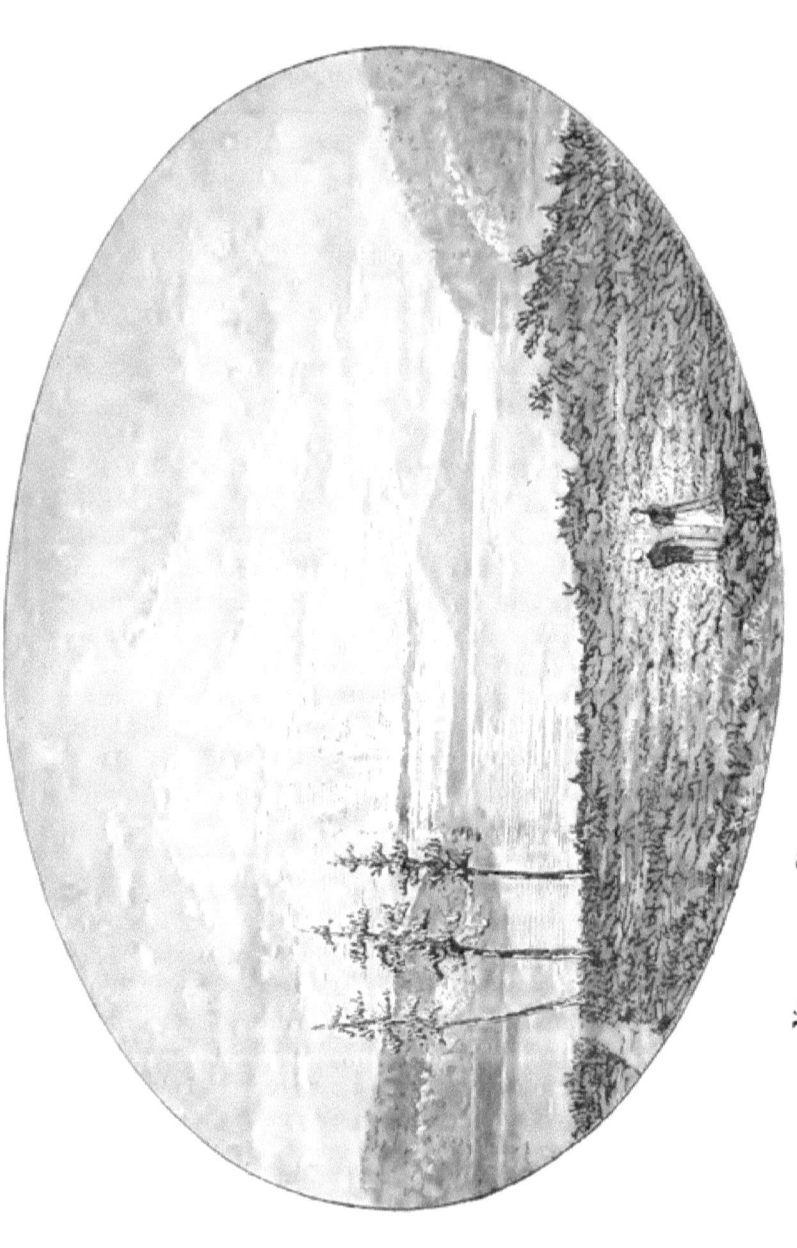

VIEW FROM PIAZZA OF MOUNT KINEO HOUSE, LOOKING WEST.

in that direction, and ascertain if possible whose fire it might be.

Over the lake and through the forest he journeyed, then up the side of the mountain, following in the direction of the light. At last he came upon a rude lodge, built of bark and skins.

Kinneho's heart beat wildly within him, as, bending over the fire, he saw the wasted form of his mother, Maquaso. Though he had known her in the days of her beauty, he did not fail to recognize, in the bent form and distorted features, his long-lost mother. He rushed forward and embraced her in his arms. She, overcome by his sudden appearance, would have sunk to the ground only for the strong arms which supported her. He hastily carried her to the lodge, bathed her face with water from a stream near by, and forced some nourishment between her lips; but all to no purpose. Her eyes had looked once more upon her son, only to close in death.

On the side of Squaw Mountain he fashioned a rude grave; heaped together a pile of stones to mark her resting-place. Each new moon he came to visit the lonely mound, and sprinkle it with tears.

In summer time a delicate white flower blooms in this forest, known as the Indian Pipe. The Indians affirm that this flower sprang from the tears of Kinneho. Wherever his tears fell, this flower is said to have appeared.

During many moons the camp-fire of Kinneho could be seen on the dark bluff. The Indians still superstitiously shunned the spot. Sometimes they crept through the forest to the shore, which is now called Pebble Beach; but when they looked upwards against the perpendicular bank of solid rock they imagined that the form of the Great Spirit was hovering over them. And they thought they heard his voice pouring down imprecations upon their heads. Sometimes, they say, Kinneho made long journeys through the forest to Mount Katahdin, whose snowy sides were plainly visible from his own mountain. During these times they missed his camp-fire by night, and his smoke by day; and then they would summon almost the requisite courage to visit the spot, when of a sudden it would again appear.

But at last the fire died out, never to be rekindled by the hand of Kinneho. In vain did they watch for its reappearance.

Stealthily they crept around to the northern side of the mountain, and up its sides, but they found not Kinneho. By the side of the spring which still bubbles up through the rocks they found a pair of moccasons; beside this a tomahawk and a few trinkets. Further on they found the traces of his fire, and the rocks charred and blackened, which even yet have not returned to their original color.

The Indians ever after believed that the mountain had opened and swallowed the form of Kinneho, and that he was doomed to remain in its bowels to the end of time. And so they called the mountain Kinneho, which in our day has been shortened to Kineo.

Such is the legend of Kineo. If any of our readers should visit the place (and we advise them to do so, if they wish to behold some of Maine's grandest scenery) they will find the tradition to be mainly as we have printed it.

The estate comprises some twelve hundred acres around the mountain, and all the small islands in the lake belong to it. It was bought by Mr. Winthrop W. Chenery, of Boston, the proprietor of the Highland Stock Farm, of Belmont, some twenty years ago. For several years he came here hunting and fishing, stopping at a small house, which soon grew by rapid additions into quite a fair-sized hotel. About ten years ago Mr. O. A. Dennen, the present superintendent, took charge of the property and the house. About six weeks after Mr. Dennen went to Kineo the hotel burned down, and between that time and 1870, when the new house was commenced, the accommodations were rather scant. This house was finished in 1874, but still proved inadequate for the increasing number of visitors; and in 1876 an annex, four stories high, was built that contained forty rooms. Again, in 1881, sixty new rooms were added, making the hotel more complete than ever before, and better able to take care of the larger number of people who came each year.

In the fall of 1882, however, the Mt. Kineo House was again destroyed by fire, and not only the hotel, but nearly every one of the out-buildings, the fire making almost a complete sweep. Undaunted by this great misfortune the owners put their shoulders to the wheel once more, and, in the spring of 1883, rebuilt the annex, the store, and several other buildings, and a limited number of people were cared for during the summer. In the fall, arrangements were perfected to again rebuild the Mt. Kineo House. A saw-mill was bought and erected near the premises, a large force of mechanics was set to work, and through the winter of 1883 and the spring of 1884 work was unceasingly pushed until the completion of the new hotel in July, which is equal to any in New England. It contains about two hundred rooms, the dining-room being a noble apartment, 51 × 110 feet, without pillar or post to mar its grand dimensions, and capable of comfortably seating four hundred people. The house is supplied with bath-rooms, electric bells, and all modern conveniences, heated by steam, and lighted throughout with gas. The rooms are large, light, and airy, reached by broad stairways or steam-elevator, and from the large windows command beautiful pictures of lake and forest, valley and mountain. The parlor, music, reception, play, reading, and dining rooms, hotel, telegraph, and post-offices, are on the lower floor.

Isolated as the Mount Kineo House is from the civilized world, the proprietor is compelled to run an extensive establishment, and keep on hand a heavy stock of supplies; hence the store, blacksmith-shop, and farm buildings,—unusual adjuncts to a hotel. A yoke of oxen, several horses, the little donkey, the children's pet (that has been upon the place for years), six cows, a large flock of sheep, numerous pigs and poultry, supply the motive-power for farm-work, and furnish all the fresh meat and chickens for table use. A large vegetable-garden furnishes the freshest and nicest of vegetables for the table in summer, and a sufficient crop of potatoes is raised to last an entire year. Besides the cultivated land around the house, a farm of forty acres has been cleared upon the northern end of the estate, with house and barn of its own, and large crops of various kinds are raised there. All the preserves and pickles used in the hotel are grown and put up upon the place. A small fleet of birch canoes and row-boats belong to the estate, and are let to summer visitors. The charge for canoes is twenty-five cents per day, and for row-boats from twenty-five to seventy-five cents per day, or three dollars by the week. A new steamer, the "Kineo," has been built this season.

The elegant little steam yacht "Day Dream" belongs to the house, and may be used by the guests for fishing or excursion parties for ten dollars per day, including the services of two men.

Capt. Daniel Brown has charge of the boat, and is a favorite with all of the *habitués* of Kineo; Joe Burnham, the engineer, is a worthy assistant of the captain, and a very pleasant fellow.

The house sets upon the end of the peninsula, and faces south, overlooking a large portion of the lake. The grounds are kept in good order, showing marks of excellent judgment and refined taste. Particular attention has been paid to drainage, and no epidemic will ever disturb the health of the patrons of Kineo. There are swings and croquet-grounds near the hotel, and lovers of base-ball have ample room to indulge in the national game. Cool and shady paths wind through the forest in different directions, furnishing romantic walks to various places of interest.

Leaving the hotel, we pass to the rear of the house and follow a path that runs along near the base of the mountain, furnishing us with grand and impressive views the entire way. Across field and pasture and forest we pursue our ramble, and after a few minutes' walk reach Cliff Beach, where we have a fine view of the "Cliff," as it frowns down upon us. Kineo Bay lies before us in all its beauty, and beyond North Bay stretches some fifteen or twenty miles away to the head of the lake. An hour may be spent very pleasantly at the Cliff. Table Rock, a favorite resort of the fly-fishermen, is but a short distance from here.

Having spent sufficient time at the Cliff, we follow along the shore of Kineo Bay, easterly, and in a few minutes reach Pebbly Beach, one of the greatest curiosities in the vicinity of the Mt. Kineo House. Several rough boulders make a divide between Cliff and Pebbly Beaches. Pebbly Beach is about a quarter of a mile long, and covered to a great depth with the handsomest pebbles we have ever seen, of every size, shape, and color. From the beach one has a magnificent view of the lake, and can be amused here for hours, either in examining and making a collection of the beautiful pebbles, or studying the charming scenery and listening to the enchanting music of the waves as they murmur and sing along the beach. From here also one obtains a view of a moose's neck and head, with branching horns and antlers, that appears on the face of the "Cliff," not far from Pulpit Rock. It can be seen to the best advantage on a bright, sunny day.

Just beyond Pebbly Beach is the Mystic Grotto. Down in a

little dell a mass of broken rock forms a natural grotto, a favorite resort for lovers of nature. Its entire seclusiveness adds to its attraction, and makes it a charming place to while away a leisure hour.

Leaving the grotto, we retrace our steps to Pebbly Beach, and there take a different path for our return. The way lies nearly the whole distance through the forest, where delicious shade and cool air are highly appreciated on a warm day. The path is good and easy to follow. About half way to the house we reach the Gold Mine, which is on the left-hand side of the path. It consists of a huge ledge of quartz rock that reaches to Pebbly Beach. Several years ago Mr. Chenery did some blasting here, and had the rock assayed, which yielded ten dollars' worth of gold to the ton. From the gold obtained he had a small pin manufactured. At some future time no doubt the mine will be further developed.

As we come out from the woods, in sight of the hotel, two little bark shanties attract our attention. These are the lodges of an Indian family of the Tomar tribe of Canada. Here they live the greater portion of the season, making canoes, baskets, and other knick-knacks from birch bark, which in summer they readily dispose of to the strangers who visit Kineo.

From Indian Lodge the path lies on the top of a gravelly ridge, and a few moments' walk brings us to the hotel.

The DEVIL'S DELIGHT is a short distance from the hotel, on the south side of Mt. Kineo. A pleasant path leads to it. Here the mountain has succumbed to the ravages of time and storm; and great masses of the rock, loosened by the frosts of winter and the lightning shafts of summer, have been torn and rent asunder, and have fallen in inextricable confusion below, where they lie in every snape, the *débris* forming a hard road over which to travel.

One wishing to take a short walk will find it a pleasant stroll to go over the grounds in front of the house, or along the beach to the "Three Sisters," a group of pines on the western shore, offering an inviting shade, where you can lounge to your heart's content, watching the sparkling waves, the blue sky, and the towering mountains.

Boat Excursions.

The excursions one may make by boat from the Mt. Kineo House are almost unlimited, and we propose to mention only the more popular ones. We will commence with those nearest the hotel. On these water-trips one has choice of canoe, row-boat, or steamer.

Leaving Kineo directly after breakfast, and crossing to the western shore of the lake, we reach the mouth of Moose River, and, passing to the left of Muskrat Island, a pleasant sail of four miles brings us to Brassau Lake. Part of the distance on the river is through rapids that furnish many picturesque views. At the foot of the first rapids you reach in going up the river is a pretty wooded islet. This was christened "Gertrude Isle," by John A. Gardner, of Providence, R.I., Sept. 13, 1878, in honor of Mrs. G. The island is a favorite place for picnics. Eating our lunch at the lake, we return to Kineo in the afternoon, having spent an enjoyable day. There is excellent fishing at Brassau, and where one takes a day for the trip there is plenty of time to try the virtue of flies and rods. Misery Stream empties into Brassau Lake about a mile from Moose River, and furnishes excellent fishing. Little Brassau, a miniature lake, lies about three miles beyond its namesake, and is noted for the fishing and hunting in its vicinity.

Baker Brook empties into Moosehead about two miles above Moose River, on the same side of the lake. A trip to the brook from Kineo gives one a sail of eight miles, and furnishes an agreeable excursion for half a day.

Tomhegan Stream, six miles distant from Kineo, is a favorite place for excursions from the hotel, and a day is needed to enjoy the trip thoroughly. It is a pretty place, and if visitors wish to camp over night they will find many pleasant spots on which to pitch their tent.

One of the most beautiful streams that empty into Moosehead is the

Socatean River,

eight miles from Kineo. It is a narrow stream, its waters deep and dark, flowing, in an irregular course, between banks thickly wooded. Four miles from the lake are Socatean Falls, of which we give an illustration. Excursions to this river from Kineo are frequent during the summer, and we know of no more enjoyable one on the entire lake. One who is pressed for time, may, by the aid of the "Day Dream" and a canoe, visit all of these places in a day.

The Moody Islands, lying south of Kineo, and but two miles distant, furnish a pleasant half-day's excursion by row-boat or canoe.

The largest of these islands is a perfect gem. Its shores are very irregular, and on the north side is a pretty cave almost landlocked. The shores are divided into sand beaches, pebble beaches, and rough boulders. The island is quite thickly wooded, some of the lumber used in the construction of the hotel having been cut upon it, and offers several inviting spots for picnics. The island narrows up in the middle, until only a few feet wide, and somewhat resembles a pair of spectacles in shape. In the spring, when the water is high, it flows across the narrow strip of beach, making two islands. The island contains a great many beautiful mosses and wild flowers, and guests from the hotel frequently devote a day to its exploration, taking their dinner with them. The smaller Moody Island is a few rods south of the large one, and is partially wooded. On the back side of it the rock has peeled off in layers, leaving a perpendicular wall from two to eight feet high, and some rods in length. At the head of a little pebbly beach, at the western end of this island, is a large boulder known as Eagle Rock. The white gulls that are seen about the lake build their nests and raise their young on these islands.

One of the most pleasant and popular trips from Kineo is a sail to Kineo Bay. Leaving the hotel, our course lies around the point, following the shore, and passing Kineo landing and the farm; next we double Hardscrabble, a reef of rocks at the northwest corner of the shore; pursuing our way we round the eastern shore and enter Kineo Bay; here we visit Pulpit Rock and the Cliff, and make a landing on the side of the old mountain, whose lofty top projects several feet beyond us, overhanging the waters of the lake, black as night and of unknown depth. It is a place where visitors find a feeling of awe instinctively creeping over them, as they gaze at the majestic mountain above them, and at the dark pool beneath. Several slides on this side of the mountain have left a mass of broken and splintered rock at the water's edge, on which a few hardy trees struggle for an existence.

There is a remarkable echo here, the solid sides of the moun-

SOOATEAN FALLS.

[From *Harper's Magazine*

tain throwing back clear and distinct the least noise or sound. The "Day Dream" often runs in here to try her whistle, for the amusement of excursionists.

Cowan's Cove

is a little over two miles south-east of the Mount Kineo House, and is a charming place. The cove runs in from the lake about two miles. There is an island at the entrance known as Mutton Chop Island, a lovely place for a picnic. About half way to the head of the cove, another island, the smaller of the two, rises abruptly from the middle of the water, and is called Boulder Island, from the number of large boulders that are found upon it. Both of these islands are wooded, and one wishing to take dinner on either of them will find plenty of driftwood for fires. There is good fishing in this cove, and if you do not wish to take dinner away from the hotel half a day is ample for the excursion.

The West Outlet

is two miles south-west of the Mount Kineo House, and a trip to it forms a pleasant half-day's excursion. A short arm of the lake makes in here. The entrance is narrow and shallow; passing through you enter a small bay, circular in shape, and almost completely landlocked. There is a small island near the middle of the bay. The bottom here is very rocky, and furnishes good fishing. The water at the mouth of this outlet never freezes hard, and the steamers are anchored here in the fall when they go into winter quarters.

One of the prettiest trips that can be made on the "Day Dream" is that to the Kennebec Dam, at the East Outlet. The course lies down the lake from the hotel, past the Moody Islands, and Sloop Island, then between Sanbar and Hogback Islands, then by Spider, Snake, and Black Islands on the right, and Squaw Point on the left, reaching the wharf at the dam. There is excellent fishing anywhere in this vicinity. The river is quite wide, and about a mile below the dam are some picturesque rapids. An old road runs along the north bank of the river to Gooderich's farm, two miles beyond. It is a fair road to walk over; and after the first day of September one will find good partridge-shooting, as the cover in the vicinity is unusually fine.

On the right of the little beach, at the foot of Mount Kineo, is a large ledge that rises almost perpendicularly from the lake. Upon the southern side of this is the figure of an Indian chief, about eight or ten inches high, painted in a color resembling red ochre. This picture has been there for years, and neither time nor storms seem to have any effect upon it. It was no doubt the work of Indians many generations ago. Capt. Brown, of the "Day Dream," first discovered the painting.

For an excursion of several days, Spencer Pond offers many attractions. It is one of the remotest points on the lake, and its outlet, a mile and a half long, empties into Spencer Bay, fifteen miles from Kineo. Its shores are wild and marshy, and the vegetation about them partakes of a tropical character. It is an excellent fishing spot, and a favorite resort for ducks. Partridges are abundant in the vicinity. The bottom of the pond is muddy, and pond-lilies grow luxuriously in some parts of it.

Spencer Mountain,

about a mile distant, offers a chance for persons to try their muscle and courage in its ascent. It is difficult of access, and but few sportsmen have ever reached its summit. Old Ellis, a noted trapper, is said to have been the first white man to stand upon its top.

Little Spencer, a miniature pond, nestles among the hills a mile distant to the north, connected with the larger pond by a small brook.

The Roach Ponds are reached from Lily Bay, and several days are needed to visit them. Parties making this excursion can procure accommodations at Roach River Farm, and will find the present occupant a capital story-teller and an obliging host.

Ascent of Mount Kineo.

The ascent of Mount Kineo is easily made, and no one who visits the hotel thinks of leaving without climbing the mountain, if able to bear such a jaunt. One might as well visit Niagara and not go out to view the Falls.

A boat-ride of a mile brings us to Kineo landing, a small, gravelly beach on the western side of the mountain. Stepping from the boat we notice a sign-board, warning persons not to roll stones down the eastern side of the mountain, which overhangs Kineo Bay. This is to guard people who may be on the water below from accident; it is a very sensible precaution, and should be strictly observed by all who visit the top of the mountain.

The path leads from the beach up the base of the mountain, swinging off to the southern side and following the verge of the precipice to the summit; at times a safe distance away from it, at others uncomfortably near for timid persons, or those with weak nerves. In some places it is smooth, in others rough, but never very difficult. It will take from half an hour to an hour to reach the top, and ladies suitably dressed can go up as easily as gentlemen. In the depression between the two crests an ice-cold spring of sparkling water, pure and clear, bubbles up through the sand from beneath a mossy rock, and flows westward. Many, after their weary climb, assuage their thirst from this welcome gift of nature.

The toil of the ascent is scarcely noticed, so busily engaged are we in catching glimpses of the picture around us, which, like some dissolving view, changes with each onward step. Now we stop for a moment to scan the silvery lake, whose sparkling bosom is decked with islands of emerald green. Then we gaze in admiration upon the mountains miles away, whose summits, clear and well-defined, tower thousands of feet above the sea.

Onward we pursue our way, and finally reach the summit, the goal of our ambition. Here the scene, in all its wild beauty and majestic grandeur, bursts upon us. We stand in mute admiration, and catch the inspiration of the place. How can we describe it, when no pen can do it justice? The blue sky above us curtained with fleecy clouds; the distant mountains, some so far away that their outlines are scarcely perceptible; the sloping sides of nearer hills wooded to the top; a continuous forest, wild and dense, broken only by two or three small clearings within the whole range of our vision; northward, the lake ending against the sky, a line of tall trunks apparently forming a barrier to those who would penetrate the distant wilderness; southward, the lake gemmed with islands, and finally closed in by surrounding mountains, concealing from our view the country beyond. North Bay, the North-East and North-West Carries, Brassau Lake, Moose

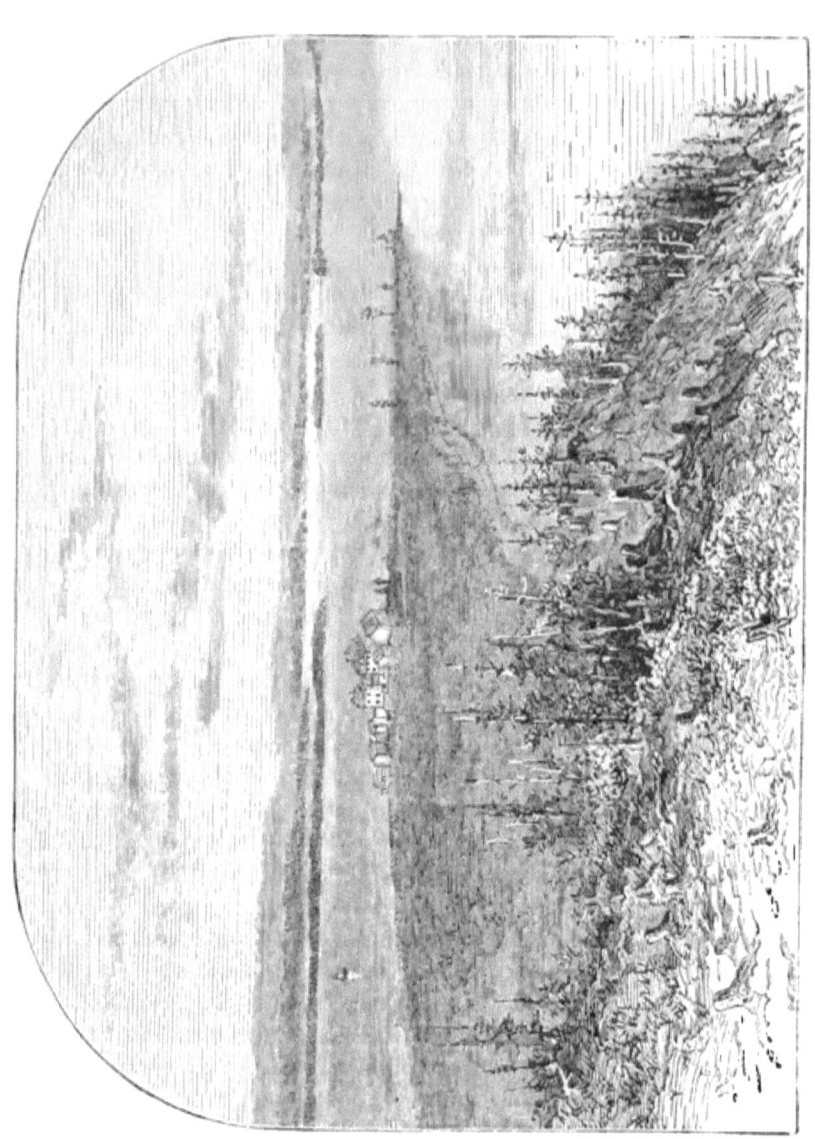

VIEW FROM MOUNT KINEO.

[From Harper's Magazine

River, the West and East Outlets, Lily Bay, Spencer Bay, Kineo Junior, the Twin Spencers, Mount Katahdin, the Lily Bay Range, Old Squaw, Bald Head, Misery Mountain, and many others are seen from the top of Kineo.

At several different places on its summit embryo monuments mark the spot where former visitors have attempted to leave some token of their presence.

If one has the nerve, and is foolhardy enough to make the attempt, he can crawl out upon the crumbling edge of the precipice that overhangs Kineo Bay, and drop a stone that will strike the water thirty feet from the base of the mountain. A single slip here would in a moment send a soul into eternity, — a single false step put one beyond the aid of man. It is a spot one naturally shrinks from, as if afraid some invisible spirit might hurl him into the abyss below. Far beneath, the screaming eagles guard their young among the frowning cliffs, and laugh to scorn any attempt at capture.

Many hours may be delightfully and profitably spent on Mt. Kineo, and we advise all who make the ascent to take lunch with them, and devote a day to it, confident that they will be well satisfied with the time spent in the trip. The descent of the mountain is a little easier than the ascent, and is made much quicker.

A friend of the writer, who made the ascent of Kineo some years ago, thus relates his experience: —

"After dinner a party of us attempted to scale the front of the precipice. It seems, when viewed from the house, to be but a few rods distant; but we found it to be nearly a mile. Its south and east sides are perpendicular, and varying from two to eleven hundred feet in height. It is composed of greenstone porphyry, much resembling flint, except in its color, which is light-green, and is the material from which most of the Indian arrow-heads are made. We attempted the ascent towards the west end, where the perpendicular is about four hundred and fifty feet. After a severe scramble we succeeded in getting up nearly to the top, when we were brought to a halt by a wall of rock, so compact that we could neither get our fingers or toes into it. Here was a fix. It was comparatively safe to climb up, for we could see what we were laying hold upon, although at times we were spread out face to the ledge, like a person being crucified, without room to turn either way; but the backing down was quite another thing. Backing down is always disagreeable; but in this instance it was particularly so. Above was but fifty feet to the top, but this distance was impassable. Below was four hundred feet, and a splendid chance to fall. After a hard scramble we succeeded in getting down with whole necks, which was more than I expected. Being determined not to give up the ascent of the mountain we returned to the house, procured a sail-boat, and went around by the lake to the north-west end; from this point, after a scramble of a mile and a half, we reached the summit, just previous to which we discovered, within a few feet of the brink of the precipice, a clear, beautiful spring of the most delicious water that I ever tasted. One of our party drank immoderately of it, stopping between each draught to comment upon the difference between it and the rusty Cochituate we were accustomed to drink in Boston.

"The view from the summit well repaid us for the trouble we had taken to get there. Far away to the north and south stretched the beautiful lake, broken into a thousand bays and inlets, and dotted with islands wooded to the water's edge. The country, as far as the eye could see, was covered with one vast, interminable forest in every direction, broken only by mountains and valleys, which, furrowed by the rays of the setting sun, just disappearing behind a long range of blue mountains, far in the hazy distance, formed a gorgeous spectacle, and one that I shall not soon forget.

"Southward could be seen the magnificent lake, now calm and glassy as a mirror, with every tint and hue of the sunset sky reflected from its bosom, stretching far away until lost by its windings among the islands and forest; while in the south-east stood the Spencer Mountains, like two brothers, side by side, and just far enough away to give them a rich, rosy tint; the contrast between them and the dark, heavy forest from which they arose was extremely beautiful.

"More to the northward and nearly east from us stood Mount Katahdin, solitary and alone in its noble grandeur, towering high above all others in the view; its summit seemed divided into two peaks, each appearing as if trying to outdo the other in height, its distance giving it a deep violet color. Nearer to us, but distant four or five miles, was another mountain about the height of

Kineo, and like all the others covered with forest, except the south part of its summit, which was a perpendicular precipice of two or three hundred feet. Below us lay the narrow neck of land connecting Mount Kineo with the eastern shore of the lake.

"Looking northward we again saw the lake stretching away in that direction for twenty miles; unlike the southern half it is clear of islands, except a few small ones near the western shore. The country to the northward of the lake is more even, and as far as could be seen with a glass it was covered with the same interminable forest; the predominance of evergreen in which imparts to the scene a dark, sombre effect, appearing strange to eyes unaccustomed to such a view.

"Turning to the westward our gaze is arrested by long ranges of mountains, their distances indicated by their different tints of color, varying from a delicate rosy hue to a deep blue, and sometimes gray; these being beautifully relieved by a flood of golden light from the setting sun, whose rays filled the whole western sky and gave to the landscape an appearance of enchantment. Nearer to us could be seen Moose River winding its way among the trees until it empties into the lake directly opposite Kineo. Still further west glowed the charming Brassau Lake like a sea of gold embosomed in the forest. Altogether the scene was beautiful beyond description. It was rendered more impressive by the strange silence that pervaded everything. None of the sounds one is accustomed to hear in a civilized region: no sound of voices, or the ring of the artisan's hammer; no bells, or the shrill scream of the locomotive, — nothing but silence everywhere. From the spot where we stood a descent of about fifty feet brought me to the brink of a precipice, seven hundred and fifty feet in height, perpendicular from the lake on the left and the forest on the right.

"I sat upon the brink of the cliff and amused myself with dropping stones over into the lake and noting the time of their descent. There was one in our party I could not induce to look over the brink. He complained of a curious morbid impulse or desire to jump over. I have heard others complain of the same sensation when standing upon high places. When I first looked over a feeling of awe crept over me at the dizzy height, but I had no disposition to jump over.

"We amused ourselves part of the time with rolling large stones over to the right, and listening to the crash as they fell into the forest. The ground at this place was covered with large mountain blueberries. We stowed away as many as our capacity would allow. While eating the berries we espied a birch canoe put off from the landing to bring us back to the house, and we started down to the lake, arriving at the shore just in season to meet our conveyance. The process of getting seated in a birch-canoe without getting spilled out is a very delicate one. We accomplished it, however, after several attempts, in a very successful manner for greenhorns, the guide said. Our tiny bark sped swiftly over the placid water, propelled by the strong arms of the guide, and we landed at the hotel just in season for supper, and well pleased with our ascent of Mount Kineo."

The Guides and Fishing.

At the Mt. Kineo House one can obtain the best of guides. They are practical woodsmen, good-natured, tough, and hardy, and will use their best endeavors to please. They can tell you all about the fishing and hunting, and show you to any place you may wish to visit.

Their terms are $3.00 per day while about the hotel, they boarding themselves. On river trips, that necessitate camping out, they have $3.00 per day and their board. They furnish canoe, tent, and cooking-utensils; the party engaging them finds the provisions. They are intelligent and wide-awake, capital story-tellers, successful hunters, and expert fishermen. They are very skilful in handling a canoe, and it is no more for them to pole up a bad rapid in a birch than it would be for an ordinary boatman to go over the same distance in dead water.

The fishing in the vicinity of Kineo is as good as in any part of the lake. Table Rock, near the end of the Cliff, is a great resort for fly-fishermen, and large quantities of trout are caught there in June and September. For deep-water fishing, a buoy is anchored out in the lake in sixty feet of water, half a mile west from the hotel. This spot is kept well-baited, to attract the fish. The fishing-parties fasten their boats to this buoy, and then indulge in the sport. The laker, the spotted brook-trout, and white fish, are all caught at this place. The laker is a species of trout, possessing a forked tail, with no red spots on the belly, and sometimes attains a weight of twenty-five or thirty pounds. The white fish averages a pound and a half in weight, although some have been caught double that weight, and are considered very nice eating. Although rather oily in taste, some prefer them to trout. When the fishermen return to the hotel it is customary to place the fish in pans on the piazza, where they can be seen by all, and a strong rivalry exists to see who will bring home the largest number.

Bait-fishing is best from April to June, deep-water fishing in July and the early part of August, and fly-fishing the last of August and through September. Both flies and bait are used at all seasons. The speckled brook trout are the best to eat, and the most gamy to catch, and vary in weight from a quarter of a pound to four or five pounds.

In addition to the fishing about Kineo, one can visit the Outlet, Moose River, Brassau Lake, Misery Stream, Baker Brook, Tomhegan, Socatean River, and many other places, from which they are almost certain to return with a good string of trout.

The Hunting.

Between the hotel and Kineo Bay there is a piece of woodland, about two miles long and a mile wide, that furnishes good cover for partridges, and many are found here through September and October. There is scarcely a day in the fall that some of these birds do not find their way to the hotel table, having passed through the skilful hands of the admirable cook that caters to the inner wants of the guests at Kineo, and prove a welcome addition to the bill of fare.

We make an extract from an article published in the August (1875) number of "Harper's Magazine," on Moosehead Lake, which pretty well covers the above heading. The only point in which we differ from the author of the extract below is in his locating the game at such a distance from Moosehead, as numbers of deer, caribou, and other game are shot each year in close proximity to the lake shore.

"Many people are disappointed with the hunting. They come expecting to find bears without searching for them, and to kill partridges by the dozen with a single charge of buck-shot. The game around the lake has been greatly killed off, and one must go long distances to find what he wishes. The real hunter goes where the game is, and the guides are chiefly engaged during the winter in hunting expeditions. They usually go in pairs, warmly dressed, but not burdened with equipments, and are often absent a month or six weeks from home. They carry a gun, an axe, a dipper, matches, a few pounds of hard bread, and make their tent each day at nightfall. One prepares logs for the camp-fire, while the other with his snow-shoes digs down to the ground, and makes a place eight feet square, which is filled with fir-boughs at the bottom and sides. A fire is built in the middle, and they lie down, one on each side, without more covering than the clothes worn during the day. The only caution is to keep your feet warm. Thus men, with the thermometer down to zero, go from Greenville down the West Branch to Ripogum's, and even over to Katahdin and up to Chamberlain Farm, in search of moose, bears, and caribou. They often strike a trail, and turn in at the logging-camps, where one is always sure of a generous welcome.

"The game back in the woods is abundant. Moose ten years ago were very plenty, but have been so much killed off that they are seldom found except around Katahdin and further north and west. They live in winter on browse and fir-boughs, in summer on blue-joint and lilies; are short-sighted and strong-scented, and are best shot near the streams and lakes. Bears are hunted chiefly in September and October. They feed on ants, berries, and honey-trees, prowl around the camps, and are found in the fall by the streams and on the burned lands. They are human enough to be exceedingly fond of rum and molasses, and are often trapped or shot in this way. Masterman, the hero of bear-shooting, says that he never had one face him yet. The black-cats live on hedgehogs, mice, and various small game, inhabit the roughest parts of the mountains, and are not easily trapped, often biting off their toes in order to escape. The beavers live together in families of from two to twelve. The Indians watch and shoot them at night. To catch them you have to set your trap in ten inches of water, so as to take their hind-legs. The musk-rats are taken in traps, or in their holes in the bank. The mink is chiefly caught in traps at dead-falls. The otter, furnishing the best fur, live on fish, and are generally trapped. Deer are numerous, live much like the moose, and are hunted in the same way. The caribou, a species of deer, are plenty, and very hard to kill.

They live principally on mosses and browse, and are still-hunted. For bird game, bald-eagles are plenty, but not often killed; partridges are numerous, and hunted in October; and black-duck shooting is good in September and October. The loons defy the skill of the hunter. They are the evil spirits of the lake. Their cry sounds like the mocking laughter of demons, and is heard at all times, day and night. They are about the size of a goose, but heavier, always in motion, and seldom caught alive. They are shot with a rifle, but are so quick in their movements that hardly one shot in a thousand takes effect. All this hunting is at your hand, if you are patient and can wait for it. It is obviously out of reach for those who spend but a week at the lake, and live at Mount Kineo. In the autumn sportsmen abound, and excursions with guides to all accessible points, until the end of October, are the order of the day. Even then life does not depart from the lake. The lumbermen succeed the sportsmen, and twelve hundred men pass up into the woods and back again to the towns below before the summer visitors come again. In these grand old forests Maine finds her chief source of wealth."

Distances from Mount Kineo House to places of interest.

Moose River, 2 miles by boat.
West Outlet, 2 " " "
Baker Brook, 4 " " "
Tomhegan, 6 " " "
Socatean, 8 " " "
Kennebec Dam, East Outlet, 8 miles by boat.
Brassau Lake, 6 miles by canoe.
Spencer Bay to Narrows, 9 miles by boat.
North-west Carry, 20 miles by boat.
North-east Carry, 20 " " "
Cliff, by boat, 6 miles.
Westerly Point, by boat, 1½ miles.
Cliff Beach, by path, 1 mile.
Indian Lodge, by path, ½ mile.
Echo Point, by path, 1½ miles.
Pebble Beach, by path, 1½ miles.
Gold Mine, by path, 1 mile.
Cliff Rock, by boat from Cliff Beach, ½ a mile.

Moody Islands, 2 miles, by boat.
Sand bar, 4 miles, by boat.
Summit of Mt. Kineo from landing, 1½ miles.
Devil's Delight, by path, 1 mile.
Mystic Grotto, by path, 1½ miles.
Cowan's Cove, by boat, 3 miles.
Duck Cove, by boat, 6 miles.
Hatching House, by path, 2 miles.
Hatching House, by boat, 6 miles.

During the spring of 1880 the proprietors of the Mount Kineo House built several bath-houses on the beach near the hotel, an improvement that was warmly commended by the guests, especially the women and children.

At the same time several miles of carriage-road were constructed, and one can now take a team at the hotel and pass an hour very pleasantly in driving about the vicinity.

Mr. Dennen has talked some of building a rough road, sufficiently good for buckboard travelling through the woods from the Mount Kineo House to the base of Spencer Mountain, a distance of about twelve miles. Should this ever be done, an excursion to the Spencer Mountain would be one of the most popular that could be made from the hotel, and hundreds would make the ascent of those sightly and symmetrical peaks. The long and arduous trip to be made now, before one even reaches the base of the mountains, deters nearly everybody from making the trial, and I believe only one lady has ever had the courage and determination to attempt it.

In October, 1879, Mrs. George H. Witherle, of Castine, Me., accompanied by her husband and a guide, made the ascent, and reached the top of the highest peak of the Spencer Mountains. She has the honor of being the first white woman who ever stood on the summit of Spencer Mountains, although several ladies have ascended Katahdin.

During the fall of 1879 Mr. Dennen made another effort to improve the attractiveness of Mount Kineo to visitors, by having a hatching-house for the propagation of trout and land-locked salmon erected on a small stream emptying into Kineo Bay, about two miles from the hotel. It was constructed under the superintendence of Henry O. Stanley, of Dixfield, Me. The building is sixteen feet by thirty feet, and contains eight troughs, eighteen feet in length by sixteen inches in width, capable of accommodating five hundred thousand eggs. There is also room to add more troughs if needed, and by the addition of wire-bottomed trays, such as are used at the United States Hatching Works at Grand Lake Stream, to double the capacity of the house. Mr. Dennen also had a small but comfortable house built on the opposite side of the stream from the Hatching Works for the use of Capt. Brown, who takes charge of the hatching during the winter. The grounds in the vicinity of the buildings have been improved, and the hatching-house and its surroundings will in future become a favorite resort for the visitors to Mount Kineo. A good path leads from the hotel to the hatching-house, and the walk is a pleasant one. As the buildings stand but a few rods from the lake shore, they can be reached easily by boat if one desires a water trip, although the distance by water is more than double the land route. Moosehead Lake will now not only have half a million trout eggs yearly hatched and turned into her waters, but will also add salmon to restock the exhausted waters of the Kennebec.

Many thousand of the speckled brook trout and land-locked salmon are turned out of the Mount Kineo Hatching-house each year, thus largely increasing the number of fish in the lake, and guaranteeing to fishermen a good catch in the future.

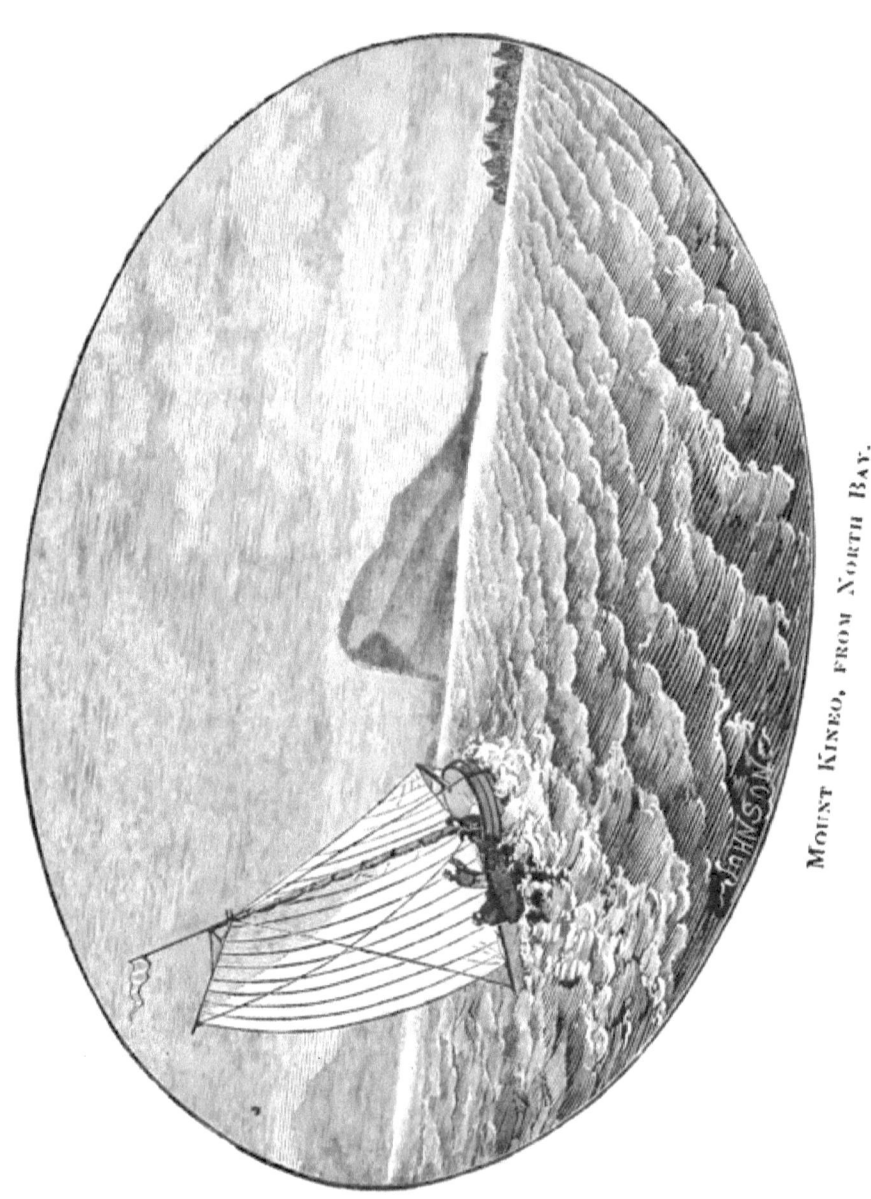

MOUNT KINEO, FROM NORTH BAY.

CHAPTER VIII.

Two Routes from Boston to Moosehead Lake via the Forks of the Kennebec and Moose River. — First Route via Oakland and North Anson.

Leave Boston in the morning at 9.00, via Eastern, or Boston and Maine Railroads, connecting at Portland with the Maine Central Railroad, the great thoroughfare for pleasure-travel through the State of Maine. The train for Oakland leaves Portland, via Lewiston, on arrival of trains from Boston, arriving at Oakland at 4.45 P.M.

At Oakland you change cars, taking the train over the SOMERSET RAILWAY for North Anson, twenty-five miles distant, which place you reach at 6.05 P.M. Baggage is checked through from Boston to North Anson.

If you have time to spare *en route*, you can spend a few days at Oakland very pleasantly. It is a pretty place, has some fine scenery, and contains a small but well-kept and comfortable hotel, the LAKE HOUSE, located on the main street, but a short distance from the railroad.

The Dunn Edge-Tool Company furnish the principal industry of the place, and their buildings are situated at the outlet of Lake Messalonskee, about a quarter of a mile from the depot. Their shops are very extensive, giving employment to one hundred and seventy-five persons, and they turn out one hundred and twenty-five dozen scythes and twenty dozen axes each working-day, besides tools of other descriptions. Water, of which they have an ample supply, furnishes the motive-power, and a walk through the long line of buildings is an interesting and instructive one. In one shop you can see the iron and steel in the rough, and trace it step by step through all the different processes, until it becomes a finely tempered axe or scythe, ready for market. J. Ayer, Esq., the President of the Somerset Railway, and R. B. Dunn, Esq., are the principal owners. The company also own another similar establishment at Fayette. W. M. Ayer, Esq., Superintendent of the Somerset Railway, is also connected with the Dunn Edge-Tool Company.

Messalonskee Lake is nine miles long and one mile wide, and contains several islands. It is a very pretty sheet of water, and offers strong inducements to those who like bathing, boating, and fishing. The little steam-launch Ina runs on the lake during the summer, and can be hired for excursions. Several miles of woodland border on the lake, offering charming places for picnic and camping-out parties.

Below the Edge-Tool Company's dam, Messalonskee Stream runs through a deep and precipitous gorge, forming heavy falls and rapids. The entire fall is sixty feet or more, in two nearly perpendicular pitches, the first about fifty feet and the second about twenty. This gorge or cañon is perhaps an eighth of a mile long, the banks being about seventy feet high at the upper end, and decreasing gradually to about three feet at the lower. The walls are formed of slate rock, and in some places they nearly overhang the water. Its average width is about forty feet. There is a pretty growth of mixed woods on each side of the stream. It is a charming spot, and formerly was much resorted to by picnic parties; but a few years ago a young lady fell into the rapids and was drowned, and now the place is rather shunned by such gatherings. Visitors would do well to be careful in visiting the falls and cascade, for a single careless step might place them beyond the reach of earthly aid.

There are many beautiful drives in the vicinity of Oakland, and good teams may be obtained at the hotel.

The train for North Anson leaves the station on arrival of the Maine Central from Portland, running through Oakland, Norridgewock, Old Point, Madison, and Anson, crossing the Kennebec River twice, introducing the traveller to some really fine scenery, and arrives at North Anson, the present terminus of the road, at 6.05 P.M. There is some talk of continuing the road to Solon within the next year or two, that being the original objective point.

In leaving Oakland the road rises by a heavy grade to the high land in Norridgewock; the rest of the distance the grades are quite easy. The road makes some sharp turns, disclosing, as it sweeps around the bends, lovely views of the river, with its frequent rapids and falls.

Norridgewock, one of the earliest settled towns in Maine, was once the shire town of Somerset County, but through the influence of ex-Gov. Coburn and brother the county seat was changed to Skowhegan, new buildings being erected in the latter town and presented to the county by the enterprising Coburns, to whom many places in Maine owe much of their prosperity. Norridgewock, while being one of the prettiest towns in Maine, has the additional charm of an interesting historical record in connection with the Indians. The Norridgewock tribe, an offshoot of the once powerful Abenahies, who at one time owned all the land from the Penobscot Valley to Salmon Falls River, formerly owned the lands in the vicinity of Norridgewock and Madison. Their encampment was near the river bank, in what is at present an open field, known by the Indian name of Old Point, and only a few miles above the present site of Norridgewock village. This field, however, is in the present town of Madison, which was once a part of Norridgewock.

The only remaining memento that now marks the spot where once clustered the wigwams of the "Norridgewogs" is a granite monument erected to the memory of Sebastian Râle, a French priest of the Jesuit order, who came among the Indians at Old Point about the beginning of the year 1689. This monument is in plain sight from the cars on the left side as you go to North Anson.

The priest learned their language, manners, and customs, and, having once obtained a controlling ascendancy over them, was not slow to use it by inciting the Indians against their English neighbors, and they harassed the settlers in that vicinity. This led to their destruction, and the death of the scheming and meddlesome fanatic at their head. On the 19th day of August, 1724, a detachment of four companies, consisting of two hundred and eight men, left Fort Richmond, under the guidance of three Mohawk Indians. The troops were commanded by Captains Moulton, Harmon, Bourne, and Bane. They worked their way up the Kennebec as far as Taconnet, where they left their boats with a guard of forty men, and the remainder proceeded up the river.

Arriving at Skowhegan, Harmon, with sixty men, crossed the stream at the great eddy, for the purpose of cutting off reinforcements from other tribes, while Moulton, after leaving ten men in Skowhegan to guard the baggage, proceeded with the remaining ninety-eight to Old Point. Marching cautiously through the woods, he reached the high lands overlooking the village on August 24th. He attacked the foe at once, and the Indians, taken by surprise, were all slaughtered, the priest among them. A very interesting account of early Norridgewock and this battle will be found in the second part of Whittier's poem of "Mogg Megone."

At Norridgewock the road crosses the Kennebec, which we see for the first time, and runs up to Madison, on the right bank of the river, where it crosses again and continues to North Anson, on the left side. The road runs mostly through cleared land, across which you obtain some fine views of the distant mountains towering up in the Dead River country; but occasionally it strikes a pretty piece of forest, and in some places it runs so near the river as almost to overhang it.

North Anson, a busy little town, is built on both sides of the Carabasset, a noisy stream, broken by rapids which empties into the Kennebec at this point. A fine view of Mount Abraham and the twin peaks of Mount Bigelow, that tower up to the west, may be had from the village. One can have supper here and go on to Solon the same evening, seven miles distant, or can stop here over night and leave for Solon the next morning by stage or private conveyance.

From North Anson to the Forks of the Kennebec is forty miles, and teams connect in the morning at Solon with the stage from Skowhegan, and go on. Returning, teams connect at Solon with stage from the Forks, arriving in North Anson in time for the morning train for Oakland. Fare from Oakland to North Anson is $1.00; from North Anson to Solon, 50 cents. One can procure a team at reasonable rates to carry them from North Anson to the Forks the same night.

To Dead River.

Stages leave North Anson daily on arrival of train, and reach North New Portland, eight miles distant, in time for supper at the DIRIGO HOUSE, Viles Brothers, proprietors, where you stop over night. Leaving North New Portland the next morning, a ride of twelve miles brings you to Lexington, where there is a good hotel. The stage only stops here long enough to change the mails. Beyond the village the road enters the woods, running over high land, and thence through a wild and romantic pass in the mountains to Dead River, a distance of ten miles, arriving at the PARSONS HOUSE, S. A. Parsons, proprietor, in time for dinner.

This hotel is pleasantly situated near the river, and has accommodations for seventy-five people. The rooms are well furnished, and the table excellent. There is a good livery stable connected with the house, and teams of all descriptions can be procured.

A good road runs through the woods from Parsons' hotel to Carry Pond, four miles distant, where is some of the best trout-fishing in the State. All kinds of wild game are thick in this vicinity, including moose and bears. Guides, canoes, and provisions can be obtained in the village, for camping-out trips, and as this place is off the beaten track of sportsmen, good hunting and fishing may be found with but slight trouble, and within short distances of the village.

A stage leaves Parsons' hotel three times a week for Eustis, seventeen miles distant, a pretty little village, having two good hotels, situated in close proximity to excellent fishing and hunting grounds.

The stage fare from North Anson to Dead River is $2.25, and from Dead River to Eustis, $1.25.

Second Route, via Waterville and Skowhegan.

Between Portland and Waterville one has choice of two routes (see Chapter III.), the two trains arriving at Waterville only five minutes apart. A through car runs from Portland to Skowhegan over both routes. The train from Skowhegan leaves Waterville at 4.55 P.M., or on arrival of the morning trains from Boston, reaching Skowhegan, nineteen miles distant, at 6.00. The road follows the west bank of the Kennebec, crossing the river at Skowhegan village, over a high bridge, from which one gazes down into the yawning chasm below on a mass of foaming rapids. The ride up the river is very pleasant, the stream being in sight a good part of the way. Fairfield is the first station after leaving

Hotel Haselton, Skowhegan, Maine.

Waterville; then comes Somerset Mills, Pishon's Ferry, and Skowhegan.

The night train from Boston fails by an hour to connect with the stage. But where there are six persons on board who are going up the river the stage will wait for them, if the proprietors are previously notified.

Skowhegan is a beautiful and thriving town, and has a large lumbering interest. There are many pleasant drives in the vicinity, and the falls in the Kennebec, above the bridge, are one of the principal attractions. Ex-Governor Coburn is one of the wealthiest men in the place, and has done much towards building it up. A small steam-launch runs on the river above the falls, making three trips a day, each way, between Skowhegan and Norridgewock, five miles. The town rejoices in a first-class hotel, the HOTEL HESELTON, but a stone's throw from the depot, containing one hundred nicely furnished rooms, besides billiard-room and dance-hall. A well-supplied table, with the best the market affords, is one of the features of the establishment, and the proprietor, Mr. F. B. Heselton, spares no pains to make the visits of his guests pleasant. A large livery-stable is connected with the house, and one can hire teams of any description.

From Skowhegan to the Forks of the Kennebec, forty-six miles, there is an excellent stage-line, owned and operated by E. G. Coffin, who runs first-class stages each way, daily, excepting Sunday. He has two excellent and careful drivers, I. S. Young and Charles Moore, who, besides being good whips, are very agreeable story-tellers.

The stage leaves the Hotel Heselton at seven o'clock in the morning, stopping for dinner at Bingham, and reaching the Forks at five o'clock. The road is good the entire distance. The first three miles is up hill, and by looking back you obtain a fine view of the village left behind. Once on top of the hill you will notice Madison Pond to the right, four miles from Skowhegan. This pond is a beautiful sheet of water, covering about two thousand acres, and is well stocked with several kinds of trout. There are sail and row boats on this lake that may be hired of W. D. Hayden, whose house stands by the stage-road, but a short distance from the pond. Visitors to Skowhegan will find a drive to the pond and back a pleasant way of spending a day. Passing through Madison, this pond is in sight for several miles. Between Madison and Solon you pass over Robbins Hill, ten miles from Skowhegan, and from this sightly elevation you have one of the finest views to be obtained on the entire route. Mountain after mountain sweeps upward all about you, Moxie Mountain being prominent in the north. Fifteen miles from Skowhegan you reach Solon village, a charming little place, and here you catch sight of the river, which you have not seen before since you started, for while you drove north, the river made a bend to the west. The stage stops a few moments at the Carratunk House, a large and comfortable hotel, kept by J. H. Gray. Falls Brook, a small, swift stream, runs through the centre of the village and empties into the Kennebec. Carratunk Falls, half a mile from the hotel, are well worth seeing. There is good fishing in this vicinity, and the village is a pleasant place for people to pass a few weeks in summer. From here to the Forks the Kennebec is in sight all the way on your left, the road following it quite closely. In the early summer, when the logs are floating down stream, and tumbling over the rapids and falls, followed by the river-drivers, some in batteaux, and others along the shore on foot, the picture is lively and animated.

From Solon to Bingham, eight miles, the scenery is very fine; and, indeed, it improves with each mile as you ascend the river. Along this distance are some very good farms. Reaching Bingham, twenty-three miles from Skowhegan, the stage leaves you at the STAGE HOUSE, the largest of the two hotels, where you procure a good dinner, for which you are well prepared after your morning's drive. This house is kept by Mr. John Frain, a wide-awake and attentive landlord, who will look carefully after your wants should you sojourn with him for a while. There are good fishing and hunting in this vicinity, and guides may be obtained at reasonable rates. The Austin Stream, flowing through this village to the Kennebec, is well stocked with trout.

After dinner you leave Bingham, which, by the way, is the terminus of the telegraph line, behind, and pursue your journey northward. Above Bingham the hills rapidly attain the dignity of mountains, and approach nearer to the river, leaving only a narrow valley. A chain of mountains run from Bingham to the Forks, on either side of the river, and the stage rattles along their base, there being in many places barely room for the road between the river and mountains. The river in this vicinity is more crooked, and as the stage follows its curves, now through some piece of woods, and then across "dug-ways" on the very edge of the bank, beautiful changes in the landscape appear every moment. At some of these "dug-ways" a wooden rampart of logs had to be built on the side next the river, before the road, narrow as it is, could be constructed. An exhilarating feeling of excitement takes possession of you as you are swung around the first of these high curves, the horses on the gallop; but several repetitions lessens the novelty of the situation, and it finally becomes an old story.

Four miles from Bingham village you pass Baker Mountain on the right. Here you will notice some holes in the side of the mountain, made by New York parties, who wasted time and money digging here for gold in 1852. It is said they took out some quartz that assayed forty dollars to the ton; and parties living in the vicinity claim that the mountain is rich in other minerals, if not in gold. Iron ore is plainly to be seen from the road.

Eight miles from Bingham village you reach CARNEY'S HOTEL, a popular resort for sportsmen, standing a few feet back from the road, at the base of a mountain. There is first-rate sporting in this vicinity, both with rod and gun, and Mr. Carney can furnish guides. He is also well acquainted with the country himself, and occasionally takes a tramp with those who stop at his house. Gold has been found in a small stream that runs near the hotel, and this part of the State may one day be as well known to miners as the Blue Hill district. Pleasant Ridge Ponds, and Carrying Place Ponds, both great fishing resorts, are only a few miles from Carney's. A short distance above the hotel the driver will point out to you, on the opposite side of the river, a level plateau, where Arnold's army encamped during the wearisome march to Canada in the winter of 1775. One of his men died at this place, and was buried near the river, a simple stone marking the spot. From here Arnold went across to the Carrying Place Ponds, which he crossed to Dead River, camping there some time, and then proceeded up the north branch, through Chain Ponds, into Canada.

Passing through Moscow, the last incorporated town in this direction, you reach the little village of Carratunk, crossing Pleasant Pond Stream, that empties into the Kennebec. This stream is the outlet of Pleasant Pond, one of the prettiest sheets of water in Maine. The pond, where there is a small settlement, is three miles from the river, and is reached by a good road. It is nestled in among high mountains that nearly surround it. The bottom of the pond is covered with white sand, and so clear and limpid is the water, that in some places, where it is eighty feet deep, you can see small pebbles as plainly as if they were in the bed of a shallow brook. The trout taken here are of a peculiar color, and very delicate flavor, and there are plenty of them. A road runs from the head of the pond to Mosquito Pond, four miles beyond.

From Carratunk to the Forks it is nine miles, the country growing wilder as you proceed. The greater part of the way the road is dug from the side of the mountain, and sometimes you have the towering pines on one side of you and the rushing river on the other, and both so near that you can almost reach out with either hand and touch them. In some places the road literally overhangs the river, and should anything happen to your team, at such a point, you would be sure of a ducking, if nothing worse. But the entire distance from Skowhegan to the Forks the road-bed is good, and the scenery is delightful. Skilful drivers, replete with good stories, add to the pleasures of the drive; and when you are set down at the FORKS HOTEL, you will agree with me in saying that you have had the pleasantest ride you ever took in your life. You will also be agreeably surprised to find such a hotel as you see here, way up in the woods. The house was built in 1875 by Ex-Governor Coburn, and Mrs. Joseph Clark is the present proprietor. There are but few hotels in the State that will surpass it for size, comfort, and convenience. The rooms are large, and handsomely furnished, the parlor containing a nice piano. Water is carried to each of the three flats, and the house contains modern conveniences, unlooked for in such a place. The hotel stands on the bank of the East Branch (the main Kennebec), and in sight of the West Branch (Dead River), and the rooms all command fine views. The two branches unite a short distance below the hotel; and a little way below the Forks our artist made the sketch, an engraving of which graces the following page. This house has accommodations for one hundred guests, and it is almost useless to say that Mrs. Clark's table is unexceptionable. During their season, fish and game are served on the table in abundance. The Forks are the centre of one of the greatest sporting regions of the State, and the scenery in the vicinity is charming. Mrs. Clark can supply plenty of guides, at reasonable prices, who know the country thoroughly, and who can furnish you with good sport. Trout have been taken in the East Branch, but a few rods from the hotel, weighing as high as three pounds.

Moxie Falls and Pond

are the great attractions to strangers visiting the Forks; the first, on account of its beauty; the second, for its excellent fishing. A ride or walk of three miles and you reach the falls, having a perpendicular drop of ninety-five feet. This is one of the grandest and highest cataracts in the State. The channel at the head of the falls is not over twenty feet wide, thus increasing the velocity of the water as it makes its final plunge over the ledges, to the boiling caldron beneath. The direct fall of the water has worn a deep hole in the rock below, and logs coming down the stream disappear from sight for several seconds after leaping the falls. By changing your position from point to point a great variety of views may be obtained. This is a splendid place to take trout at some seasons of the year.

Moxie Stream, on which the falls are located, empties into the East Branch, a mile or so above the hotel.

Moxie Pond, four miles above the falls, is about ten miles long and a mile wide, and is surrounded by a thick forest. On your way to it you pass another fall known as Rankin's Falls, about fifteen feet high. This pond is full of trout, and a fisherman was never known to leave it without fish if he tried to get them. At the dam at the outlet of the pond Frank Heald has a camp, and keeps a boat on the pond. The shores of the pond are wild and romantic, and offer many pretty spots for camping. A small stream, known as Baker Brook, empties into the head of the pond, and Mosquito, Alder, and Sandy Brooks, in the vicinity, furnish good fishing. Deer and caribou haunt the locality, and blueberries and cranberries are plenty about the shores of

The Forks of the Kennebec.

the pond. Two miles below the outlet there is a farm, where Tom Morris has a camp. From the Forks two roads run to the pond, one on each side of Moxie Stream. The one on the south side is the shortest, being only five miles. There are other streams and ponds in this vicinity, too numerous to mention, all furnishing good trout fishing, whose location may be learned from the guides.

From the Forks to Indian Pond is fifteen miles; thence ten miles to Moosehead Lake. The best road is on the left bank of the Kennebec.

On the return trip from the Forks the stage reaches Skowhegan in time to connect with the night train for Boston. Excursion tickets are now sold from Boston to the Forks and return for $13.00. From Portland and return, $10.00.

A stage-line runs from the forks to Hilton's, in Sandy-Bay Township, a distance of forty-five miles, where it connects with the Canada stage for St. Joseph, fifty-five miles beyond, where connection is made with the Quebec Central Railway for Point Levis, opposite Quebec.

Between the Forks and Adams', Parlin Pond, the stage runs daily, excepting Sunday, each way. Between Adams' and Hilton's, in Sandy Bay, the stage runs three times a week, leaving Adams' every Tuesday, Thursday, and Saturday, returning on Monday, Wednesday, and Friday.

At seven in the morning the stage starts for Moose River, and, bidding adieu to the Forks Hotel and its hospitable landlady, you resume your journey. Crossing the Kennebec, over a covered wooden bridge, the road follows the east bank of Dead River for a mile, and then turns sharply to the right, while the river sweeps to the left. In the next ten miles the road rises over eleven hundred feet; but the ascent is gradual, there being but few steep pitches. The land is rough and poor, and is better adapted to the lumberman than farmer. Occasionally you obtain good views of distant mountains, but the woods are so thick for several miles that you do not obtain many extended views. This ride through the woods is delightful; you see some excellent timber along the road, and cross several small streams. Five miles from the Forks you pass a small hotel, kept by E. G. Smith, and just beyond this house the road enters a forest that continues unbroken for the next ten miles, and in this distance you do not see a house. Although the land is rising all the time, the road runs up hill and down.

Reaching the top of Johnson Mountain you obtain a splendid view of Bald Mountain higher up on the left. As you near the limit of the woods you will notice an immense boulder on the right side of the road, weighing many tons. It has been split in two, probably by the action of the frost, leaving a gap about five feet wide. It is said that a number of years ago a man in Canada stole several hundred dollars in gold, and fled to Maine with it. Fearing detection, on his way through these woods he hid the money beneath this rock, intending to return when the excitement had passed, and recover it. In the meantime he was taken ill; and on his death-bed told the story of his guilt, and gave the location of the stolen money. Whether this story is true or false, it is evident that some one has believed it, as the earth has been dug over all around the rock; but I believe the hidden treasure has never yet been discovered.

Emerging from the woods, you catch sight of PARLIN POND, sixteen hundred and ten feet above tide-water. It is three miles long and about a mile wide, and is charmingly located, being surrounded by high mountains. It furnishes fine trout fishing. As you reach the pond you will notice a little patch of cleared land on the left side of the road. An old man, seventy years of age, formerly resided here summers, spending his winters at Moose River. He was accidentally drowned in the pond a few years ago, while fishing, by falling out of a canoe.

Midway of the pond, on the left of the road, is a farm, formerly owned by J. Bean. This property has been bought by Mr. A. F. Adams, one of the most enterprising men in this vicinity, who has built a new hotel on the site of the old house, and fitted it up in good shape, for the entertainment of sportsmen and tourists, and here you take dinner. This is one of the prettiest places I have ever seen. The location of the house is admirable, and from the piazza you obtain a wide-spread view, for many miles, of mountain and forest. The most prominent peaks in the vicinity are Bean Mountain and Hurricane Mountain; the summit of the latter honored by a fine trout pond. From the house to this pond is only six miles. Directly in front, but a few rods from the hotel, is the beautiful lakelet before spoken of. Mr. Adams thinks of putting a small steam-launch on the pond for the use of fishermen and tourists who stop with him.

A road runs from the dam, at the foot of Parlin Pond, down to Long Stream, then up to Long Pond. There is first-rate trout fishing at the dam at Parlin Pond; also at Long Pond. From the hotel to Long Pond is only six miles, with a good road or path all the way. Besides the bodies of water mentioned, there are other ponds and streams in this vicinity, well stocked with trout, that are known to Mr. Savage. There is also good shooting here in the fall. Guides may be hired for $1.50 per day.

The PARLIN POND HOUSE is well kept by Geo. W. Savage, the present proprietor, the rooms being neat and pleasant, and the table well supplied. There is a bowling-alley and croquet-ground near the house; also a livery-stable, supplied with horses and vehicles. Mr. Savage keeps boats and canoes on Parlin Pond, and will carry you back and forth in a team, if you do not wish to walk, without any charge; or if you want to fish up Moose River he will send you up on his stage, boat and all. He is one of the most pleasant and obliging landlords I have ever met.

The post-office at Parlin Pond is in the hotel, thus making it very convenient for those stopping at the house.

Leaving the Parlin Pond House after dinner, the stage conveys you to Moose River, in Holden Plantation, fifteen miles distant. Beyond the hotel the land rises, and a four miles' ride brings you to the top of a lofty eminence in Jackman-town, known as LOOK-OUT HILL, twenty miles from the Forks. The small cluster of buildings here, including the hotel and post-office, are owned mostly by Mr. Adams, of the Parlin Pond House. This hill is one of the prettiest and most sightly places on the road, and the landscape pictures offered here are very inviting. From Adams', the road for several miles is up hill and down, and then crosses a mountain known as Owl's Head. Most of the distance is through the woods. Climbing another hill, you leave the forest behind, and as you descend this last hill have a fine view of Moose River Valley, and the village; also the long range of mountains, fifteen miles away, that divide Maine from Canada. The land at Moose River is better than any you have seen since leaving Carratunk, and the farmers raise good crops.

You arrive at Moose River about three o'clock, and the stage leaves you at the COLBY HOUSE, kept by Mrs. Nancy Colby, a comfortable little hotel, standing close to the river, on the north bank. A new house is to be built here the present season.

If you wish to go beyond Moose River, keep your seat, while the stage continues on to Hilton's, in Sandy Bay Township, fifteen miles distant, which place you reach about six o'clock. Here you stop over night, at a good hotel, kept by Mr. A. F. Adams. The Canada stage leaves Sandy Bay for St. Joseph, Monday, Wednesday, and Friday, connecting with the Quebec Central Railway for Quebec, the following morning; returning leaves St. Joseph, Tuesday, Thursday, and Saturday mornings. The fare is $2.50 each way.

From Hilton's, Sandy Bay, to St. Georges, Canada, is thirty-two miles; stage fare, $1.50. At St. Georges is a good hotel, kept by Michael Mchail, located near the gold mines. At this house you take dinner. From St. Georges to St. Joseph is twenty-three miles; stage fare, $1.00. Stop over night, and take the cars next morning for Point Levi, opposite Quebec; distance, forty-five miles; time, about three hours; fare, $1.25.

The fare from the Forks to Adams is $1.25; to Moose River, $2.00; to Hilton's, Sandy Bay, $2.50. This road from Skowhegan is the regularly travelled highway from Maine to Canada, and is in first-rate condition the entire distance to St. Joseph. This is a delightful trip in summer, and you can make the tour to Quebec this way, returning by the Grand Trunk Railway, in five or six days.

Moose River Village

contains another small hotel besides the one mentioned, two stores, twenty or thirty houses, post-office and custom-house, the latter being in the Colby House. Guides, canoes, and provisions for camping out may be obtained here. This village is the centre of a large and wide-spread hunting and fishing region. As your route lies down the river, I will give you an idea of the country above. For this information I am indebted to Joseph A. Newton, a first-rate fellow and capital guide, a resident of Moose River Village. He is thoroughly posted on the country in this vicinity, as well as the Moosehead Lake Region, and his services can be

MOOSEHEAD LAKE AND VICINITY.

obtained at any time, when not engaged, for $2.00 per day. This price includes canoe and camp kit.

Leaving the Colby House, you paddle under the bridge and up Moose River for fifty rods, when you reach Wood Pond, six miles long. Turning to the left, you follow its eastern shore four miles, to the head of the pond. Pat Kenny has a farm and house here; also boats and canoes. He will act as guide, if you require one. Little Wood and Big Little Wood Ponds lie west of Wood Pond and are reached by a mile and a half carry from Wood Pond to Little Wood. Crossing Little Wood, you paddle up Wood Stream, a mile and a half, to Big Little Wood, two miles and a half long and a mile wide. A road runs from the head of this pond to the village, and one can visit it on foot, if preferable. There is good fishing in all these ponds, trout being plenty. From the head of Wood Pond you paddle a mile up the river, reaching Attean Pond, about seven miles long. It has a large number of islands, and is surrounded by a hard-wood forest. Its shores are very pretty. A good carry, a mile and a quarter long, runs from its western end to Holeb Pond. Crossing this pond, three miles long, you run down its outlet, Holeb Stream, one mile long, to Moose River. Or, if there is not water enough in the stream for a canoe, carry across this mile. From the mouth of Holeb Stream, down Moose River, to the Colby House is twenty-five miles, with only two short carries; that around Holeb Falls being half a mile long, and the second, at Attean Rips, only a few rods. Both the carries are on the right of the river going down. If you choose, you can go from the Colby House to the head waters of Moose River, some fifty miles, in a canoe, by making a few carries.

Leaving the comfortable hotel at Moose River bridge, you paddle down the river for several miles, when you reach Long Pond. The river is deep and there is not much of a current. The banks are low, and most of the land on either side has been cleared and cultivated. As you paddle out on the pond you will notice two farms on the left shore that, like almost everything else in this country, belong to the Coburns. Redman lives on the first, and Demo on the second. As you paddle down the lake, you catch glimpses of wooded mountains to the south. The shores of the lake are pretty, wooded most of the distance, and offer many

LONG POND OUTLET, MOOSE RIVER.
(From sketch by W. M. Todd.)

inducements to campers. Long Pond is nine miles long and from one-fourth of a mile to two miles wide, and contains several islands. It is irregular in shape, and the narrows almost cut it in two. On your way down you pass the Upper Churchill Stream, about two miles from Moose River, and the Lower Churchill, about three miles from the outlet. These streams empty into the pond on the northern side. Parlin Stream, the outlet of Parlin Pond, empties into Long Pond on the south side, about opposite of the Lower Churchill. There is good fishing in all these streams and in the pond. In the fall of 1879 a large dam was built at the outlet of Long Pond, raising the water several feet. The pond narrows up at the lower end, and the banks are high. From the dam down to Little Brassau is six miles, the stream being navigable for canoes. You will have to carry around the Rolling Dam, near Coburn's hay farm, and perhaps around Stony Brook Rapids also. A good road runs from the outlet of Long Pond, down the left bank of the river, to Little Brassau, and about a mile beyond. There are one or two wet places on it; but the most of the way it is dry walking. Continuing on from Little Brassau, three miles of good water bring you to the western shore of Brassau Lake. A mile below Little Brassau, you pass Tom Fletcher Brook, a good fishing-ground, on the left. This vicinity is also a favorite camping-ground. Brassau Stream, emptying into the head of the lake, and Misery Stream, at the foot, are both good trout streams. At the foot of the lake is a long sand beach, known as "Misery Sands."

From Moose River you cross the lake in a south-easterly direction, and four miles' paddling brings you to the outlet, near an old hay farm, about a mile from the foot of the lake. From the lake to Gertrude Island, a distance of about three miles, you will find some pretty lively water, there being rapids most of the way. Sam's Pitch and the Dam are the worst places, and unless you have a guide, or are an experienced canoeman, you will find it safer and pleasanter to let your canoe down with a rope, while you scramble along the rocks. From the island to the lake you have good water and a swift current. The distance is two miles. As you leave Moose River you will find shoal water, and you had better keep well over to the right. From the outlet to the Mount Kineo House is two miles, the hotel being in sight from the mouth of the river. If you reach the lake at night or in a fog, steer a due east course, and you will come out all right. An old tote road runs the entire distance from Brassau Lake to Moosehead Lake. It follows the north bank of the river, starting from near the outlet of Brassau, and coming out on Coburn's hay farm, opposite Mount Kineo. The distance this way from Moose River village to the Mount Kineo House is about thirty-three miles, and from Skowhegan one hundred and eight. This is by far the prettiest way of reaching the Mount Kineo House, although it takes longer than by the rail and stage routes. There is no difficulty at all in ladies going this way, several having made the trip already. Although there are seventy-five miles of staging, it is over one of the best and most picturesque roads in New England, and there is more of interest to be seen on the way than by any other route. The trip from Boston to Mount Kineo via the Forks and Moose River, can be made in three days, or you can be as much longer as you please. The time is not far distant when this will be one of the most popular routes to the Mount Kineo House and Moosehead Lake.

CHAPTER IX.

From Kineo to the Head of the Lake.

The steamer "Wm. Parker," Capt. Charles Robinson, makes regular trips from Greenville to the head of the lake, touching at Kineo every Tuesday and Friday. Charlie is a son of Captain Thomas, and a worthy "chip of the old block." Pleasant, agreeable, and efficient, it is a pleasure to sail with him. Leaving the steamboat wharf near the hotel, we round the point, and, studying the frowning peaks of old Kineo, as we sail along, suddenly discover a face in profile, on the edge of the middle cliff, at once grand and impressive. There it stands, as it has stood for ages, outlined sharp against the sky, bold and defiant, overlooking with calm dignity the intrusion of civilization upon its wild retreat. This Old Man of the Mountain is fully equal to that of Franconia or Dixville Notch, and is one of the greatest curiosities that Kineo possesses. The right location from which to see it is about half way between the point of the peninsula on which the hotel stands, and the little beach where you land to ascend the mountain. To our left on the western shore are two clearings, where two men, by the names of Caldor and Thompson, are redeeming farms from the wilderness. Moose River empties into the lake about opposite Mount Kineo, two miles from the hotel. Just above the river is the Coburn hay-farm. On our right, Westerly Point and Kineo Farm are noticed, and passing Hard Scrabble, a ledge of rock on the western shore of Kineo, we enter North Bay, which stretches away beyond us for a distance of nearly twenty miles, until apparently lost in the forest. So flat is the land at the North-east Carry, that from this distance the trees appear to rise directly from the water. A nearer approach dispels the illusion.

Farm Island, on our left, comprises about twelve hundred acres of wild woodland, and is owned by John Eveleth, of Greenville. Baker Brook, four miles, and Tomhegan Stream, six miles, from Kineo, empty into the lake on the western side. On our right, five miles above Kineo, is a clearing known as the Shaw Farm,

RAPIDS ON MOOSE RIVER, OUTLET OF BRASSAU LAKE.

In this vicinity, also, you will notice a mountain to the east, called Kineo Junior. As we get higher up the lake, its resemblance to Old Kineo is very striking. Steaming on, the boat passes Socatean River on our left, eight miles from Kineo. A short distance above, Socatean Point makes into the lake, and, a couple of miles beyond, Moose Brook enters the lake. Centre Island is passed on our left, and off on the eastern side of the lake are Big and Little Duck Coves. About half-way between Mount Kineo and the head of the lake we obtain a fine view of the Spencer Mountains, one of the prominent landmarks to the eastward, the nearest peak presenting an almost perpendicular wall of barren rock.

Above Moose Brook the shore makes a curve, forming W Point, and near this is W Farm. Beyond here an arm of the lake extends some distance into the wilderness, and at the head of it is the North-west Carry. Marsh Lane, an old guide and lumberman, lived here for many years, and his shanty still stands. Marsh is dead — peace to his ashes! — but his son Ferdinand, a smart, energetic fellow, has erected a comfortable camp here, where good entertainment is offered to sportsmen, and also keeps a team to haul canoes and supplies across the carry, which is a mile and a half long.

Carry Brook empties into the lake near Lane's, and parties going up the West Branch usually paddle up the brook a distance of three miles, where they make a landing, and only have a few rods to carry before striking Penobscot. Williams Stream enters the lake just above W Farm.

In coming out from the North-west Carry, Mount Kineo looms up to the south-east, while Kineo Junior is directly before us, and one cannot help but noticing the similarity of appearance between the two. On the back side Kineo Junior overhangs the land just as its prototype does the water. Continuing on our course we notice an island near the mouth of the North-west Arm, of considerable size, that has never been named. We can now discern the sand beach at the head of the lake, and the long pier running out for several hundred yards into the water, where the steamer stops. A few moments more, and we arrive at the North-east Carry, where steamboat navigation ceases.

Parties going down the West Branch stop here, and cross the Carry, which is two miles and forty rods long. Simeon Savage

Ox-Railroad Train leaving the Station.
(From sketch by W. M. Tidd.)

has a house here for the accommodation of sportsmen, and keeps a team to haul baggage and stores across to the river.

Years ago there used to be an ox-railroad on this carry, built by Major Strickland, a prominent lumber operator of Bangor. Although partially destroyed by fire, traces of it are still visible, and in some places the rails and cross-ties still remain as originally laid down. A friend of the author, who visited Moosehead when this railroad was in operation, and to whom we are indebted for our engraving, thus speaks of it: —

"We arrived at the head of the lake at twelve o'clock, noon, having run twenty miles, nearly, in a straight line with a free wind. The water around the north shore is very shallow, and the bottom is sandy. Here is an old pier built five hundred feet out into the lake, to accommodate the steamer in landing stores for the lumbermen. On the top of this pier is a wooden railroad, built of logs, the top and outside being hewn to guide the wheels. This road is two miles in length, and has its other terminus at the west branch of the Penobscot River, where there is a shanty which is a depot of supplies for the lumbermen, who go into the woods in the fall. The proprietor of this establishment has a primitive sort of a car, with wooden wheels, with which he conveys freight, and passengers, if they are not in a hurry. The motive-power upon this road consists of a single ox, or, as the conductor and engineer say, 'bullgine,' who travels upon a flooring laid of poles upon the cross-ties between the rails. The 'bullgine' is attached to the car by means of a yoke and two poles serving as shafts, with hooks at their ends. The style of the depot at this end of the road will be understood by the sketch. A small part of the roof is covered with hemlock bark, and the rest is open for ventilation, I suppose. The proportions and style of architecture are carefully preserved in the picture."

Winthrop thus speaks of this railroad in his "Life in the Open Air": —

"The steamboat dumped us and our canoe on a wharf at the lake-head about four o'clock. A wharf promised a settlement, which, however, did not exist. There was population, — one man and one great ox. Following the inland-pointing nose of the ox, we saw, penetrating the forest, a wooden railroad. Ox-locomotive, and no other, befitted such rails. The train was one great go-cart. We packed our traps upon it, roofed them with our birch, and without much ceremony of whistling moved on. As we started so did the steamer. The link between us and the inhabited world grew more and more attenuated. Finally it snapped, and we were in the actual wilderness.

"I am sorry to chronicle that Iglesias hereupon turned to the ox, and said impatiently: —

"'Now, then, bullgine!'

"Why a railroad, even a wooden one, here? For this: the Penobscot, at this point, approaches within two and a half miles of Moosehead Lake, and over this portage supplies are taken conveniently for the lumbermen of an extensive lumbering country above, along the river. Corduroy railroad, ox-locomotive, and go-cart train up in the pine woods were a novelty and a privilege. Our cloven-hoofed engine did not whir turbulently along, like a thing of wheels. Slow and sure must the knock-kneed chewer of cuds step from log to log. Creakingly the train followed him, pausing and starting, and pausing again with groans of inertia. A very fat ox was this, protesting every moment against his employment, where speed, his duty, and sloth, his nature, kept him bewildered by their rival injunctions.

"Whenever the engine driver stopped to pick a huckleberry, the train, self-braking, stopped also, and the engine took in fuel from the tall grass that grew between the sleepers. It was the sensation of sloth at its uttermost.

"Iglesias and I, meanwhile, marched along and shot the game of the country, namely, one *Tetrao Canadensis*, one spruce-partridge. making in all one bird, quite too pretty to shoot with its red and black plumage. The spruce-partridge is rather rare in inhabited Maine, and is malignantly accused of being bitter in flesh, and of feeding on spruce-buds to make itself distasteful. Our bird we found sweetly berry-fed. The bitterness, if any, was that we had not a brace.

"So, at last, in an hour, after shooting one bird and swallowing six million berries, — for the railroad was a shaft into a mine of them, — we came to the terminus. The chewer of cuds was disconnected, and plodded off to his stable. The go-cart slid down an inclined plane to the river, the Penobscot.

"We paid quite freely for our brief monopoly of the railroad to the superintendent, engineer, stoker, poker, switch-tender, brakeman, baggage-master, and every other official in one. But who would grudge his tribute to the enterprise that opened this narrow vista through toward the Hyperborians, and planted these not once crumbling sleepers, and not once rickety rails, to save the passenger a portage? Here, at Bullgineville, the pluralist railroad manager had his cabin and clearing, ox-engine-house, and warehouse.

"To balance these symbols of advance, we found a station of the rear-guard of another army. An Indian party of two was encamped on the bank. The fusty sagamore of this pair was lying wounded; his fusty squaw tended him tenderly, minding, meanwhile, a very witch-like caldron of savory fume. No skirmish, with actual war-whoop and shien of real scalping-knife had put this prostrate chieftain *hors du combat*. He had shot himself cruelly, by accident. So he informed us feebly, in a muddy, guttural *patois* of Canadian French. This aboriginal meeting was of great value; it helped to eliminate the railroad."

CHAPTER X.

Camping Out.

PEOPLE who do not object to roughing it a little, and who would like to see the real inside, as it were, of woods life, should obtain a guide and the necessary outfit, and visit some of the lakes beyond Moosehead, indulging in a couple of weeks' camping. A person who has tried it thus gives his experience: "The scene from camp that night was beautiful. The wooded western slope of Kineo stood out in wonderful strength and color. The mottled sky reflected the sunlight upon the distant foliage with exquisite softness. The lake was smooth like a mirror, and the islands seemed like enchanted land. The fish leaped from the water as if to express their delight. The ripples glistened in the lessening light, and the shifting clouds every moment changed shape and color. The distant mountains took the departing rays with a kind of grand repose. The semi-human cry of the loons broke the universal stillness and solitude of the hour. It seemed a time when Nature and God could most fitly hold communion together. The scene was changed with the dawn of another day. Long before sunrise I looked out upon the lake and sky. The artist had preceded me, and rose at two o'clock to watch the auroral display. The coming on of day was an event by itself. Dark and stern, the distant hills were outlined against the reddening sky. The rising mist just touched the tranquil lake, and the chill of morning was visible in your breath. Not a leaf stirred; not a sound came from the forest. Nature was in silent prayer to her Maker. The delightfulness of the scene grew every moment. Dark recesses were visible on the wooded hill-sides, and the foliage showed light and shade. The forest seemed to be waking up. The fish again leaped from the surface of the lake.

"Shoots of light started out from the mountain's edge. The changes were quicker and brighter. The magician's hand was visibly shifting the scene. The mountains glowed with golden light. The ruddy beams shot across to the western hills, and peak answered greeting to peak. The great orb of day lifted up his disk above the mountain's edge, and poured his glory into the darkness across the lake and into the forest, until the water itself became the mirror of the day, and the darkness fled in silent retreat through the forest. One could not help thinking of those words which expressed this glory under other scenes in the beginning of the world : 'And the evening and the morning were the first day.'

"The forest itself has a charm which grows upon you. Here are the grand old primitive forests of New England; but if you think to see sentinels which have been standing for many centuries, and which seem to have come down from an ancient and honorable past, you will be disappointed. The lumberman's axe has searched out the largest and best trees, far inland from every stream and pond, through the entire Maine forest, and the big trees of other days are now as rare as the moose which once stood proudly beside them. In places where you would like to feel that no one has been before you, you will presently find some mark that man has preceded you and cut down a tree, or killed a moose, or made a camp. There is an impression, too, that trees simply grow old and do not die, and many expect to find them vigorous in a green old age. This is a mistake. You cannot go a rod into the forest from the edge of the lake, in any place but the very few clearings, without treading upon the moss-buried shapes of venerable spruce and pines, or climbing over the huge forms which are waiting the gentle process of decay; and the very soil beneath your feet is the departed life of fallen trees. It is a strange, unusual feeling to thus walk amidst life and death through the forest. It is like life, only you don't see a grave at every step, or find life so often locked hand in hand with death. The silence, the solitude, the sense of your own individual existence, come over you wonderfully; you grow conscious almost of your own shadow. The birds which in our common woods fly from branch to branch and make the trees vocal with their songs do not penetrate these wilds. You may see a heron or an eagle, the woodpecker, the kingfisher, and the hawk, but the domestic birds all prefer to keep closer to the habitation of man. The few voices which you hear are foreign, and communicate insensibly the feeling of wildness and isolation which, hour by hour, in a recess of the forest a mile from shore, grows to be almost painful. To spend a few days here alone seems like living a month. The accompaniments of life are removed, and selfishness, ambition, and care have here no place; a man is most truly thrown upon his own resources. To be alone with nature, without book, without work, without care, without the slightest hindrance to wandering at your own sweet will, with a heart which beats 'true to the kindred points of heaven and home,' and to be for this purpose in the very heart of the Moosehead forests, is more than all the trout-fishing, and almost the rival of the matchless views which meet the eye.

"These experiences in their fulness can only be obtained by camping out. Pitching your tent in the wilderness is the favorite way of spending vacation among younger men; and anywhere from fifty to a hundred persons may be found any day from July to October encamped here and there around this magnificent lake. They come in parties of four and six and eight, bringing their equipments and boarding themselves — as often encamping without guides as with them. The fun of these outdoor experiences is immense. The cooking is of a rare sort: pork and potatoes and hard-tack, and fish if you can catch them. If the appetite were not sharpened by exercise in the fresh, clear air, nothing would be eaten, the cooking by men, unless they are professionals, being anything but congenial to the stomach; yet the zest of the thing, the attempt to take care of one's self, the hearty effort at good-nature, which alone can keep such a company in good spirits, overcome everything, and the *cuisine* is made the best of.

"It takes a good guide to give camping out a genuine flavor. You can pitch a canvas tent without trouble, but the backwoodsman makes his tent for the place where he stops, and cuts his garment according to the cloth. Our party of six — an artist, a doctor, an ex-minister, two boys, and a priest — engaged one of the oldest and most characteristic guides for our camping out. The splendid steamer 'Governor Coburn,' on her trip to the lake, left us at the Northwest Carry, in the midst of a shower, to take care of ourselves. We could stay at Marsh Lane's cabin, which offered fair accommodations, or camp out. We chose the woods. The guide, Skipper Sam, had pitched his tent and made his bed with the wild beasts often before. He and his stout wife, in the early part of their fifty years' sojourn at the lake, had made extensive journeys through Northern Maine in search of gold, and knew all about the woods. The skipper chose the Gothic form of architecture in the construction of our camp, and began the tent, as Agassiz used to draw pictures of fishes, from an existing ideal in his own mind. Three forked sticks were speedily driven into the ground, and a pole was laid in the forks, this was the upper edge. The batteau sail covered one side; the bark of hemlock trees, peeled off in large sheets and lapped, sheathed the other; the ends were left open for ventilation; spruce and fir boughs were arranged on the ground for our bed; bark was stretched across the ridge-pole to keep out the impending rain; a big fire was made outside; our kettles and pans and accoutrements were hung up on the broken limbs of the nearest trees; and as darkness walled us in, our humble home in cheerfulness, in simplicity, in adaptation of means to ends, was very like a Scotch kitchen.

"Supper that night was not a distinguished meal. We roasted a few trout, holding them by wooden spits over the fire, and hardtack and tea completed the humble fare. It was served on a big log, the party sitting around on stumps and rocks, hungry and thankful. The lake was at once well and wash-basin. The skipper cleaned his dishes with Indian's soap — rubbing them in the sand. The first night of camping-out is like the day of one's marriage; you are on your best behavior. The only light was the camp-fire. A quiet smoke, a few yarns, a good toasting of one's several sides as one shifted from one seat to another, and we turned in for the night. The artist, true to his instinct, had camped out on the Saranac lakes for his wedding-tour, and turned in with a familiar air, as if it were pleasure. It was my lot to lie next to the wilderness; my pillow was a bag of potatoes. Rolling myself up in an army blanket, I lay down to sleep; but sleep fled before anxious fears. What if a bear should come down from yonder mountain and just bite my leg off for his supper? What if some of the lesser fry should try their hand on me — squirrels search my pockets, wood-mice crawl into my boots and vary my slumbers with a new sensation? There is a time when every man is a coward, and my time had come. Like many a coward, however, I said nothing, and soon lost myself in sleep. Slumber is sweet out in these pine and spruce forests. The aroma of the trees fills the air; the silence is profound; the wild game is harmless; the security is complete; and nothing but a man's own sins need keep him awake. And just here is the tonic of the woods. Your life is completely changed; your thoughts are taken up with things about you; your observing faculties are exercised within a small but fresh range; you have to learn, if the lesson is new, to be a good fellow; and so camping-out becomes a quick test of character, no less than a wonderful renewing power for a worn-out man.

"It was a study to see how each man in the party took to his own special liking.

"The boys were fast for hunting, and brought in hawks, partridges, and squirrels. The artist had a general disposition to enjoy himself, and didn't fish, didn't hunt, didn't tell stories; but he was thoroughly genial, and we all liked him. The doctor talked 'shop' a little, and theology more, and told stories, and developed a character of growing interest each day. The ex-minister had a solemn way about him which was very impressive. He was great with the rod, and supplied the table with trout. The priest had a passion for paddling a canoe, for entering into various experiences, and for finding out everything. He could tell stories, but didn't fish or shoot; was, in fact, resting from his parish cares, and glad to be much alone. He and the artist took rambles into the thicket, and had much in common. Skipper Sam, a genuine character, made great fun. Clad in homespun, the stub of a pipe in his mouth, his ancient felt hat half concealing his hair, now sprinkled with gray, his eyes under the grim brows twinkling with humor, he liked nothing better than to sit by the hour together, taking a puff from his pipe, and spitting at the fire, amidst his wonderful yarns. You could set him a-going as you do a clock, and he was always ready for a little bigger story than the one last told.

"The climax of our camping-out was reached one evening at Marsh Lane's. We had broken camp and gone over to old Marsh's to spend the night, taking our supper at his cabin. The night was clear, and the stars shone brightly. Marsh's log-cabin is the rudest possible specimen of the backwoods hotel, and being at the Carry which strikes the old Canada road, and the last house before you reach the north-west boundary line of the State, takes the men who come and go both ways. Captain Smart, of the West

Branch drive, was waiting to enter the interior with a party prospecting for lumber, and the party had come up from Kineo in a canoe just before sunset, and encamped on the further side of the bay. Skipper Sam built of drift-wood and broken stumps a famous fire upon the beach, and our own party sat down on seats which nature had provided, to wear away the hours till the time for turning in. Every man looked rougher than his wont in the red light, Skipper Sam the roughest of all. We had lighted our pipes, had extemporized comfortable seats, and were warming up for good talking, when the dip of paddles announced the arrival of the exploring party from the other side, — two Boston men interested in lumber, with the elder Masterman, a famous hunter, as their guide. Marsh Lane, a six-footer, slightly bent with years, a grim, old man, a settler of thirty-five years ago, well known as a capital guide and hunter, presently straggled in, smoking his pipe, silent, moody, with his dog behind him. His cook, a queer specimen of humanity, dragged himself along in the rear, — a man who works hard for his board and clothes, and is too shiftless to do better. It was one of those rare gatherings where every man was unlike his fellow, and each was anxious to have his own say. Skipper Sam was in his element. He piled the fagots upon the fire till the flames shot up high into the air and glared out upon the darkness of the lake. He was allowed to be the master of ceremonies, and his own doings and sayings were the chief entertainment of the evening. Conversation and story-telling had become quite brisk before our visitors came, and were more brisk afterward. The topics, as was natural, were chiefly hunting and fishing, and the adventures which grow out of life in the woods; and the two guides, stimulated by the attentive listeners, soon began a race to see which could tell the biggest story. It was first trout-fishing, then moose-hunting, then bear-hunting; then the habits of the moose were discussed. Questions increased the number and rapidity of the stories of personal adventure. Old Marsh Lane puffed away at his pipe, discharging tobacco-juice furiously at the end of a long story, attentive, not dropping even a word. Skipper Sam walked up and down the narrow beach, too excited to sit down. Neither guide could wait till the other had finished his story before he began one of his own, and each, by gesticulation and raising of

CAMP AT HEAD OF LAKE. [*From Harper's Magazine.*

his voice, tried to gain exclusive attention. Personal adventures from the lips of one who had killed two hundred bears, told in the picturesque and earnest manner which takes hold of your imagination, made the stories of Masterman intensely interesting; and if the skipper told whoppers, it was a pardonable offence in one who could not bear to be outdone.

"Thus these naturally silent men of the woods kept our whole party on the *qui vive* till a late hour over their simple and thrilling narratives. Suddenly the talk ended. It was good-night all around. Rough forms retreated into the darkness, a canoe touched the lake, the dip of the paddles soon died away in the distance, and one after another our own party disappeared into the cabin, each rolling himself up in a blanket for the night, leaving the ex-minister and the priest to keep the fire, and watch for the expected steamer, if she should come in the night. Even they finally searched in vain for the soft side of a bed of rocks, and sought shelter in the camp. The morning disclosed six strange shapes in as many different directions imbedded in the straw, and the guide stoutly insisted that he had slept soundly under his canoe on the rocks. With the morning came the steamer, and after a breakfast, to which we did ample justice, we went on board. Thus ended our camping out. We were glad to have it begin, and more glad to have it end, and to return to civilized life."

CHAPTER XI.

The head of the Lake and its Surroundings — Where to go — What to see — Fishing, Hunting, etc.

For several years there has been a good hotel needed at the North-east Carry, and this want has now been supplied. In August, 1878, Mr. Simeon Savage, for several years one of the proprietors at the Lake House, Greenville, bought the Carry House at the head of the lake, formerly kept by John Ross; also, the land connected with the house, comprising about six hundred acres. A marked change immediately took place in the management of the hotel, particular attention being paid to the furnishing of the rooms and table. Good beds, clean and well-furnished rooms, and a carefully served table, are now offered to the lake travel. Mrs. Savage, with her former experience in the largest hotel in Greenville, manages the house-keeping admirably. Mr. Savage has commenced a series of improvements, that if carried forward to a successful conclusion will make the WINNEGARNOCK HOUSE one of the most desirable stopping-places in the entire Moosehead Lake region. Since the house came into his possession, the dining-room has been enlarged to double its former capacity, and several more rooms have been finished, making in all fourteen sleeping rooms, with good accommodations for twenty to twenty-five guests.

The hotel is a two-story-and-a-half building, with piazza in front, and office, dining-room, parlor, etc., on the ground floor; all the sleeping-rooms are above.

The grounds around the house have been cleared of the *débris* that formerly littered the premises, and present a tidy and attractive appearance, to which they had long been strangers. The hotel stands at the head of the lake, on the east side of the carry road, near the steamboat wharf, and a few rods from a beautiful sand-beach, three miles in extent, offering as good facilities as the sea-shore for riding, walking, and bathing. A short distance from the hotel a bath-house has been erected over a large ledge on the beach, for the accommodation of the guests.

The views from the piazza of the WINNEGARNOCK are equal to any about the lake. Commencing on the left, the eye rests upon range after range of mountains, that, upheaved against the sky, sweep around in a semi-circle nearly to the extreme right of the hotel. Lobster Mountain, the Spencer Mountains, Kineo Junior, Mount Kineo, Blue Ridge, Squaw Mountain, the Misery Mountains, Bald Mountain, the twin Bigelows, and numerous others, all lend their aid to form a picture of unsurpassed loveliness.

Sitting upon the piazza of the hotel, while a heavy south wind is blowing, and watching the white-capped waves as they roll over and over, finally to dash themselves amid a mass of snowy foam, on the hard, sandy beach, with a roar like distant thunder, you can easily imagine yourself at the sea-coast, and the waste of water before you a part of old ocean.

At the farther end of the sand beach, on the eastern side of the house, is a long strip of pebbly beach, where one can find pretty pebbles, of all sizes and colors. Along the beach, for several hundred yards from the shore, the water is quite shoal, furnishing an excellent chance for ladies unaccustomed to a canoe to master the art of paddling, with no greater danger to fear than a ducking, if the canoe should happen to upset, as it probably will.

From the front of the hotel an unbroken view of the lake is obtained for over twenty miles. Behind it a dense forest extends nearly to the Penobscot. Through this the carry-road penetrates to the river, like a cañon through a mountain. In coming up the lake, this road is visible soon after passing Kineo, a cut or notch in the woods giving its location.

A croquet-ground and bowling-alley furnish healthy and pleasant amusement for the guests of the house. Mr. Savage has also horses and a handsome barouche for riding parties, who, by combining the beach and carry-road, can take a drive, if they desire, of nearly ten miles. This is the only place in the lake region, after leaving Greenville, where one can indulge in driving to any extent.

Row-boats and canoes are kept on the lake by Mr. Savage, for fishing and excursions; also, on the West Branch at the end of the carry-road, at the head of Seboomook Falls, and at Lobster Lake.

A short distance from the hotel blueberries grow in unlimited numbers, and hundreds of people flock to the head of the lake, during the season, to gather them. Two hundred bushels have gone down on the steamer on one trip, which gives one something of an idea of the number picked. Raspberries and wild strawberries are also very plenty in the vicinity.

A person stopping at the WINNEGARNOCK HOUSE has almost an unlimited number of excursions to choose from. You can visit Norcross Brook, Williams Stream, Duck Cove, the North-west Carry, and various other places on the lake, and take from half a day to two or three days in making the excursion, as your time or inclination will allow. Two miles down the lake you obtain the best view of Mount Katahdin to be had anywhere around Moosehead.

For river excursions you may visit Seboomook Falls, Russell Stream, Elm Stream, the Moosehorn, or Lobster Lake; any of these can be done in a day; but your pleasure will be increased if you can take more time, and camp out a night or two. And, by the way, the cream of camping out is all in the first three days.

For longer trips that will necessitate camping out or stopping at some farm-house, you can go up the West Branch to Nulhedus, or beyond, or down the river to Chesuncook, Ripogenus, Mount Katahdin, Chamberlain Lake, Caucomgomoc, and other places as your fancy or pleasure may dictate.

Lobster Lake

Is visited by a great many people each summer, and is one of the prettiest sheets of water in Maine. Leaving the Winnegarnock House you cross the carry, and paddle down the West Branch for two miles to Lobster Stream, that enters the river from the right. A rocky bar extends across the mouth of the stream, making shoal water for a short distance. There is a small island in the Penobscot, opposite the mouth of the Lobster. Our way lies up the latter, and we follow it to the lake, a distance of two miles. The banks are muddy, and from four to six feet high. For the first mile on each side of the stream there is a heavy growth, consisting of poplars, white birch, fir, spruce, elms, and alders; the next half mile there is only a belt of trees skirting the stream, with bogs and swamps behind. As you begin the last half mile, the most of the trees disappear, leaving only a few alder bushes, an occasional elm, and coarse grass. The river is deep, and rather crooked. About half way between the Penobscot and the lake, an abrupt turn in the river discloses Lobster Mountain, looming up directly in front of you, a round-topped peak, thickly wooded to its summit, the foliage dark-green. A little farther on you catch a glimpse of Spencer Mountain.

The windings of the river hide the lake until you are close to it, and when you reach it the first exclamation is one of delight; hemmed in on three sides by mountains, on the fourth, bordered by meadow and hill. There are a great many sand beaches around the lake, and these are divided from each other, at irregular intervals, by bold, rocky headlands, that produce a very picturesque effect. There are several islands in the lake; none, however, very large. The growth around the shores consists of fir, spruce, poplar, white birch, Norway pine, etc.

Some of the rocky ledges dividing the sand-beaches are a great curiosity. They appear to be composed of layers of stone similar to slate; near the water they are furrowed, and worn full of holes, looking as if a huge cable chain had been laid out in regular rows upon the beach. I thought at first that these holes were caused by the motion of the water; but it cannot be, from the fact that the same ledges, twenty and thirty feet above the lake, are bored with similar holes, resembling the work of woodpeckers on old dead trees.

These dividing headlands are covered mostly with Norway pine and cedars, and are luxuriously carpeted with moss. They extend back several hundred feet from the lake, and have the appearance of horsebacks. A geologist would find much to interest him in an examination of these ledges.

On the eastern shore of the lake, just above an island, and directly opposite to Lobster Mountain, there is a place where two of these headlands are together, as usual dividing two sand-beaches. The headlands are about fifty feet apart at the lake shore, a deep gully between them, and as they run back from the water they come nearer together, the gully becoming more shallow. Some of the ledges about the shore are so full of holes that they resemble honeycomb more than anything else. From the tops of these ridges one obtains splendid views of the lake and mountains. The Spencer Mountains lie south-west of the lake, and Lobster Mountain, west. Kineo Junior, and several other mountains whose names we do not know, can be seen from different parts of the lake.

The land at the north and north-west end of the lake consists of swamps and meadows, and the shores are low. But all around the remainder of the lake the land is high, and in some places the mountains descend to the water. The foliage is deep and rich, the forest dense, and comprises nearly all of the different varieties of our native trees. Over some of the lower ridges near the lake shore, distant mountains are seen towering up against the sky.

This lake is one of the prettiest sheets of water we have ever seen, and it is a pity that it could not have received some name more in sympathy with its surroundings. Its name originated from the number of fresh-water lobsters found in it. They are not much larger than shrimps. "Beautiful Lake" would be far more appropriate.

Nearly all of the sand-beaches that border the lake are oval, or semi-circular, in shape. Back of these, in many places, will be found a strip of pebbles and stones from six to twenty feet wide. These rocky beaches are well worth your attention. They contain stones of all kinds, sizes, shapes, and colors. Some of these rocks are curiously indented; others are polished as highly as marble. There is a smooth stone, to be found in large quantities in some of these places, that strongly resembles hornblende; but I could not decide whether it was or not. I picked up one stone about the size of a lemon, that was almost round, and carried it off with me for a souvenir.

On my last trip to Lobster Lake I intended making a circuit of it, and exploring it thoroughly; but before we had time the wind came out strong from the north-west, kicking up a troublesome sea, and it was too rough for canoeing with any degree of comfort.

However, we crossed the lake, thereby securing a thorough wetting from the spray that occasionally flew over us, passing to the north of the peninsula that nearly cuts the lake in two, and reached the western shore. Rounding a pebbly point we entered a small bay, full of rocky islets, and followed the shore until we reached the base of Lobster Mountain. Then turning about we retraced our course to the point, and paddled along the western shore back to Lobster Stream.

On this side of the lake we found the same characteristics as on the eastern shore; bold, rocky headlands and sand-beaches alternating with each other the entire distance around to the river.

Within half a mile of the outlet, on a clear day, you can obtain a magnificent view of Katahdin. And we stopped a few moments to take a look at the mountain, rising majestically in the east, grand, impressive, sublime, — its loftiest peak just showing above a fleecy mantle of cloud, and bathed in the golden rays of an autumnal sun. The mass of feathery cloud hovered about it, as long as we were in sight, with caressing tenderness, and kissed its cold forehead as daintily as coy maiden ever touched the lips of her lover. But our time was limited; and, with a sigh of regret at leaving this beautiful sheet of water, and a kindly nod to old Katahdin, we paddled onward, and swept into the Lobster Stream.

By this time the wind had almost ceased blowing, and the river was calm and placid; its waters scarcely ruffled. As we turned out of the Lobster into the Penobscot, the declining sun met us full in the face, dazzling our eyes, and caused us to do an unusual amount of winking and blinking. Only a few expiring zephyrs swept the bosom of the West Branch, and we paddled lazily along, reaching the carry-road in an hour and a quarter from the time we left the lake. I had never passed a more delightful day, and had never seen a more beautiful sheet of water than Lobster Lake.

This locality, especially about the outlet of the lake, was once a great place for moose, and a few are still found in the vicinity. A few years ago a law was passed for their protection, and they cannot be shot until the winter of 1880. Caribou and deer are plenty around the lake, and quite a number are shot each year.

There is a second route to Lobster Lake from the Winnegarnock House, that some may prefer. A good road runs from the head of Moosehead through the woods to Lobster, coming out a little west of the outlet. The distance by the woods road is three miles. It starts from the eastern side of the beach, about a mile from the hotel. Parties can go to Lobster by way of the rivers, and return through the woods, or *vice versa*, thus giving greater variety to the trip.

The fishing in the vicinity of the WINNEGARNOCK is excellent, and

LANDING THE CANOES. [From *Harper's Magazine*

many trout are taken each season from the end of the steamboat wharf. At Norcross Brook, Centre Island, W. Ledges, Williams Stream, Russell Stream and Pond, Nulhedus, Seboomook Falls, Lobster Lake, and other places but a short distance away, known to Mr. Savage, one is always sure of a good catch.

Through September and October there is first-rate partridge shooting within a mile or two of the house; and musk-rat, mink, and otter are plenty on the West Branch. Between Lobster Stream and the Moosehead is good ground for deer and caribou, and numbers are shot there each season.

Distances from the Winnegarnock House to places of interest.

Penobscot River, by road, 2 miles.
Lobster Lake, by carriage and canoe, 6 miles.
Lobster Lake, by beach and path, through the woods, $4\frac{1}{2}$ miles.
Seboomook Falls, by carriage and canoe, 7 miles.
Russell Stream, by carriage and canoe, 4 miles.
Moosehorn Stream, by carriage and canoe, 10 miles.
Chesuncook Lake, by carriage and canoe, 22 miles.
Centre Island, by water, 4 miles.
North-west Carry and Carry Brook, by canoe or row-boat, 7 miles.
Norcross Brook, by land or water, $2\frac{1}{2}$ miles.
Williams Stream, by water, 6 miles.
Duck Cove, by water, 8 miles.

Mr. Savage charges $1.50 for hauling one canoe across the carry; two or more canoes, $1.00 each. These prices include baggage and camp-stores.

CHAPTER XII.

Tours Beyond Moosehead — Down the West Branch.

ONE of the most interesting and exciting tours that can be made beyond Moosehead Lake is the trip down the West Branch of the Penobscot, bringing one, as it does, to the most direct point from which the ascent of Mt. Katahdin can be made. A canoe is indispensable for this trip, and if you take our advice you will also engage a good guide. Good we mean in the literal sense of the word: a guide who wields a strong and skilful paddle, who knows how to handle a setting-pole, who can shoot straight, a good cook, an excellent story-teller; one strong, willing, cheerful, and courageous. This is the outline of the man you need to accompany you down the West Branch, and perchance to the summit of Katahdin. Such a guide commands good pay. But a cross-grained, lazy slouch, hired because you can get him cheap, is dear at any price. One of the best guides we know of for this trip is Charlie Nicholas, an Indian, who lives at Greenville. We can recommend him, from personal experience, as being, in the woods, "the right man in the right place."

Leaving the hospitable quarters of Mr. Savage we cross the carry, the road running through the well-cultivated farm of Joseph Morris, who has been located here since 1871. Mr. Morris makes a business during summer of entertaining sportsmen and tourists, at a reasonable price. He has plenty of teams, and is always ready to do any hauling over the carry at low rates.

A tote-road starts from the Morris Farm, and runs to Chesuncook, following the river closely all the way. People who are fond of walking can thus make the trip to Chesuncook by land, although they may have to ford some of the small streams that cross; none of them, however, are over a foot deep. The road is dry and well bushed out, and so plain it can be followed the entire distance without difficulty. It comes out at the head of Chesuncook about half a mile from the hotel. Sometimes in the fall, when the water is very low on the river, the woodsmen prefer to stretch their legs over the "tote-road," rather than double them up in a birch.

At the landing beyond Morris' we launch our canoe, and a few moments later are floating down the Penobscot. For the first two miles the river is comparatively smooth, and the water deep and black. Its banks are about six feet high, thickly covered with white and black spruce, fir, cedar, birch, maple, poplar; also an occasional oak, hemlock, ash, and elm. The common yellow lily and the fragrant pond-lilies are plenty along our course, and tempt us from time to time to pluck their white blossoms, and inhale their delicious perfume. This vicinity was once a famous hunting-ground for moose, and even now they are sometimes shot here. We saw moose tracks for some distance along the sides of this part of the river, on one of our trips to Chesuncook. The first stream we pass of any importance is LOBSTER STREAM, which comes in on the right from the south-east, two miles below the carry. There is a small island at the mouth of the stream, and the water around it is shoal. LOBSTER LAKE is about two miles from the river, and during high water the Penobscot flows back into the lake. The Lobster Stream is navigable, for canoes or boats, the entire distance to the lake. Near the mouth of the stream we obtain a fine view of the Spencer Mountains, lying east of the northern end of Moosehead.

Below the mouth of the Lobster we find some quick water, and the river narrows and widens by turns, in some places being wider than at the carry. Two miles more and we reach WARREN ISLAND, small and thickly wooded, a good camping-place. Charlie Nicholas, the guide, claims to be the first person who camped on it. The landing is on the left side. For three miles beyond it is dead water, and we paddle easily along. We have now passed the MOOSE HORN, a small stream that empties into the river from the right. It is very crooked, and only a few feet wide. In this vicinity we obtain the first view of Katahdin. One mile below is KENNEY'S RIPS. On the right-hand side of the river you will notice SEARS' CLEARING, just half way to Chesuncook. There is an old potato cellar on the clearing, in sight from the river, that offers a shelter if you are caught in a rain. Lazy people are in the habit of camping there.

Two miles below the Moose Horn we reach the RAGMUFF, a

winding stream that comes in on the left. It is generally good fishing-ground at the mouths of these small streams. Leaving Ragmuff — singular name by the way — we pass over some long rips, and notice the LITTLE RAGMUFF, a narrow, crooked stream that empties into the Penobscot on the left. A short distance beyond the banks of the river improve in appearance, the blue clay changing to gravel, boulders, and ledges. From time to time you will notice on the side of the river piles of muscle-shells, or fresh-water clams. These are left by musk-rats, who bring the clams from the bottom of the river, and, after opening them and eating the meat, leave the shells behind to mystify voyagers.

We have now reached the BIG ISLAND, partially cleared for a farm, and passing to the right of it have another stretch of rapids. Then we pass the FOX HOLE, another good place for fishing; there is also a good camping-place near here on the left side of the river. A short distance below, we reach another island. Passing to the left of this, we notice on the left bank of the stream, about opposite of the middle of the island, a cold spring, — a good place to stop a few moments if you are thirsty. There is first-rate fishing in this vicinity.

About three-quarters of a mile below here is a stretch of dead water; passing over this, you come to another island, covered with coarse grass, and ornamented with a few scraggy elms. At the head of this island, on the left bank of the river, is an attractive place to camp, and, judging from the looks of the ground, a great many parties have camped there. During the spring and summer it is good fishing in this locality. The river is perhaps thirty rods wide here, and its shores are covered with elms, poplars, and birches.

From this point islands increase in number, the most of them being small, and covered with coarse grass and alders. The ROCKY RIPS are the next rapids. Running these without difficulty, you reach the Pine Stream dead water. Passing PINE STREAM, flowing in from the right, three miles above the lake, a few strokes of the paddle and you are at the head of PINE STREAM FALLS. Here are the most considerable rapids between the two lakes, but they are easily run by an experienced canoe-man.

Between the falls and the lake you pass fifteen or twenty islands. The land on each side of the river below the falls is low and meadowy, covered with swamp-grass, and a dismal-looking growth of trees, the most of which have been killed by the frequent rise of the water. In the spring, during high water, the lake flows back nearly to the foot of the falls.

Approaching the lake, you pass two piers, a boom being strung across, below them, to hold the logs when they come down the river. A short distance beyond you glide by two log shanties — the outposts of Chesuncook settlement, situated on the right bank of the river. These houses are occupied by French Canadians, who are generally squatters. The banks of the river below these cabins have been cleared, and you soon shoot out into the lake, turn the barren point on your right hand, and head for the Chesuncook Farm House, a quarter of a mile below the mouth of the river on the southern side of the lake.

On entering the lake, where the stream runs south-easterly, we obtained a good view of the mountains about Katahdin, apparently twenty-five miles or more away. The twenty miles of the Penobscot, between Moosehead and Chesuncook lakes, are comparatively smooth, and a great part dead-water; in some parts it is shallow and rapid, with rocks or gravel-beds, where you can wade across. There is no expanse of water, but very little break in the forest, and the meadow only shows here and there. There are no hills near the river, nor within sight, except one or two distant mountains seen in a few places. The banks are from six to ten feet high, but occasionally rise gently to higher ground. In several places the forest on the bank is only a thin strip, letting the light through from some alder swamp or meadow behind.

Between the North-east Carry and the lake there are several small streams emptying into the Penobscot from each side. They are of little account, being dry during the latter part of the summer, and are not shown on the maps.

There is quite a settlement at Chesuncook, the population numbering nearly eighty people, most of whom are French Canadians. The hotel stands upon a hill, about a hundred feet above the lake, and has accommodations for perhaps twenty people. It commands a very fair view of Katahdin, and a number of other mountains; also six or eight miles of the lake. There is one store at Chesuncook Lake, belonging to Mr. Hatheway, the proprietor of the hotel. The stock is similar to that generally kept in a country store. A school is kept here sometimes during a few months of winter, but there is neither church nor chapel. There are a number of good fishing resorts within a circle of five miles from the hotel, and guides and canoes can be obtained of the proprietor, if desired.

CHESUNCOOK Lake extends north-west and south-east, and is seventeen miles long and two wide in the broadest part; there are no islands in it, and, generally speaking, it is a shoal lake; the upper end especially so. Parties on their way down the West Branch, who have occasion to linger in this vicinity, will find the Chesuncook Farm house a comfortable place to stop at. The Caucomgomoc flows into the lake about two miles above here. Theodore Winthrop, in his "Life in the Open Air,"[1] thus relates his experience on Chesuncook and Ripogenus: —

"Chesuncook is a 'bulge' of the Penobscot; so much for its topography. It is deep in the woods, except that some miles from its opening there is a lumber-station, with house and barns. In the wilderness, man makes for man by a necessity of human instinct. We made for the log houses. We found there an ex-barkeeper of a certain well-known New York cockney coffee-house, promoted into a frontiersman, but mindful still of flesh-pots. Poor fellow, he was still prouder that he had once tossed the foaming cocktail than that he could now fell the forest-monarch. Mixed drinks were dearer to him than pure air. When we entered the long, low log-cabin, he was boiling doughnuts, as was to be expected. In certain regions of America every cook who is not baking pork and beans is boiling doughnuts, just as in certain other gastronomic quarters *frijoles* alternate with *tortillas*.

"Doughnuts, like peaches, must be eaten with the dew upon them. Caught as they come bobbing up in the bubbling pot, I will not say that they are despicable. Woodsmen and canoemen, competent to pork and beans, can master also the alternative. The ex-barkeeper was generous with these brown and glistening langrage-shot, and aimed volley after volley at our mouths. Nor was he content with giving us our personal fill; into every crevice of our firkin he packed a pellet of future indigestion. Besides this result of foraging, we took the hint from a visible cow that milk might be had. Of this also the ex-barkeeper served us out

---

[1] Published by James R. Osgood & Co., Boston.

galore, sighing that it was not the punch of his metropolitan days. We put our milk in our teapot, and, thus, with all the ravages of the past made good, we launched again upon Chesuncook.

"Chesuncook, according to its quality of lake, had no aid to give us with current. Paddling all a hot August mid-day over slothful water would be tame, day-laborer's work. But there was a breeze. Good! Come, kind zephyr, fill our red blanket-sail! Cancut's blanket in the bow became a substitute for Cancut's paddle in the stern. We swept along before the wind, unsteadily, over Lake Chesuncook, at sea in a bowl, — 'rolled to starboard, rolled to larboard,' in our keelless craft. Zephyr only followed us, mild as he was strong, and strong as he was mild. Had he been puffy, it would have been all over with us. But the breeze only sang about our way, and shook the water out of sunny calm. Katahdin to the north, a fair, blue pyramid, lifted higher and stooped forward more imminent, yet still so many leagues away that his features were undefined, and the gray of his scalp undistinguishable from the green of his beard of forest. Every mile, however, as we slid drowsily over the hot lake, proved more and more that we were not befooled, — Iglesias by memory and I by anticipation. Katahdin lost nothing by approach, as some of the grandees do; as it grew bigger, it grew better.

"Twenty miles, or so, of Chesuncook, sun-cooked Chesuncook, we traversed by the aid of our blanket-sail, pleasantly wafted by the unboisterous breeze. Undrowned, unducked, as safe from the perils of the broad lake as we had come out of the defiles of the rapids, we landed at the carry below the dam at the lake's outlet.

"The skin of many a slaughtered varmint was nailed on its shingle, and the landing-place was carpeted with the fur. Doughnuts, ex-barkeepers, and civilization at one end of the lake, and here were musk-rat skins, trappers, and the primeval. Two hunters of moose, in default of their fern-horned, blubber-lipped game, had condescended to musk-rat, and were making the lower end of Chesuncook fragrant with muskiness.

"It is surprising how hospitable and comrade a creature is man. The trappers of musk-rats were charmingly brotherly. They guided us across the carry; they would not hear of our being porters. 'Pluck the superabundant huckleberry,' said they, 'while we, suspending your firkin and your traps upon the setting-pole, tote them, as the spies of Joshua toted the grape-clusters of the Promised Land.'

"Cancut, for his share, carried the canoe. He wore it upon his head and shoulders. Tough work he found it, toiling through the underwood, and poking his way like an elongated and mobile mushroom through the thick shrubbery. Ever and anon as Iglesias and I paused, we would be aware of the canoe thrusting itself above our heads in the covert, and a voice would come from an unseen head under its shell, 'It's soul-breaking, carrying is!'

"The portage was short. We emerged from the birchen grove upon the river, below a brilliant cascading rapid. The water came flashing gloriously forward, a far other element than the tame, flat stuff we had drifted slowly over all the dullish hours. Water on the go is nobler than water on the stand; recklessness may be as fatal as stagnation, but it is more heroic.

"Presently, over the edge, where the foam and spray were springing up into sunshine, our canoe suddenly appeared, and had hardly appeared, when, as if by one leap, it had passed the rapid, and was gliding in the stiller current to our feet. One of the muskrateers had relieved Cancut of his head-piece, and shot the lower rush of water. We again embarked, and, guided by the trappers in their own canoe, paddled out upon Lake Ripogenus.

"Ripogenus is a tarn, a lovely oval tarn, within a rim of forest and hill; and there behold, *O gioja!* at its eastern end, stooping forward and filling the sphere, was Katahdin, large and alone.

"But we must hasten, for day wanes, and we must see and sketch this cloudless summit from *terra firma*. A mile and half way down the lake, we landed at the foot of a grassy hill-side, where once had been a lumberman's station and hay-farm. It was abandoned now, and lonely in that deeper sense in which widowhood is lonelier than celibacy, a home deserted lonelier than a desert. Tumble-down was the never-painted house; ditto its three barns. But, besides a camp, there were two things to be had here, — one certain, one possible, probable even. The view, that was an inevitable certainty; Iglesias would bag that as his share of the plunder of Ripogenus. For my bagging, bears, perchance, awaited. The trappers had seen a bear near the barns. Cancut, in his previous visit, had seen a disappearance of bear. No sooner had the birch's bow touched lightly upon the shore than we seized our respective weapons,— Iglesias his peaceful and creative sketch-book, I my warlike and destructive gun,— and dashed up the hill-side.

"I made for the barns to catch bruin napping or lolling in the old hay. I entertain a *vendetta* toward the ursine family. I had a *duello*, pistol against claw, with one of them in the mountains of Oregon, and have nothing to show to point the moral and adorn the tale. My antagonist of that hand-to-hand fight received two shots, and then dodged into cover and was lost in the twilight. Soon or late in my life, I hoped that I should avenge this evasion. Ripogenus would, perhaps, give what the Nachehese Pass had taken away.

"Vain hope! I was not to be an ursicide. I begin to fear that I shall slay no other than my proper personal bearishness. I did my duty for another result at Ripogenus. I bolted audaciously into every barn. I made excursions into the woods around. I found the mark of the beast, not the beast. He had not long ago decamped, and was now, perhaps, sucking the meditative paw hard-by in an arbor of his bear-garden.

"After a vain hunt, I gave up Beast and turned to Beauty. I looked about me, seeing much.

"Foremost I saw a fellow-man, my comrade, fondled by breeze and brightness, and whispered to by all sweet sounds. I saw Iglesias below me, on the slope, sketching. He was preserving the scene at its *bel momento*. I repented more bitterly of my momentary falseness to Beauty while I saw him so constant.

"Furthermore, I saw a landscape of vigorous simplicity, easy to comprehend. By mellow sunset the grass slope of the old farm seemed no longer tanned and rusty, but ripened. The oval lake was blue and calm, and that is already much to say; shaddows of the western hills were growing over it, but flight after flight of illumined clouds soared above, to console the sky and the water for the coming of night. Northward, a forest darkled, whose glades of brightness I could not see. Eastward, the bank mounted abruptly to a bare, fire-swept table-land, whereon a few dead trees stood, parched and ghostly skeletons draped with rags of moss.

"Furthermost and topmost, I saw Katahdin twenty miles away, a giant undwarfed by any rival. The remainder landscape was only minor and judiciously accessory. The hills were low before it, the lake lowly, and upright above lake and hill lifted the mountain pyramid. Isolate greatness tells. There were no underling mounts above this mountain-in-chief. And now on its shoulders and crest sunset shone, glowing. Warm violet followed the glow, soothing away the harshness of granite lines. Luminous violet dwelt upon the peak, while below the clinging forests were purple in sheltered gorges, where they could climb nearer the summit, loved of light, and lower down gloomed green and sombre in the shadow.

"Meanwhile, as I looked, the quivering violet rose higher and higher, and at last floated away like a disengaged flame. A smouldering blue dwelt upon the peak. Ashy gray overcame the blue. As dusk thickened and stars trembled into sight, the gray grew luminous. Katahdin's mighty presence seemed to absorb such dreamy glimmers as float in limpid night-air; a faint glory, a twilight of its own, clothed it. King of the day-lit world, it became queen of the dimmer realms of night, and like a woman-queen it did not disdain to stoop and study its loveliness in the polished lake, and stooping thus it overhung the earth, a shadowy creature of gleam and gloom, an eternized cloud.

"I sat staring and straying in sweet reverie, until the scene before me was dim as metaphysics. Suddenly a flame flashed up in the void. It grew and steadied, and dark objects became visible about it. In the loneliness — for Iglesias had disappeared — I allowed myself a moment's luxury of superstition. Were these the Cyclops of Katahdin? Possibly. Were they Trolls forging diabolic enginery, or Gypsies of Yankeedom? I will see, — and went tumbling down the hillside.

"As I entered the circle about the cooking-fire of drift-wood by the lake, Iglesias said, —

"'The beef-steak and the mutton chops will do for breakfast; now, then, with your bear!'

"'Haw, haw!' guffawed Cancut; and the sound, taking the lake at a stride, found echoes everywhere, till he grew silent and peered suspiciously into the dark.

"'There's more bears raound'n yer kin shake a stick at,' said one of the muskrateers. 'I wouldn't recommend yer to stir 'em up naow, haowlin' like that.'

"'I meant it for laffin',' said Cancut, humbly.

"'Ef yer call that 'ere larfin', couldn't yer cry a little to kinder slick daown the bears?' said the trapper.

"Iglesias now invited us to *chocolat à la crème*, made with the boon of the ex-barkeeper. I suppose I may say, without flattery, that this tipple was marvellous. What a pity Nature spoiled a cook by making the muddler of that chocolate a painter of grandeurs. When Fine Art is in a man's nature, it must exude, as pitch leaks from a pine-tree. Our musk-rat hunters partook injudiciously of this unaccustomed dainty, and were visited with indescribable Nemesis. They had never been acclimated to chocolate, as had Iglesias and I, by sipping it under the shade of the mimosa and the palm.

"Up to a certain point an unlucky hunter is more likely to hunt than a lucky. Satiety follows more speedily upon success than despair upon failure. Let us thank Heaven for that, brethren dear. I had bagged not a bear, and must needs satisfy my assassin instincts upon something with hoofs and horns. The younger trapper of musk-rat, being young, was ardent, — being young, was hopeful, — being young, believed in exceptions to general rules, — and being young, believed that, given a good fellow with a gun, Nature would provide a victim. Therefore he proposed that we should canoe it along the shallows in this sweetest and stillest of all the nights. The senior shook his head incredulously; Iglesias shook his head noddingly.

"'Since you have massacred all the bears,' said Iglesias, 'I will go lay me down in their lair in the barn. If you find me cheek-by-jowl with Ursa Major when you come back, make a pun and he will go.'

"It was stiller than stillness upon the lake. Ripogenus, it seemed, had never listened to such silence as this. Calm never could have been so beyond the notion of calm. Stars in the empyrean and stars in Ripogenus winked at each other across ninety-nine billions of leagues as uninterruptedly as boys at a boarding-school table.

"I knelt amidships in the birch with gun and rifle on either side. The pilot gave one stroke of his paddle, and we floated out upon what seemed the lake. Whatever we were poised and floating upon he hesitated to shatter with another dip of his paddle, lest he should shatter the thin basis, and sink toward heaven and the stars.

"Presently the silence seemed to demand gentle violence, and the unwavering water needed slight tremors to teach it the tenderness of its calm; then my guide used his blade, and cut into glassiness.

"We crept noiselessly along by the lake-edge within the shadows of the pines. With never a plash we slid. Rare drops fell from the cautious paddle and tinkled on the surface, overshot, not parted, by our imponderable passage. Sometimes from far within the forest would come sounds of rustling branches or crackling twigs. Somebody of life approaches with stealthy tread. Gentlier, even gentlier, my steersman. Take up no pearly drop from the lake, mother of pearliness, lest, falling, it sound too loudly. Somewhat comes. Let it come unterrified to our ambush among the shadows by the shore.

"Somewhat, something, somebody, was coming, perhaps, but some other thing or body thwarted it and it came not. To glide over glassiness while uneventful moments link themselves into hours is monotonous. Night and stillness laid their soothing spell upon me. I was entranced. I lost myself out of time and space, and seemed to be floating unimpelled and purposeless, nowhere in Forever.

"Somewhere in Now I suddenly found myself.

"There he was. There was the moose trampling and snorting hard by, in the shallows of Ripogenus, trampling out of being the whole nadir of stars, making the world conscious of its lost silence by the death of silence in tumult.

"I trembled with sudden eagerness. I seized my gun. In another instant I should have lodged the fatal pellet, when a voice whispered over my shoulder, 'I kinder guess yer've ben asleep an' dreamin', ha'n't yer?'

"So I had.

"Never a moose came down to cool his clumsy snout in the water, and swallow reflections of stars. Never a moose abandoned dry-browse in the bitter woods for succulent lily-pads, full in their cells and veins of water and sunlight. Till long past midnight we paddled, and watched, and listened, whisperless. In vain. At last, as we rounded a point, the level gleam of our dying camp-fire athwart the water reminded us of passing hour and traveler duties, of rest to-night and toil to-morrow.

"My companions, fearless as if there were no bears this side of Ursa Major, were bivouacked in one of the barns. There I entered skulkingly, as a gameless hunter may, and hid my untrophied head beneath a mound of ancient hay, not without the mustiness of its age.

"No one clawed us, no one chawed us, that night. A Ripogenus chill awakened the whole party with early dawn. We sprang from our nests, shook the hay-seed out of our hair, and were full-dressed without more ceremony, ready for whatever grand sensation Nature might purvey for our æsthetic breakfast.

"Nothing is ever as we expect. When we stepped into out-of-doors, looking for Ripogenus, a lake of Maine, we found not a single aquatic fact in the landscape. Ripogenus, a lake, had mizzled (as the Americans say), literally mizzled. Our simplified view comprised a grassy hill with barns, and a stern positive pyramid, surely Katahdin; and aloft, beyond, above, below, thither, hither, and yon, Fog, — not fog, but FOG.

"Ripogenus, the water-body, had had aspirations, and a boon of brief transfiguration into a cloud-body had been granted it by Nature, who grants to every terrestrial essence prophetic experiences of what it one day would be.

"In short, and to repeat, Ripogenus had transmuted itself into vapor, and filled the valley full to our feet. A faint wind had power to billow this mist-lake, and drive cresting surges up against the eastern hill-side, over which they sometimes broke, and, involving it totally, rolled clear and free toward Katahdin, where he stood hiding the glows of sunrise. Leagues higher up than the mountain rested a presence of cirri, already white and luminous with full daylight, and from them drooped linking wreaths of orange mist, clinging to the rosy-violet granite of the peak.

"Up clomb and sailed Ripogenus and befogged the whole; then we condescended to breakfast.

"Singularly enough, mill-dams are always found below mill-ponds. Analogously in the Maine rivers, below the lakes, rapids are. Rapids too often compel carries. While we breakfasted without steak of bear, or cutlet of moose, Ripogenus grad-nally retracted itself, and became conscious again of what poetry there is in a lake's pause and a rapid's flow. Fog condensed into water, and water submitting to its destiny went cascading down through a wild defile where no birch could follow.

"The Ripogenus carry is three miles long, a faint path through thickets.

"'First half,' said Cancut, ''s plain enough; but after that 'twould take a philosopher with his spectacles on to find it.'

"This was discouraging. Philosophers twain we might deem ourselves; but what is a craftsman without tools? And never a goggle had we.

"But the trappers of musk-rats had become our fast friends. They insisted upon lightening our loads over the brambly league. This was kindly. Cancut's elongated head-piece, the birch, was his share of the burden; and a bag of bread, a firkin of various grub, damp blankets for three, and multitudinous traps, seemed more than two could carry at one trip over this longest and roughest of portages.

"We paddled from the camp to the lake-foot, and there, while the others compacted the portables for portage, Iglesias and I, at cost of a ducking with mist-drops from the thickets, scrambled up a crag for a supreme view of the fair lake and the clear mountain. And we did well. Katahdin, from the hill guarding the exit of the Penobscot from Ripogenus, is eminent and emphatic, a signal and solitary pyramid, grander than any below the realms of the unchangeable, more distinctly mountainous than any mountain of those that stop short of the venerable honors of eternal snow.

"We trod the trail, we others, easier than Cancut. He found it hard to thread the mazes of an overgrown path and navigate his canoe at the same time. 'Better,' thought he, as he staggered and plunged and bumped along, extricating his boat-bonnet now from a bower of raspberry-bushes, now from the branches of a brotherly birch-tree,—'better,' thought he, 'were I seated in what I bear, and bounding gayly over the billow. Peril is better than pother.'

"Bushwhacking thus for a league, we circumvented the peril, and came upon the river flowing fair and free. The trappers said adieu, and launched us. Back then they went to consult their traps and flay their fragrant captives, and we shot forward.

"That was a day all poetry and music. Mountain airs bent and blunted the noonday sunbeams. There was a shade of delicate birches on either hand, whenever we loved to linger. Our feather-shallop went dancing on, fleet as the current, and whenever a passion for speed came, after moments of luxurious sloth, we could change floating at the river's will into leaps and chasing, with a few strokes of the paddle. All was untouched, unvisited wilderness, and we from bend to bend the first discoverers. So we might fancy ourselves; for civilization had been here only to cut pines, not to plant houses. Yet these fair curves, and liberal reaches, and bright rapids of the birchen-bowered river were only solitary, not lonely. It is never lonely with Nature. Without unnatural men or unnatural beasts, she is capital society by herself. And so we found her, — a lovely being, in perfect toilet, which I describe, in an indiscriminating, masculine way, by saying that it was a forest and a river and lakes and a mountain and doubtless sky, all made resplendent by her judicious disposition of a most becoming light. Iglesias and I, being old friends, were received into close intimacy. She smiled upon us unaffectedly, and had a thousand exquisite things to say, drawing us out also, with feminine tact, to say our best things, and teaching us to be conscious, in her presence, of more delicate possibilities of refinement and a tenderer poetic sense. So we voyaged through the sunny hours and were happy.

"Yet there was no monotony in our progress. We could not always drift and glide. Sometimes we must fight our way. Below the placid reaches were the inevitable 'rips' and rapids; some we could shoot without hitting anything; some would hit us heavily, did we try to shoot. Whenever the rocks in the current were only as thick as the plums in a boarding-school pudding, we could venture to run the gauntlet; whenever they multiplied to a schoolboy's ideal, we were arrested. Just at the brink of peril we would sweep in by an eddy into a shady pool by the shore. At such spots we found a path across the carry. Cancut at once preceded to bonnet himself with the trickling birch. Iglesias and I took up the packs and hurried on with minds intent on berries. Berries we always found, — blueberries covered with a cloudy bloom, blueberries, pulpy, saccharine, plenteous.

"Often, when a portage was not quite necessary, a dangerous bit of white water would require the birch to be lightened. Cancut must steer her alone over the foam, while we, springing ashore, raced through the thick of the forest, tore through the briers, and plunged through the punk of trees older than history, now rotting where they fell, slain by Time, the giganticide. Cancut then had us at advantage. Sometimes we had laughed at him, when he, a good-humored malaprop, made vague clutches at the thread of discourse. Now suppose he should take a fancy to drop down stream and leave us. What then? Berries then, and little else, unless we had a chance at a trout or a partridge. It is not cheery, but dreary, to be left in pathlessness, blanketless, guideless, and with breadths of lake and mountain and Nature, shaggy and bearish, between man and man. With the consciousness of a latent shudder in our hearts at such a possibility, we parted brier and bramble until the rapid was passed, we scuffled hastily through to the riverbank, and there always, in some quiet nook, was a beacon of red-flannel shirt among the green leaves over the blue and shadowy water, and always the fast-sailing Cancut awaiting us, making the woods resound to amicable hails, and ready again to be joked and to retaliate.

"Such alternations made our voyage a charming olla. We had the placid glide, the fleet dash, the wild career, the pause, the landing, the agreeable interlude of a portage, and the unburdened stampede along-shore. Thus we won our way, or our way wooed us on, until, in early afternoon, a lovely lakelet opened before us. The fringed shores retired, and as we shot forth upon wider calm, lo, Katahdin! unlooked for, at last, as a revelation. Our boat ruffled its shadow, doing pretty violence to its dignity, that we might know the greater grandeur of the substance. There was a gentle agency of atmosphere softening the bold forms of this startling neighbor, and giving it distance, lest we might fear it would topple and crush us. Clouds, level below, hid the summit and towered aloft. Among them we might imagine the mountain rising with thousands more of feet of heaven-piercing height; there is one degree of sublimity in mystery, as there is another degree in certitude.

"We lay to in a shady nook, just off Katahdin's reflection in the river, while Iglesias sketched him. Meanwhile I, analyzing my view, presently discovered a droll image in the track of a land-avalanche down the front. It was a comical fellow, a little giant, a colossal dwarf, six hundred feet high, and should have been thrice as tall, had it had any proper development, — for out of his head grew two misdirected skeleton legs, 'hanging down and dangling.' The countenance was long, elfin, sneering, solemn, as of a truculent demon, saddish for his trade, an ashamed, but unrepentant rascal. He had two immense erect ears, and in his boisterous position had suffered a loss of hair, wearing nothing save an impudent scalp-lock. A very grotesque personage. Was he the guardian imp, the legendary Eft of Katahdin, scoffing already at us as verdant, and warning that he would make us unhappy, if we essayed to appear on Brocken heights without initiation?

"'A terrible pooty mountain,' Cancut observed; and so it is.

"Not to fail in topographical duty, I record, that near this lakelet flows in the river Sowadehunk, and not far below, a sister streamlet, hardly less melodiously named, Ayboljockameegus. Opposite the latter we landed and encamped, with Katahdin full in front, and broadly visible."

CHAPTER XIII.

The Ascent of Mount Katahdin — Four Different Accounts.

The ascent of Katahdin is usually made from some point near the Sourdnahunk Stream. Having never made the ascent of the mountain, we relate the experience of several who have. We quote the following from Springer's "Forest Life and Forest Trees":— [1]

"Our travelers, after having made the ascent of the river to the proper point, and made the necessary arrangements for their journey up the mountain, 'entered the slide at eight o'clock,' A.M., in the early part of September, and found its ascent quite steep, 'though not difficult or dangerous at all when one takes time.'

"On almost all sides of the mountain there is a short, tangled growth of alders and white birch coming up between the rocks. These, being kept down by the winds, grow into an almost impassable bramble. At a distance it has a beautiful, smooth appearance, like a green, grassy hill, or what one of the company called a 'piece of oats.' The slide serves as a path up through all this tangle, reaching to the top of the south-eastern ridge of the mountain, which is above all timber growth, making about one-third of the whole perpendicular height of Katahdin, to which the ascent of the brook below would add another third.

"Although it was hard climbing, we ascended pretty fast, and the clear morning air gave an indescribable beauty to the prospect below. The most pleasing was the constant change and variety caused by our rapid ascent. It was known that the mountain, at this season of the year, is frequented by bears in pursuit of cranberries; but we did not see any, though our gunner had enjoined silence in hopes of obtaining a shot. I remained with the rear, to see all up safe. The most zealous 'went ahead,' and

---

[1] Published by Harper & Brothers, New York.

were soon out of sight, until, near the head of the slide, we heard them from the distant topmost peaks calling out, 'Come on, ye braves!' At this distance they looked very small in stature. From the head of the slide we turned to the left, and ascended north-west to the first and most eastern peak: by this time our comrades had reached the most western. We here paused to view our position. It is, perhaps, the most favorable spot for surveying the whole structure. From thence the principal peaks are in a curved line, going south-west, then west and north-west. The second peak, called by us the 'Chimney,' is near the first, but separated by a sharp cut, one hundred and fifty or two hundred feet deep, and nearly square in its form. We had seen one of our comrades upon its summit, else we might not have attempted the ascent. His zeal seemed to blind him to danger, for, when questioned on our return, he could neither tell *when* or *how* he ascended. Our first plan was to pass around the base without going over the top; but this we found impossible, and were about to give up, when one pointed out a diagonal course, where, by taking a few pretty long steps, he thought we could ascend. I tried first, and succeeded, and all followed but two. From the 'Chimney' we went from one hammock to another, making, on the whole, a gradual ascent, till we reached the middle of the principal peaks, a distance of nearly half a mile. There we met our comrades on their return from the western peak, and all sat down to rest. Here we found a monument that had been erected by some former visitor, but was overgrown with moss, appearing lonely, as if it had seen no relations for years. On the first and most eastern peak all the monuments which I had made the year previous looked new and fresh. It is not easy to decide which of the two (the western and middle peaks) is highest. Judgment was given in favor of the middle one.

"While sitting on the south side of the monument, at twelve o'clock, we put the thermometer in a favorable place, and it went up to 84°. At the same time, on the north side, and six feet from us, water was freezing, and the snow dry and crusty. Near by the monument a rock stood in its natural position, having a sharp peak in the top. This was the highest one of the kind. Of this about four inches were broken off, and one of the company carried it home with the conviction that we had lowered the height

INSPECTION OF A DAY'S FISHING.

of Katahdin to that amount. About two, P.M., we returned to the eastern peak. It may be well to pause here and take a resurvey of the scene thus far presented, and as much more as can be viewed from the point.

"From this eastern peak a spur makes out eastward one mile. Half a mile down, however, it divides, and a branch runs to the north-east to the same distance. On the south-west, across the cut, is the 'Chimney.' From this the line of peaks and hammocks curves to the west till it reaches the middle and highest peak. From one hammock to the other there are, in all, thirty rods of narrow passes. Some of them are so narrow that a man could drop a stone from either hand, and it would go to unknown depths below. In some places the only possible way is over the top, and only one foot wide. For a great part of the time the wind blows across these passes so violently that the stones themselves have to be firmly fixed to keep their places. It seemed remarkable, as if for our convenience, that the day of our visit was still and quiet. From the middle peak the line curves to the north-west, to the further monument. From this point a branch makes down to the south-west, having on it some extensive table-lands, while the top ridge or curve turns directly north with the 'sag.' At the bottom of the 'sag' we come upon a wide flat, which runs north half a mile, and stretches out to a considerable width. At the northern extremity of the flat the ridge curves to the east, and rises to a peak about equal in height to the eastern peak of the northern wing. This is probably the highest of the northern peaks, from which a spur makes down, a little south of east, to within one quarter of a mile from the one that comes from the southern wing. All this nearly includes a deep basin, with walls almost perpendicular, and in some places apparently two thousand feet high.

"To survey the bottom of this basin I have since made a separate journey. It contains, perhaps, two hundred acres, covered with large square blocks of granite that seem to have come from the surrounding wall. There are in all six lakes and ponds, varying in size from two to ten acres. One of them I crossed on ice the 15th of October.

"From its outlet inward to the south-west is about a mile, where there is a small lake of clear water which has no visible outlet. So far as I can learn, I was the first human visitor to this fabled residence of the Indians' Pamolah. It is not strange that a superstitious people should have many traditions of his wonderful pranks, and be kept away from close engagements with such a foe. When we reached the lake on our way to Katahdin, it is easy to see the origin of those fears which the Indians are said to have respecting the mountain as the residence of Pamolah or Big Devil. Clouds form in the basin, and are seen whirling out in all directions. Tradition tells a 'long yarn' about a 'handsome squaw' among the Penobscots, who once did a great business in *slaying* her thousands among the young chiefs of her nation, but was finally taken by Pamolah to Katahdin, where he now protects himself and his prize from approaching Indians with all his artillery of thunder and hail.

"The Indian says that it is 'sartin true, 'cause handsome squaw always ketch em deble;' whether this be true or not, the basin is the birthplace of storms, and I have myself heard the roar of its winds for several miles. But on the 15th of October, when I entered it and went to the upper lake, all was still as the house of nymphs, except when we ourselves spoke, and then the thousand echoes were like the response of fairies bidding us welcome. In this way the music of our voices would find itself in the midst of a numerous choir singing a '*round.*'

"The upper lake, which I visited and went around, has an inlet, a white, pearly brook, coming out nearly under the 'Chimney' and running a short distance through alders and meadow grass. It has no visible outlet; but on the north side it seems to ooze out among the rocks. We can trace this water-course curving to the east of north till it reaches the lower and largest lake, from which flows a brook sufficiently large for trout to run up. This brook curves to the south, running into West Branch, and is called Roaring Brook. The mountain around this basin is in the form of a horse-shoe, opening to the north-east. From the peak on the northern wing there is another deep gorge, partly encircled with a curving ridge, which some would call another basin. On the north side of this gorge there is a peak nearly equal in height to the one on the south of it, but considerably further east, making this northern basin or open gorge open to the south-east. These two basins, from some points of view, seem to be one. From the last-mentioned peak the mountain slopes off from one peak or shoulder to another, perhaps three miles, before it reaches the timber growth. Some of the branches of the Wassataquoik come from this northern part, but some of them from the basin or southern part of Katahdin.

"Rough granite, moss-covered rocks are spread over its whole surface from the short growth upward. Blueberries and cranberries grow far up the sides. At the time of our visit considerable snow lay on its summits and lined the walls of the great basin. The party, of course, found plenty of drink. The Avalanche Brook, having its source about the middle of the slide, furnished water pure as crystal. The ascent was attended with some danger and fatigue. But what a view when the utmost heights are gained! What a magnificent panorama of forests, lakes, and distant mountains! The surface of the earth, with its many-tinted verdure, resembled, in form and smoothness, the swelling sea. In the course of the forenoon, light fogs from all the lakes ascended, and, coming to Katahdin, intertwined themselves most fantastically above our heads, then settled down and dispersed. But what can be fitly said about the vast expanse of the heavens, to be seen from such an elevation, especially when the sun goes down, and the glowing stars appear in silent majesty? All the gorgeous, artificial brilliancy of man's invention is more than lost in the comparison. Language has no power to describe a scene of this nature. The height of Katahdin above the level of the sea is five thousand three hundred feet. Its position is isolated, and its structure an immense curiosity. From its summit very few populous places are visible, so extensive is the intervening wilderness. On its sides the growth of wood is beautiful, presenting a regular variation in altitude and size all the way up to the point where it ceases.

"The great basin described by Mr. Keep was to none of us an inferior object of interest. Want of time and strength prevented our descent into it. It is open to general inspection from all the heights around it. The day being quiet, the view was divested of much of its terror; but we could readily believe it the abode of all the furies in a storm, and where the polar monarch has his chief residence in Maine. We called to each other across the basin, and echo answered 'Where!' in earnest. The air was exhilarating, as may be supposed, but the effect not as sensible as we anticipated.

"The whole party returned to the head of the slide at three P.M., and engaged in picking cranberries. These grow on all parts of the mountain above the timber region, and no doubt annually yield many thousand bushels. 'They grow on vines among the rocks, and are commonly called the mountain or highland cranberry. They are smaller than the meadow cranberry, but of a better flavor.'

"At four o'clock six of the party went down to the camp to prepare fuel for the Sabbath. Our guide and the gunner remained at the head of the slide all night, and kept a fire with old roots; yet it was presumed that they had now and then a *little cold* comfort. The result of their stay is thus set forth by Mr. Keep:—

"'On Sabbath morning the eastern horizon was clear of clouds, and we looked anxiously for the sun. Just before it came up, a bright streak appeared of silver whiteness, like the reflected light of the moon. We could see the further outline of land quite plain, and for a short distance beyond was this silvery streak. Soon a small arc of the sun appeared above this bright line. I was hardly able to control my emotions while the whole came in sight. On Saturday night, about sundown, our view of the country around was more distinct and enchanting — a boundless wilderness in all directions, much of the view being south of the lakes. Of the latter, not far from two hundred are to be seen dotting the landscape. In one of them we can count one hundred islands. Soon after sunrise on Sabbath morning we went down to the camp to spend the day with the company.'

"That holy morning found us refreshed, and somewhat prepared to appreciate our peculiar circumstances. The weather was charming. The air resounded with the pleasing murmur of the Avalanche Brook, as it flowed down over its bed of rocks; nor was the song of birds denied us. Gentle breezes stirred the beautiful foliage of the circling woods. Impressive stillness reigned, and the whole scene was adapted to waken happy and exuberant emotions.

"Early we mounted some rock on the bank of the stream toward the rising sun, and overlooking a vast region of country, and there poured forth sacred melody to our hearts' content. The echo was glorious. Verily we thought our 'feet were set in a large place;' and we could readily imagine that the wide creation had found a tongue with which our own exulted in unison.

"At the hour appointed we assembled in the camp, and engaged in the exercises of a religious conference. It was good to be there. The scene finds its portraiture in the words of Cowper: —

>" ' The calm retreat, the silent shade,
>   With pray'r and praise agree,
> And seem by Thy sweet bounty made
>   For those who follow Thee.
>
>" ' Then, if Thy spirit touch the soul,
>   And grace her mean abode,
> Oh, with what peace, and joy, and love
>   She there communes with God!'

"It is not too much to say that we enjoyed a measure of such experience. The day — the place — the topics of remarks — the songs of Zion — all encircled by a kind Providence, and made effective by the presence of God, will ever be worthy of a grateful remembrance.

"In the afternoon, by request, Rev. Mr. Munsell addressed us from the 11th verse of the 145th Psalm: 'They shall speak of the glory of thy kingdom, and talk of thy power.' Our position added deep interest to the theme of discourse, and naturally furnished much ground for illustration. Indeed, the entire services of the day were attended with peculiar influences, being had under circumstances so widely different from the ordinary life of the company.

"That Sabbath was our delight, even in the face of a possible deficiency in food. But the course adopted imparted bodily rest and a peaceful mind.

"We had traveled with burdens on our backs twenty-five miles — crossed several streams — climbed rough hills — walked on rocky places — tumbled over huge trunks of fallen trees — crowded through plenty of jungle — waded the Avalanche Brook — and all this in forbidding weather; but, aside from the glorious view on the summit of Katahdin, our toil found its recompense in the novelty and influence of a Sabbath observance on such an elevation, and amid the wild scenes and solitudes of a mountain forest.

"Scarcity of food, and the engagements of some of the party, made it necessary on Monday morning to start for home. We left the camp about half-past nine, following down the brook to the point from whence we ascended, and then direct to the lake.

"'At this time,' says our guide, 'we fell into much confusion on account of two of the company who were missing, — the gunner and Mr. Meservey, for whom we made search; but in vain. Few can imagine our feelings save those who have heard the cry of *lost* coming up from the deep gloom of the wilderness in the native tone of some wanderer calling for help. After consultation, it was resolved that we must leave the ground for home, hoping for the best. We left at one, and came to the lake at four P.M., and here, to our great joy, we saw a smoke on the opposite side, near the outlet, and at five rejoined our missing companions. They had caught trout enough for us all, weighing from one to three pounds. With these, and cranberry-sauce in plenty, also bread, pork, and tea, we made merry around a cheerful fire. That night, however, a storm of rain coming up, found us poorly prepared.'

"In this connection an incident may be related. Just before our arrival, while the gunner was fishing, suddenly two moose bounded furiously into the lake, and appeared to be swimming toward him. Though all along desirous of an interview, their visit was rather too startling. He scampered, with all haste to the shore, seized his gun and fired, but the balls would not go through the '*law*,' which, at that season, afforded protection, and so the moose escaped.

"The night just referred to was a time of *realities*. Truth proved 'stranger than fiction.' Amid anxiety for the lost, the axe had been left on the mountain. A pile of logs lay near the outlet of the lake. With some of these our missing companions had made a fire; some formed the floor of the camp, and others, used as rafters, were covered with boughs for protection, but not from rain. On the above floor (the spot allowing no other), no boughs at hand could make a downy bed. Every one found out that he was composed of flesh and bones. It also became difficult to regulate the fire, so that the heat was often intense. Contrary winds would ever and anon drive the smoke into the camp, and thus cause great involuntary weeping. The scene was *felt*, and few could find sleep without stealing it. It was visible darkness all around. Toward midnight the rain commenced. One of the party, writing to another from Lincoln in December, says, 'Old Mount Katahdin from this place looks dreary enough. Its snow-capped top often reminds me of our amusing adventures; but nothing in all our travels affords more amusement in moments of meditation than the night on the Pond Dam. That old plaid cloak, dripping in the rain; its occupant upon a log without the camp, singing, "The morning light is breaking," when it was only one o'clock; and then again, "He shall come down like rain," etc., — all together have left an impression on my mind not soon to be effaced.'

"The occupant of that 'cloak,' unable to sleep, conversed with the 'daughters of music,' and was prompted to sing the night out and the morning in; and as the rain increased, the whole crew joined heartily in the chorus. Our departure from such lodgings was very early. Beneath continual droppings from the trees and bushes, we pressed through an obstinate pathway, and arrived at the Wassataquoik camp at half-past nine. This march was really toilsome, but brought us out at the desired point. After a long rest, we followed the old supply road most of the way, forded the Wassataquoik, and came out opposite Mr. Hunt's, whence the bateaux took us across the East Branch. This was a little past four o'clock P.M. Our appearance was far from beardless, our 'externals' somewhat ragged and torn, and our appetites keen as a 'Damascus razor.' 'Mine host' and family received us most cordially, having felt some anxiety in our absence. They made us joyful around a full table of good things. On the day following, Wednesday, we passed to Mr. Cushman's, and on Thursday took conveyances for home."

Another visitor[1] to this point of attraction observes: —

"While I was engaged in noting the bearings of this mountain, the clouds suddenly darted down upon its summit, and concealed it from view, while we could observe that a violent snow-squall was

---

[1] Dr. Jackson.

paying homage to Pomola, the demon of the mountain. Presently the storm ceased, and the clouds, having thus paid their tribute, passed on, and left the mountain white with snow. This took place on the 20th of September.

"Crossing the lake — 'Millnoket, a most beautiful sheet of water, containing a great number of small islands, from which circumstance it takes its name' — we reached the carrying-place at the head of a long creek, where we pitched our camp amid a few poplar trees, which were of second growth, or have sprung up since the forests were burned. The want of good fuel and of boughs for a bed was severely felt, since we were obliged to repose on naked rocks, and the green poplar trees appeared to give more smoke than fire. The night was cold, and the wind violent, so that sleep was out of the question. Early in the morning we prepared to carry our boats over to Ambijejis Lake, and the labor was found very difficult, since the water was low, and we had to traverse a long tract of boggy land before reaching the other lake.

"Tracks of moose and caribou abound in the mud, since they frequent the shallow parts of the lake, to feed upon the lily-pads or the leaves of the Nuphan lutea, which here abound. A noble-looking caribou suddenly started from the woods, and trotted quietly along the shores of the lake quite near us; but we were not prepared to take him, and he presently darted into the forest and disappeared.

"Our provisions having been reduced, owing to the circumstance that our journey proved much longer than we had anticipated, I thought it necessary to put the whole party on a regular allowance, which was mutually agreed to. Our Indian, Neptune, succeeded in catching half-a-dozen musquash, which we were glad to share with him, and a few trout which were also taken, and served to save a portion of our more substantial food. At Pock-wock-amus Falls, where the river rushes over a ledge of granite, large trout are caught abundantly, and we stopped a short time to obtain a supply. They are readily taken with a common fishing-hook and line, baited with a piece of pork, or even with a slip of paper, which is to be trailed over the surface of the water. Some of the trout thus caught would weigh from three and a half to four pounds.

"On the 22d of September we prepared ourselves for ascending the mountain, taking with us our tent, a few cooking utensils, and all the food remaining, except a small quantity of Indian cornmeal, which we concealed on the island for use on our return.

"Our party, all clothed with red flannel shirts, and loaded with our various equipments, made a singular appearance as we landed on the opposite shore and filed into the woods.

"Having reached a height where the forest-trees were so diminutive that we could not camp any higher up for want of fuel, we pitched our tent. This place is about half-way up the mountain. From it we have an extensive view of the surrounding country.

'Leaving our camp on the mountain side at seven A.M. we set out for the summit of Katahdin, traveling steadily up the slide, clambering over loose boulders of granite, trap, and graywacke, which are heaped up in confusion along its course. We at length reached a place where it was dangerous longer to walk on the loose rocks, and, passing over to the right-hand side, clambered up among the dwarfish bushes that cling to the side of the mountain.

"Two of our party became discouraged on reaching this point, and there being no necessity of their accompanying us, they were allowed to return to camp. The remainder of our ascent was extremely difficult, and required no small perseverance. Our Indian guide, Louis, placed stones along the path, in order that we might more readily find the way down the mountain, and the wisdom of this precaution was fully manifested in the sequel. At ten A.M. we reached the table-land which forms the mountain's top, and ascends gradually to the central peak. Here the wind and driving snow and hail rendered it almost impossible to proceed, but we at length reached the central peak. The true altitude of Mt. Katahdin, above the level of the sea, is a little more than one mile perpendicular elevation. It is, then, evidently the highest point in the State of Maine, and is the most abrupt granite mountain in New England.

"Amid a furious snow-storm we set out on our return from this region of clouds and snow. Louis declared that Pomola was angry with us for presuming to measure the height of the mountain, and thus revenged himself. 'Descending, we had nearly gone astray, and might have descended on the wrong side, had it not been for the precaution of Louis, before named. Clouds and darkness hung upon the mountain's brow, and the cold blasts almost deprived us of breath. Incrusted with snow, we carefully slid upon the surface of the rocks.' 'We tumbled down some large blocks of granite, that descended with a terrible fracas, dashing the rocks into fragments as they bounded along.' 'Our party encamped upon the mountain side, and passed a sleepless night, without food, and amid a driving snow-storm.'

"Early next morning we struck our tent and descended the mountain; but so enfeebled had we become by hunger, privations, and fatigue, that it was with difficulty we could carry ourselves and burdens. Every now and then our knees would give way beneath us, and cause us to fall upon the ground. When we reached the base of the mountain, we discovered some wild choke-cherries hanging in bunches from the trees, which the bears had often climbed and broken for the fruit. Felling one of these cherry-trees, we ate the astringent fruit, and were in some measure resuscitated in strength, so as to march with renewed vigor. A bed of blueberries also presented itself, and we stopped to dine upon them. 'Proceeding on, we met two of our company, who had passed down the night before, who had cooked all the Indian meal that we had left at our old camp on the island, and brought the cakes for our relief. On our way down the river we fortunately met two young men ascending the stream in a canoe, on an exploring expedition; we induced them to sell us twenty biscuits, which, being two to a man, on short allowance, we hoped to be able to reach Nickatow. On our way down we met another crew, who supplied us with the necessary rations to reach Nickatow, where, on our arrival, we obtained all that was necessary for the comfortable prosecution of our down-river journey.'"

We give another account, taken from Thoreau's "Maine Woods":—[1]

"By six o'clock, having mounted our packs and a good blanketful of trout, ready dressed, and swung up such baggage and provision as we wished to leave behind, upon the tops of saplings, to be out of the reach of bears, we started for the summit of the

---

[1] Published by James R. Osgood & Co., Boston.

mountain, distant, as Uncle George said the boatmen called it, about four miles, but as I judged, and as it proved, nearer fourteen. He had never been any nearer the mountain than this, and there was not the slightest trace of man to guide us farther in this direction. At first, pushing a few rods up the Aboljacknagesic, or 'open-land stream,' we fastened our bateau to a tree, and traveled up the north side, through burnt lands, now partially overgrown with young aspens and other shrubbery; but soon, recrossing this stream, where it was about fifty or sixty feet wide, upon a jam of logs and rocks, — and you could cross it by this means almost anywhere, — we struck at once for the highest peak, over a mile or more of comparatively open land, still very gradually ascending the while. Here it fell to my lot, as the oldest mountain-climber, to take the lead. So, scanning the woody side of the mountain, which lay still at an indefinite distance, stretched out some seven or eight miles in length before us, we determined to steer directly for the base of the highest peak, leaving a large slide, by which, as I have since learned, some of our predecessors ascended, on our left. This course would lead us parallel to a dark seam in the forest, which marked the bed of a torrent, and over a slight spur, which extended southward from the main mountain, from whose bare summit we could get an outlook over the country, and climb directly up the peak, which would then be close at hand. Seen from this point, a bare ridge at the extremity of the open land, Katahdin presented a different aspect from any mountain I have seen, there being a greater portion of naked rock rising abruptly from the forest; and we looked up at this blue barrier as if it were some fragment of a wall which anciently bounded the earth in that direction. Setting the compass for a north-east course, which was the bearing of the southern base of the highest peak, we were soon buried in the woods.

"We soon began to meet with traces of bears and moose, and those of rabbits were everywhere visible. The tracks of moose, more or less recent, to speak literally, covered every square rod on the sides of the mountain; and these animals are probably more numerous there now than ever before, being driven into this wilderness, from all sides, by the settlements. The track of a full-grown moose is like that of a cow, or larger, and of the young, like that of a calf. Sometimes we found ourselves traveling in faint paths, which they had made, like cow-paths in the woods, only far more indistinct, being rather openings, affording imperfect vistas through the dense underwood, than trodden paths; and everywhere the twigs had been browsed by them, clipped as smoothly as if by a knife. The bark of trees was stripped up by them to the height of eight or nine feet, in long, narrow strips, an inch wide, still showing the distinct marks of their teeth. We expected nothing less than to meet a herd of them every moment, and our Nimrod held his shooting-iron in readiness; but we did not go out of our way to look for them, and, though numerous, they are so wary that the unskilful hunter might range the forest a long time before he could get sight of one. They are sometimes dangerous to encounter, and will not turn out for the hunter, but furiously rush upon him and trample him to death, unless he is lucky enough to avoid them by dodging round a tree. The largest are nearly as large as a horse, and weigh sometimes one thousand pounds; and it is said that they can step over a five-feet gate in their ordinary walk. They are described as exceedingly awkward-looking animals, with their long legs and short bodies, making a ludicrous figure when in full run, but making great headway nevertheless. It seemed a mystery to us how they could tread these woods, which it required all our suppleness to accomplish, — climbing, stooping, and winding, alternately. They are said to drop their long and branching horns, which usually spread five or six feet, on their backs, and make their way easily by the weight of their bodies. Our boatman said, but I know not with how much truth, that their horns are apt to be gnawed away by vermin while they sleep. Their flesh, which is more like beef than venison, is common in the Bangor market.

"We had proceeded on thus seven or eight miles, till about noon, with frequent pauses to refresh the weary ones, crossing a considerable mountain stream, which we conjectured to be Murch Brook, at whose mouth we had camped, all the time in woods, without having once seen the summit — and rising very gradually, when the boatmen, beginning to despair a little, and fearing that we were leaving the mountain on one side of us, for they had not entire faith in the compass, McCauslin climbed a tree, from the top of which he could see the peak, when it appeared that we had not swerved from a right line, the compass down below still ranging with his arm, which pointed to the summit. By the side of a cool mountain rill, amid the woods, where the water began to partake of the purity and transparency of the air, we stopped to cook some of our fishes, which we had brought thus far in order to save our hard bread and pork, in the use of which we had put ourselves on short allowance. We soon had a fire blazing, and stood around it, under the damp and sombre forest of firs and birches, each with a sharpened stick, three or four feet in length, upon which he had spitted his trout, or roach, previously well gashed and salted, our sticks radiating like the spokes of a wheel from one centre, and each crowding his particular fish into the most desirable exposure, not with the truest regard always to his neighbor's rights. Thus we regaled ourselves, drinking meanwhile at the spring, till one man's pack, at least, was considerably lightened, when we again took up our line of march.

"At length we reached an elevation sufficiently bare to afford a view of the summit, still distant and blue, almost as if retreating from us. A torrent, which proved to be the same we had crossed, was seen tumbling down in front, literally from out of the clouds. But this glimpse at our whereabouts was soon lost, and we were buried in the woods again. The wood was chiefly yellow birch, spruce, fir, mountain-ash, or round-wood, as the Maine people call it, and moose-wood. It was the worst kind of traveling, sometimes like the densest scrub-oak patches, with us. The cornel, or bunch-berries, were very abundant, as well as Solomon's seal and moose-berries. Blueberries were distributed along our whole route; and in one place the bushes were drooping with the weight of the fruit, still as fresh as ever. It was the 7th of September. Such patches afforded a grateful repast, and served to bait the tired party forward. When any lagged behind, the cry of 'blueberries' was most effectual to bring them up. Even at this elevation we passed through a moose-yard formed by a large, flat rock, four or five rods square, where they tread down the snow in winter. At length, fearing that if we held the direct course to the summit, we should not find any water near our camping-ground, we gradually swerved to the west, till, at four o'clock, we struck again the torrent which I have mentioned, and here, in view of the summit, the weary party decided to camp that night.

"While my companions were seeking a suitable spot for this

purpose, I improved the little daylight that was left, in climbing the mountain alone. We were in a deep and narrow ravine, sloping up to the clouds, at an angle of nearly forty-five degrees, and hemmed in by walls of rock, which were at first covered with low trees, then with impenetrable thickets of scraggy birches and spruce-trees, and with moss, but at last bare of all vegetation but lichens, and almost continually draped in clouds. Following up the course of the torrent which occupied this, — and I mean to lay some emphasis on this word *up*, — pulling myself up by the side of perpendicular falls of twenty or thirty feet, by the roots of firs and birches, and then, perhaps, walking a level rod or two in the thin stream, — for it took up the whole road, ascending by huge steps, as it were, a giant's stairway, down which a river flowed, — I had soon cleared the trees, and paused, on the successive shelves, to look back over the country. The torrent was from fifteen to thirty feet wide, without a tributary, and seemingly not diminishing in breadth as I advanced; but still it came rushing and roaring down, with a copious tide, over and amidst masses of bare rock, from the very clouds, as though a water-spout had just burst over the mountain. Leaving this at last, I began to work my way, scarcely less arduous than Satan's anciently through Chaos, up the nearest, though not the highest, peak. At first scrambling on all fours over the top of ancient black spruce-trees (*Abies nigra*) old as the flood, from two to ten or twelve feet in height, their tops flat and spreading, and their foliage blue, and nipped with cold, as if for centuries they had ceased growing upward against the bleak sky, the solid cold. I walked some good rods erect upon the tops of these trees, which were overgrown with moss and mountain-cranberries. It seemed that in the course of time they had filled up the intervals between the huge rocks, and the cold wind had uniformly leveled all over. Here the principle of vegetation was hard put to it. There was apparently a belt of this kind running quite round the mountain, though, perhaps, nowhere so remarkable as here. Once, slumping through, I looked down ten feet, into a dark and cavernous region, and saw the stem of a spruce, on whose top I stood, as on a mass of coarse basket-work, fully nine inches in diameter at the ground. These holes were bears' dens, and the bears were even then at home.

"This was the sort of garden I made my way *over*, for an eighth of a mile, at the risk, it is true, of treading on some of the plants, not seeing any path *through* it, — certainly the most treacherous and porous country I ever traveled.

> "'Nigh foundered on he fares,
> Treading the crude consistence, half on foot,
> Half flying.'

But nothing could exceed the toughness of the twigs, — not one snapped under my weight, for they had slowly grown. Having slumped, scrambled, rolled, bounced, and walked, by turns, over this scraggy country, I arrived upon a side-hill, or rather side-mountain, where rocks, gray, silent rocks, were the flocks and herds that pastured, chewing a rocky cud at sunset. They looked at me with hard gray eyes, without a bleat or a low. This brought me to the skirt of a cloud, and bounded my walk that night. But I had already seen that Maine country when I turned about, waving, flowing, rippling, down below.

"When I returned to my companions, they had selected a camping-ground on the torrent's edge, and were resting on the ground; one was on the sick-list, rolled in a blanket, on a damp shelf of rock. It was a savage and dreary scene enough; so wildly rough, that they looked long to find a level and open space for the tent. We could not well camp higher, for want of fuel, and the trees there seemed so ever-green and sappy, that we almost doubted if they would acknowledge the influence of fire; but fire prevailed at last, and blazed here, too, like a good citizen of the world. Even at this height we met with frequent traces of moose, as well as of bears. As here was no cedar, we made our bed of coarser feathered spruce; but at any rate the feathers were plucked from the live tree. It was, perhaps, even a more grand and desolate place for a night's lodging than the summit would have been, being in the neighborhood of those wild trees, and of the torrent. Some more aerial and finer-spirited winds rushed and roared through the ravine all night, from time to time arousing our fire, and dispersing the embers about. It was as if we lay in the very nest of a young whirlwind. At midnight, one of my bed-fellows, being startled in his dreams by the sudden blazing up to its top of a fir-tree, whose green boughs were dried by the heat, sprang up, with a cry, from his bed, thinking the world on fire, and drew the whole camp after him.

"In the morning, after whetting our appetite on some raw pork, a wafer of hard bread, and a dipper of condensed cloud or waterspout, we all together began to make our way up the falls, which I have described; this time choosing the right hand, or highest peak, which was not the one I had approached before. But soon my companions were lost to my sight behind the mountain ridge in my rear, which still seemed ever retreating before me, and I climbed alone over huge rocks, loosely poised, a mile or more, still edging towards the clouds; for though the day was clear elsewhere, the summit was concealed by mist. The mountain seemed a vast aggregation of loose rocks, as if some time it had rained rocks, and they lay as they fell on the mountain sides, nowhere fairly at rest, but leaning on each other, all rocking-stones, with cavities between, but scarcely any soil or smoother shelf. They were the raw materials of a planet dropped from an un.een quarry, which the vast chemistry of nature would anon work up, or work down, into the smiling and verdant plains and valleys of earth. This was an undone extremity of the globe; as in lignite we see coal in the process of formation.

"At length I entered within the skirts of the cloud which seemed forever drifting over the summit, and yet would never be gone, but was generated out of that pure air as fast as it flowed away; and when, a quarter of a mile farther, I reached the summit of the ridge, which those who have seen in clearer weather say is about five miles long, and contains a thousand acres of table-land, I was deep within the hostile ranks of clouds, and all objects were obscured by them. Now the wind would blow me out a yard of clear sunlight, wherein I stood; then a gray, dawning light was all it could accomplish, the cloud-line ever rising and falling with the wind's intensity. Sometimes it seemed as if the summit would be cleared in a few moments, and smile in sunshine; but what was gained on one side was lost on another. It was like sitting in a chimney and waiting for the smoke to blow away. It was, in fact, a cloud-factory; these were the cloud-works, and the wind turned them off done from the cool, bare rocks. Occasionally, when the windy columns broke in to me, I caught sight of a dark, damp crag to the right or left; the mist driving ceaselessly between it and me. It reminded me of the creations of the old epic and dramatic poets, of Atlas, Vulcan, the Cyclops, and Prometheus. Such was Caucasus and the rock where Prometheus was bound. Æschylus had no doubt visited such scenery as this. It was vast, Titanic, and such as man never inhabits. Some part of the beholder, even some vital part, seems to escape through the loose grating of his ribs as he ascends. He is more lone than you can imagine. There is less of substantial thought and fair understanding in him than in the plains where men inhabit. His reason is dispersed and shadowy, more thin and subtle, like the air. Vast, Titanic, inhuman Nature has got him at disadvantage, caught him alone, and pilfers him of some of his divine faculty. She does not smile on him as in the plains. She seems to say sternly, Why came ye here before your time? This ground is not prepared for you. Is it not enough that I smile in the valleys? I have never made this soil for thy feet, this air for thy breathing, these rocks for thy neighbors. I cannot pity nor fondle thee here, but forever relentlessly drive thee hence to where I *am* kind. Why seek me where I have not called thee, and then complain because you find me but a stepmother? Shouldst thou freeze or starve, or shudder thy life away, here is no shrine, nor altar, nor any access to my ear.

> "'Chaos and ancient Night, I come no spy
> With purpose to explore or to disturb
> The secrets of your realm, but . . .
> . . . . . . as my way
> Lies through your spacious empire up to light.'

"The tops of mountains are among the unfinished parts of the globe, whither it is a slight insult to the gods to climb and pry into their secrets, and try their effect on our humanity. Only daring and insolent men, perchance, go there. Simple races, as savages, do not climb mountains; their tops are sacred and mysterious tracts never visited by them. Pomola is always angry with those who climb to the summit of Katahdin.

"According to Jackson, who, in his capacity of geological surveyor of the State, has accurately measured it, the altitude of Katahdin is five thousand three hundred feet, or a little more than one mile above the level of the sea; and he adds, 'It is then evidently the highest point in the State of Maine, and is the most abrupt granite mountain in New England.' The peculiarities of that spacious table-land on which I was standing, as well as the remarkable semi-circular precipice or basin on the eastern side, were all concealed by the mist. I had brought my whole pack to the top, not knowing but I should have to make my descent to the river, and possibly to the settled portion of the State alone, and by some other route, and wishing to have a complete outfit with me. But at length, fearing that my companions would be anxious to reach the river before night, and knowing that the clouds might rest on the mountain for days, I was compelled to descend. Occasionally, as I came down, the wind would blow me a vista open, through which I could see the country eastward, boundless forests, and lakes, and streams, gleaming in the sun, some of them emptying into the East Branch. There were also new mountains in sight in that direction. Now and then some small bird of the sparrow family would flit away before me, unable to command its course, like a fragment of the gray rock blown off by the wind.

"I found my companions where I had left them, on the side of the peak, gathering the mountain cranberries, which filled every crevice between the rocks, together with blueberries, which had a spicier flavor the higher up they grew, but were not the less agreeable to our palates. When the country is settled, and roads are made, these cranberries will perhaps become an article of commerce. From this elevation, just on the skirts of the clouds, we could overlook the country, west and south, for a hundred miles. There it was, in the State of Maine, which we had seen on the map, but not much like that, — immeasurable forest for the sun to shine on, that eastern *stuff* we hear of in Massachusetts. No clearing, no house. It did not look as if a solitary traveler had cut so much as a walking-stick there. Countless lakes, — Moosehead in the south-west, forty miles long by ten wide, like a gleaming silver platter at the end of the table; Chesuncook, eighteen long by three wide, without an island; Millinocket, on the south, with its hundred islands; and a hundred others without a name; and mountains also, whose names, for the most part, are known only to the Indians. The forest looked like a firm grass sward, and the effect of these lakes in its midst has been well compared by one who has since visited this same spot, to that of a 'mirror broken into a thousand fragments, and wildly scattered over the grass, reflecting the full blaze of the sun. It was a large farm for somebody, when cleared. According to the Gazetteer, which was printed before the boundary question was settled, this single Penobscot county, in which we were, was larger than the whole State of Vermont, with its fourteen counties; and this was only a part of the wild lands of Maine. We are concerned now, however, about natural, not political limits. We were about eighty miles, as the bird flies, from Bangor, or one hundred and fifteen, as we had rode, and walked, and paddled. We had to console ourselves with the reflection that this view was probably as good as that from the peak, as far as it went; and what were a mountain without its attendant clouds and mists? Like ourselves, neither Bailey nor Jackson had obtained a clear view from the summit.

"Setting out on our return to the river, still at an early hour in the day, we decided to follow the course of the torrent, which we supposed to be Murch Brook, as long as it would not lead us too far out of our way. We thus traveled about four miles in the very torrent itself, continually crossing and recrossing it, leaping from rock to rock, and jumping with the stream down falls of seven or eight feet, or sometimes sliding down on our back in a thin sheet of water. This ravine had been the scene of an extraordinary freshet in the spring, apparently accompanied by a slide from the mountain. It must have been filled with a stream of stones and water, at least twenty feet above the present level of the torrent. For a rod or two, on either side of its channel, the trees were barked and splintered up to their tops, the birches bent over, twisted, and sometimes finely split, like a stable-broom; some, a foot in diameter, snapped off, and whole clumps of trees bent over with the weight of rocks piled on them. In one place we noticed a rock, two or three feet in diameter, lodged nearly twenty feet high in the crotch of a tree. For the whole four miles we saw but one rill emptying in, and the volume of water did not seem to be increased from the first. We traveled thus very rapidly with a downward impetus, and grew remarkably expert at leaping from rock to rock, for leap we must, and leap we did, whether there was any rock at the right distance or not. It was a pleasant picture when the foremost turned about and looked up the winding ravine, walled in with rocks and the green forest, to see, at intervals of a rod or two, a red-shirted or green-jacketed mountaineer against the white torrent, leaping down the channel with his pack on his back, or pausing upon a convenient rock in the midst of the torrent to mend a rent in his clothes, or unstrap the dipper at his belt to take a draught of the water. At one place we were startled by seeing, on a little sandy shelf by the side of the stream, the fresh print of a man's foot, and for a moment realized how Robinson Crusoe felt in a similar case; but at last we remembered that we had struck this stream on our way up, though we could not have told where, and one had descended into the ravine for a drink. The cool air above, and the continual bathing of our bodies in mountain water, alternate foot, sitz, douche, and plunge baths, made this walk exceedingly refreshing; and we had traveled only a mile or two, after leaving the torrent, before every thread of our clothes was as dry as usual, owing, perhaps, to a peculiar quality in the atmosphere.

"After leaving the torrent, being in doubt about our course, Tom threw down his pack at the foot of the loftiest spruce-tree at hand, and shinned up the bare trunk, some twenty feet, and then climbed through the green tower, lost to our sight, until he held the topmost spray in his hand. McCauslin, in his younger days, had marched through the wilderness with a body of troops, under General Somebody, and with one other man did all the scouting and spying service. The general's word was, 'Throw down the top of that tree,' and there was no tree in the Maine woods so high that it did not lose its top in such a case. I have heard a story of two men being lost once in these woods, nearer to the settlements than this, who climbed the loftiest pine they could find, some six feet in diameter at the ground, from whose top they discovered a solitary clearing and its smoke. When at this height, some two hundred feet from the ground, one of them became dizzy, and fainted in his companion's arms, and the latter had to accomplish the descent with him, alternately fainting and reviving, as best he could. To Tom we cried, 'Where away does the summit bear? where the burnt lands?' The last he could only conjecture; he descried, however, a little meadow and pond, lying probably in our course, which we concluded to steer for. On reaching this secluded meadow, we found fresh tracks of moose on the shore of the pond, and the water was still unsettled as if they had fled before us. A little farther, in a dense thicket, we seemed still to be on their trail. It was a small meadow, of a few acres, on the mountain side, concealed by the forest, and perhaps never seen by a white man before, where one would think that the moose might browse and bathe, and rest in peace. Pursuing this course, we soon reached the open land, which went sloping down some miles toward the Penobscot.

"Perhaps I most fully realized that this was primeval, untamed, and forever untamable *Nature*, or whatever else men call it, while coming down this part of the mountain. We were passing over 'Burnt Lands,' burnt by lightning, perchance, though they showed no recent marks of fire, hardly so much as a charred stump, but looked rather like a natural pasture for the moose and deer, exceedingly wild and desolate, with occasional strips of timber crossing them, and low poplars springing up, and patches of blueberries here and there. I found myself traversing them familiarly, like some pasture run to waste, or partially reclaimed by man; but when I reflected what man, what brother, or sister, or kinsman of our race made it and claimed it, I expected the proprietor to rise up and dispute my passage. It is difficult to conceive of a region uninhabited by man. We habitually presume his presence and influence everywhere. And yet we have not seen pure Nature, unless we have seen her thus vast and drear and inhuman, though in the midst of cities. Nature was here something savage and awful, though beautiful. I looked with awe at the ground I trod on, to see what the Powers had made there, the form and fashion and the material of their work. This was that Earth of which we have heard, made out of Chaos and Old Night. Here was no man's garden, but the unhandselled globe. It was not lawn, nor pasture, nor mead, nor woodland, nor lea, nor arable, nor waste land. It was the fresh and natural surface of the planet Earth, as it was made forever and ever, — to be the dwelling of man we say, — so Nature made it, and man may use it if he can. Man was not to be associated with it. It was Matter, vast, terrific, — not his Mother Earth that we have heard of, not for him to tread on, or be buried in, — no, it were being too familiar even to let his bones lie there, — the home, this, of Necessity and Fate. There was there felt the presence of a force not bound to be kind to man. It was a place for heathenism and superstitious rites, — to be inhabited by men nearer of kin to the rocks and to wild animals than we. We walked over it with a certain awe, stopping, from time to time. to pick the blueberries which grew there, and had a smart and spicy taste. Perchance where *our* wild pines stand, and leaves lie on their forest floor, in Concord, there were once reapers, and husbandmen planted grain but here not even the surface had been scarred by man, but it was a specimen of what God saw fit to make this world. What is it to be admitted to a museum, to see a myriad of particular things, compared with being shown some star's surface, some hard matter in its home! I stand in awe of my body, this matter to which I am bound has become so strange to me. I fear not spirits, ghosts, of which I am one, — *that* my body might, — but I fear bodies, I tremble to meet them. What is this Titan that has possession of me? Talk of mysteries! — Think of our life in nature, — daily to be shown matter, to come in contact with it, — rocks, trees, wind on our cheeks! the *solid* earth! the *actual* world! the *common sense!* Contact! Contact! Who are we? where are we?

"Erelong we recognized some rocks and other features in the landscape which we had purposely impressed on our memories, and, quickening our pace, by two o'clock we reached the bateau. Here we had expected to dine on trout, but in this glaring sunlight they were slow to take the bait, so we were compelled to make the most of the crumbs of our hard bread and our pork, which were both nearly exhausted. Meanwhile we deliberated whether we should go up the river a mile farther, to Gibson's clearing, on the Sowadnehunk, where there was a deserted loghut, in order to get a half-inch auger, to mend one of our spike-poles with. There were young spruce-trees enough around us, and we had a spare spike, but nothing to make a hole with. But as it was uncertain whether we should find any tools left there, we patched up the broken pole as well as we could, for the downward voyage, in which there would be but little use for it. Moreover, we were unwilling to lose any time in this expedition, lest the wind should rise before we reached the larger lakes, and detain us; for a moderate wind produces quite a sea on these waters, in which a bateau will not live for a moment; and on one occasion McCauslin had been delayed a week at the head of the North Twin, which is only four miles across. We were nearly out of provisions, and ill-prepared in this respect for what might possibly prove a week's journey round by the shore, fording innumerable streams, and threading a trackless forest, should any accident happen to our boat."

Still another account of the ascent of Katahdin we copy from "Life in the Open Air," before alluded to, the four sketches thoroughly covering the subject: —

"Next morning, when we awoke, just before the gray of dawn, the sky was clear and scintillating; but there was a white cotton night-cap on the head of Katahdin. As we inspected him, he drew his night-cap down farther, hinting that he did not wish to see the sun that day. When a mountain is thus in the sulks after a storm, it is as well not to disturb him; he will not offer the prize of a view. Experience taught us this; but then experience is only an empiric at the best.

"Besides, whether Katahdin were bare-headed or cloud-capped, it would be better to blunder upward than lounge all day in camp and eat Sybaratic dinners. We longed for the nervy climb. We must have it. 'Up!' said tingling blood to brain. 'Dash through the forest! Grasp the crag, and leap the cleft! Sweet flash forth the streamlets from granite fissures. To breathe the winds that smite the peaks is life.'

"As soon as dawn bloomed in the woods we breakfasted, and ferried the river before sunrise. The ascent subdivides itself into five zones. 1. A scantily wooded acclivity, where bears abound. 2. A dense, swampy forest region. 3. Steep, mossy mountain-side, heavily wooded. 4. A belt of dwarf spruces, nearly impenetrable. 5. Ragged rock.

"Cancut was our leader to-day There are by far too many blueberries in the first zone. No one, of course, intends to dally, but the purple beauties tempted, and too often we were seduced. Still such yielding spurred us on to hastier speed, when we looked up after delay and saw the self-denying far ahead.

"To write an epic or climb a mountain is merely a dogged thing; the result is more interesting to most than the process. Mountains, being cloud-compellers, are rain-shedders, and the shed-water will not always flow with decorous gayety in dell or glen. Sometimes it stays bewildered in a bog, and here the climber must plunge. In the moist places great trees grow, die, fall, rot, and barricade the way with their corpses. Katahdin has to endure all the ills of mountain being, and we had all the usual difficulties to fight through doggedly. When we were clumsy, we tumbled and rose up torn. Still we plodded on, following a path blazed by the Bostonians, Cancut's late charge, and we grumblingly thanked them.

"Going up, we got higher and drier. The mountain-side became steeper than it could stay, and several land-avalanches, ancient or modern, crossed our path. It would be sad to think that all the eternal hills were crumbling thus, outwardly, unless we knew that they bubble up inwardly as fast. Posterity is thus cared for in regard to the picturesque. Cascading streams also shot by us, carrying light and music. From them we stole refreshment, and did not find the waters mineral and astringent, as Mr. Turner, the first climber, calumniously asserts.

"The trees were still large and surprisingly parallel to the mountain wall. Deep soft moss covered whatever was beneath, and sometimes this would yield and let the foot measure a crevice. Perilous pitfalls; but we clambered unharmed. The moss, so rich, deep, soft, and earthily fragrant, was a springy stair-carpet of a steep stairway. And sometimes when the carpet slipped and the state of heels over head seemed imminent, we held to the baluster-trees, as one after wassail clings to the lamp-post.

"Even on this minor mountain the law of diminishing vegetation can be studied. The great trees abandoned us, and stayed indolently down in shelter. Next the little wiry trees ceased to be the comrades of our climb. They were no longer to be seen planted upon jutting crags, and, bold as standard-bearers, inciting us to mount higher. Big spruces, knobby with balls of gum, dwindled away into little ugly dwarf spruces, hostile, as dwarfs are said to be always to human comfort. They grew man-high, and hedged themselves together into a dense thicket. We could not go under, nor over, nor through. To traverse them at all, we must recall the period when we were squirrels or cats, in some former state of being.

"Somehow we pierced, as man does ever, whether he owes it to the beast or man in him. From time to time, when in this struggle we came to an open point of rock, we would remember that we were on high, and turn to assure ourselves that nether earth was where we had left it. We always found it *in situ*, in belts, green, white, and blue, a tricolor of woods, water, and sky. Lakes were there without number, forest without limit. We could not analyze yet, for there was work to do. Also, whenever we paused, there was the old temptation, blueberries. Every outcropping ledge offered store of tonic, ozone-fed blueberries, or of mountain-cranberries, crimson and of concentrated flavor, or of the white snowberry, most delicate of fruits that grow.

"As we were creeping over the top of the dwarf-wood, Cancut, who was in advance, suddenly disappeared; he seemed to fall through a gap in the spaces, and we heard his voice calling in cavernous tones. We crawled forward and looked over. It was the upper camp of the Bostonians. They had profited by a hole in the rocks, and chopped away the stunted scrubs to enlarge it into a snug artificial abyss. It was snug, and so to the eye is a cell at Sing-Sing. If they were very misshapen Bostonians, they may have succeeded in lying there comfortably. I looked down ten feet into the rough chasm, and I saw, — *Corpo di Bacco!* — I saw a cork.

"To this station our predecessors had come in an easy day's walk from the river; here they had tossed through a night, and given a whole day to finish the ascent, returning hither again for a second night. As we purposed to put all this travel within one day, we could not stay and sympathize with the late tenants. A little more squirrel-like skipping and cat-like creeping over the spruces, and we were out among bulky boulders and rough *débris* on a shoulder of the mountain. Alas! the higher, the more hopeless. Katahdin, as he had taken pains to inform us, meant to wear the veil all day. He was drawing down the white drapery about his throat and letting it fall over his shoulders. Sun and wind struggled mightily with his sulky fit; sunshine lifted off bits of the veil, and wind seized, whirled them away, and, dragging them over the spruces below, tore them to rags. Evidently, if we wished to see the world, we must stop here and survey, before the growing vapor covered all. We climbed to the edge of Cloudland, and stood fronting the semi-circle of southward view.

"Katahdin's self is finer than what Katahdin sees. Katahdin is distinct, and its view is indistinct. It is a vague panorama, a mappy, unmethodic maze of water and woods, very roomy, very vast, very simple, — and these are capital qualities, — but also quite monotonous. A lover of largeness and scope has the proper emotions stirred, but a lover of variety very soon finds himself counting the lakes. It is a wide view, and it is a proud thing for a man six feet or less high to feel that he himself, standing on something he himself has climbed, and having Katahdin under his feet a mere convenience, can see all Maine. It does not make Maine less, but the spectator more, and that is a useful moral result. Maine's face, thus exposed, has almost no features; there are no great mountains visible, none that seem more than green hillocks in the distance. Besides sky, Katahdin's view contains only the two primal necessities of wood and water. Nowhere have I seen such breadth of solemn forest, gloomy, were it not for the cheerful interruption of many fair lakes, and bright ways of river linking them.

"Far away on the southern horizon we detected the heights of Mount Desert, our old familiar haunt. All the northern semi-circle was lost to us by the fog. We lost also the view of the mountain itself. All the bleak, lonely, barren, ancient waste of the bare summit was shrouded in cold fog. The impressive gray ruin and Titanic havoc of a granite mountain-top, the heaped boulders, the crumbling crags, the crater-like depression, the long stern reaches of sierra, the dark curving slopes channeled and polished by the storms and fine drifting mists of æons, the downright plunge of precipices, all the savageness of harsh rock, unsoftened by other vegetation than rusty moss and the dull green splashes of lichen, — all this was hidden, except when the mist, white and delicate where we stood, but thick and black above, opened whimsically and delusively, as mountain mists will do, and gave us vistas into the upper desolation. After such momentary rifts the mist thickened again, and swooped forward as if to involve our station; but noon sunshine, reverberated from the plains and valleys and lakes below, was our ally; sunshine checked the overcoming mist, and it stayed overhead, an unwelcome parasol, making our August a chilly November. Besides what our eyes lost, our minds lost, unless they had imagination enough to create it, the sentiment of triumph and valiant energy that the man of body and soul feels upon the windy heights, the highest, whence he looks far and wide, like a master of realms, and knows that the world is his; and they lost the sentiment of solemn joy that the man of soul recognizes as one of the surest intimations of immortality, stirring within him, whenever he is in the unearthly regions, the higher world.

We stayed studying the pleasant solitude and dreamy breath of Katahdin's panorama for a long time, and every moment the mystery of the mist above grew more enticing. Pride also was awakened. We turned from sunshine and Cosmos into fog and Chaos. We made ourselves quite miserable for naught. We clambered up into Nowhere, into a great, white, ghostly void. We saw nothing but the rough service we trod. We pressed along crater-like edges, and all below was filled with mist, troubled and rushing upward like the smoke of a volcano. Up we went, — nothing but granite and gray dimness. Where we arrived we know not. It was a top, certainly; that was proved by the fact that there was nothing within sight. We cannot claim that it was the topmost top; Kinchinjinga might have towered within pistol-shot; popgun-shot was our extremest range of vision, except for one instant, when a kind-hearted sunbeam gave us a vanishing glimpse of a white lake and breadth of forest far in the unknown North toward Canada.

"When we had thus reached the height of our folly and made nothing by it, we addressed ourselves to the descent, no wiser for our pains. Descent is always harder than ascent, for divine ambitions are stronger and more prevalent than degrading passions. And when Katahdin is befogged, descent is much more perilous than ascent. We edged along very cautiously by remembered landmarks the way we had come, and so, after a dreary march of a mile or so through desolation, issued into welcome sunshine and warmth at our point of departure. When I said 'we,' I did not include the gravestone pedler. He, like a sensible fellow, had determined to stay and eat berries rather than breathe fog. While we wasted our time, he had made the most of his. He had cleared Katahdin's shoulders of fruit, and now, cuddled in a sunny cleft, slept the sleep of the well-fed. His red shirt was a cheerful beacon on our weary way. We took in the landscape with one slow, comprehensive look, and, waking Cancut suddenly (who sprang to his feet amazed, and cried 'Fire!') we dashed down the mountain-side.

"It was long after noon; we were some dozen miles from camp;

we must speed. No Glissade was possible, nor plunge such as travelers make down through the ash-heaps of Vesuvius; but, having once worried through the wretched little spruces, mean counterfeits of trees, we could fling ourselves down from mossy step to step, measuring off the distance by successive leaps of a second each, and alighting on moss yielding as a cushion.

"On we hastened, retracing our footsteps of the morning across the avalanches of crumbled granite through the bogs, along the brooks; undelayed by the beauty of sunny glade or shady dell, never stopping to botanize or to classify, we traversed zone after zone and safely ran the gauntlet of the possible bears on the last level. We found lowland Nature still the same; Ayboljockameegus was flowing still; so was Penobscot; no pirate had made way with the birch; we embarked and paddled to camp.

"The first thing, when we touched *terra firma*, was to look back regretfully toward the mountain. Regret changed to wrath when we perceived its summit all clear and mistless, smiling warmly to the low summer's sun. The rascal evidently had only waited until we were out of sight in the woods to throw away his night-cap.

"One long rainy day had somewhat disgusted us with the old hemlock-covered camp in the glade of the yellow birch, and we were reasonably and not unreasonably morbid after our disappointment with Katahdin. We resolved to decamp. In the last hour of sunlight, floating pleasantly from lovely reach to reach, and view to view, we could choose a spot of bivouac where no home-scenery would recall any sorry fact of the past. We loved this gentle gliding by the tender light of evening over the shadowy river, marking the rhythm of our musical progress by touches of the paddle. We determined, too, that the balance of bodily forces should be preserved; legs had been well stretched over the bogs and boulders; now for the arms.

"Never did our sylvan sojourn look so fair as when we quitted it, and seemed to see among the streaming sunbeams in the shadows the hamadryads of the spot returned, and waving us adieux. We forgot how damp and leaks and puddles had forced themselves upon our intimacy there; we remembered that we were gay, though wet, and there had known the perfection of Ayboljockameegus trout.

"As we drifted along the winding river, between the shimmering birches on either bank, Katahdin watched us well. Sometimes he would show the point of his violet-gray peak over the woods, and sometimes, at a broad bend of the water, he revealed himself fully, and threw his great image down beside for our nearer view. We began to believe him, to disbelieve in any personal spite of his, and to recall that he himself, seen thus, was far more precious than any mappy dulness we could have seen from his summit. One great upright pyramid like this was worth a continent of groveling acres.

"Sunset came, and with it we landed at a point below a lakelike stretch of the river, where the charms of a neighbor and a distant view of the mountain combined. Cancut, the Unwearied, roofed with boughs an old frame for drying moose-hides, while Iglesias sketched, and I worshipped Katahdin. Has my reader heard enough of it, — a hillock only six thousand feet high? We are soon to drift away, and owe it here as kindly a farewell as it gave us in that radiant twilight by the river.

"From our point of view we raked the long stern front tending westward. Just before sunset, from beneath a belt of clouds evanescing over the summit, an inconceivably tender, brilliant glow of rosy violet mantled downward, filling all the valley. Then the violet purpled richer and richer, and darkened slowly to solemn blue, that blended with the gloom of the pines and shadowy channeled gorges down the steep. The peak was still in sunlight, and suddenly, half-way down, a band of roseate clouds, twining and changing like a choir of bacchantes, soared around the western edge and hung poised above the unillumined forest at the mountain-base; light as air they came and went and faded away, ghostly, after their work of momentary beauty was done. One slight maple, prematurely ripened to crimson and heralding the pomp of autumn, repeated the bright cloud-color amid the vivid verdure of a little island, and its image wavering in the water sent the flame floating nearly to our feet.

"Such are the transcendent moments of nature, unseen and disbelieved by the untaught. Iglesias having an additional method of preservation, did not fail to pencil rapidly the wondrous scene. When he had finished his dashing sketch of this glory, so transitory, he peppered the whole with cabalistic cipher, which only he could interpret into beauty."

THE CAMPER-OUT. [From Harper's Magazine.

CHAPTER XIV.

Down the West Branch — *(concluded)*.

LEAVING the Sourdnahunk Stream, signifying "running between mountains," we pass Murch Brook and the Aboljacknagesic, mountain streams, abreast of Katahdin, and paddle easily along, the current assisting our onward progress. We run the rapids awhile, then make a carry of about half a mile around Ayboljockameegus Falls. Launching our birch again, we pursue our way down the river, occasionally startled by the scream of a bald eagle, cleaving the air above us, or of the fish-hawks, who, from force, are obliged to furnish him with many a meal. The scenery is never tame, the air is pure and sweet, and as we drift along we experience the fulness of delight. There is something in this wilderness that throws a charm about one whether he will or not. But again we hear the musical murmur of swift water, and we make another landing to the carry around Pockwockomus Falls. This carry is about half a mile in length, rough and rocky, and, like the Aybol. Carry, is on the right side of the river.

Floating down the stream again, we pass several poke logans — an Indian term. These are little inlets, generally swampy, that lead nowhere in particular. If you run into one you have to retrace your course the same way. Once in a while we passed a "run-round" leading off from the river, but always coming in again. These are the *bête noir* of the inexperienced voyager. Along this part of the river there are several islands, covered with coarse grass, and for several miles along the banks there is more or less wild meadow-land. Katepskonegan Lake and Falls are next reached. The lake is three miles long, shallow and weedy, suggestive of pickerel. The falls are of some little magnitude, and quite romantic. At the foot of the falls large numbers of trout have been caught. After crossing the carry, on the right, a mile long, we again embark, and float swiftly along the beautiful river whose bosom has borne us so long that we have come to regard it as a friend, and love it none the less for its changeable moods.

Beyond here you find plenty of swift water, and occasional rapids and falls, part of which can be run by experienced persons, but at some you are obliged to make carries. Reaching Ambejejus Falls, two miles beyond Passamagamock Falls, we halt, and our canoe is once more taken out, and over the carry we go The old song, which says that " Jordan is a hard road to travel," is very applicable to the Ambejejus carry; for if that is not "a hard road to travel," then you never saw one. But the bitter and the sweet alike must have an end, and finally you dump the last of your load at the lower end of the carry, and a deep sigh of satisfaction involuntarily wells up from your heart. This carry is on the left, and is half a mile long. After a slight rest our bonny bark is again launched on the stream, and, nodding to old Katahdin, who is still in sight, our paddles dip and on we float. Mile after mile is passed. From river to lake, from lake to river again, from the calmest and smoothest of water to the swift rapids flecked with foam, — the charm of the hour being largely due to this agreeable variety that follows one from sunrise to sunset.

We once more change from river to lake. From Penobscot to Pamedomcook, one of the most irregular lakes in the Maine wilderness. Midway of the southern shore of Pamedomcook Lake, a stream a mile and a half long flows into Jo Mary Lake. A carry road runs from lake to lake on the easterly side of the river. Plying our paddles, we follow the easterly shore of the largest lake we have seen since leaving Chesuncook, passing several islands on our way, and reach the North Twin Lake, a much smaller sheet of water. Paddling through this and down the river you reach a dam and a house. Meals can be obtained here if desired. Crossing Quakish Lake, then down the river a mile, brings you to a carry on the left-hand side of the Penobscot. The carry road is two miles long, and ends at a farm on Millnokett stream. Here you can procure a team to haul your baggage and canoes across, and by making this overland trip, and then sailing down Millnokett stream, you reach the Penobscot again, having saved ten or twelve miles of rough water. Beyond this there are several small bulges in the river, and through all these we pursue our way, until we finally reach Mattawamkeag, where we stop to look around a little, stopping there over night if we have the time. If you wish you can end your trip here, and take the cars of the Maine Central Railroad for Bangor. But, if you are not yet tired of the canoe, you can continue on down the river, passing Winn, Lincoln, Enfield, Passadumkeag, and other places, until you reach the dams at Oldtown, twelve miles from Bangor, where canoe navigation ceases, and where you will reluctantly say farewell to the faithful birch, in which you have floated from the deepest wilds of the forest to the civilization of a town.

During a trip between Moosehead and Oldtown a person will learn enough about a canoe to be of great service in his next voyage. You will also see some of the most beautiful parts of the State, and obtain a good idea of how Eastern Maine looks. Such a trip will occupy about ten days. You can make it some shorter or considerable longer, as your inclination may dictate. You should leave behind all useless luggage, and take only such articles as are absolutely necessary. After carrying over two or three portages you will be surprised to find out how many things you have taken that at the start you thought you could not get along without, but which, from personal experience on carries, you would afterward gladly dispense with. A light axe, gun, ammunition, fishing-tackle, matches, pepper, salt, coffee, sugar, condensed milk, tin cup, knife, spoon, frying-pan, small iron kettle, coffee-pot, compass, needles, thread, and buttons, are all you need on a long cruise in the woods. And the above list of articles might easily be cut down half if necessity required it.

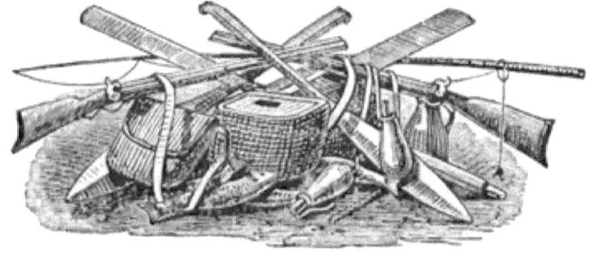

CHAPTER XV.

Tours Beyond Moosehead — Down the East Branch of the Penobscot — Up the Penobscot.

In giving an idea of the excursion down the East Branch of the Penobscot, we will only briefly allude to that part of the country that we have already been over on the trip down the West Branch.

As before, you cross the north-east carry, and, launching upon the West Branch, follow it to Lake Chesuncook. Reaching this beautiful sheet of water, you turn northward, and cross the upper end of the lake; from here, looking south-east, the eye takes in the whole length of the lake, the forest beyond, and Jo Mary Mountain, the most distant object visible. Crossing the lake is a pleasant change, after floating down a river where one's range of vision is obscured by the forest along its bank. The open expanse of water, across which one can look for miles, the wide sweep of sky, and the enlarged landscape, is preferable on some accounts to the contracted space of the river. And no small part of the preference for the change comes from the ease with which you paddle over the smooth surface of the lake. Where before was care and excitement, is now peace and careless indolence. No furious rapids or impassable falls endanger your lives or impede your progress. But with your voices attuned to song, you ply your paddles, keeping time with your music, and mile after mile is easily if not speedily accomplished.

Passing the Caucomgomoc stream, which empties into Chesuncook on your left, you continue your way. The stream flows from Caucomgomoc Lake, which lies about ten miles north-west of the head of Chesuncook. Turning north-easterly you enter the Umbazooksus, ten miles long, a sluggish stream, with considerable meadow-land on either side. Along the edge of the meadow, extended a belt of dead trees, killed by the back-water from the dam at the foot of Chesuncook. As you ascend the Umbazooksus, it contracts much in width, but little in depth, and finally the

MOOSEHEAD LAKE AND VICINITY.

paddle gives place to the setting-pole. Several miles more of poling, with now and then a short carry, by way of amusement, and you reach Umbazooksus Lake, possibly four or five miles long, stretching north-westerly from the outlet. A good road runs on the right up to the lake. Pursuing your way across the northeast end of the lake, you arrive at the Mud Pond carry.

Umbazooksus Lake is the head of the Penobscot in this direction, and Mud Pond is the nearest bend of the Allaguash, one of the principal sources of the St. John River. Hodge, who went through this way to the St. Lawrence in the service of the State, calls the portage here a mile and three-quarters long, and states that Mud Pond is fourteen feet higher than Umbazooksus Lake. Mud Pond is considerably more than half way from Umbazooksus to Chamberlain Lake, into which it empties. This is one of the worst carries there is in the State, wet, muddy, and boggy. Large boulders and dead falls covered with slippery moss add to the attractiveness (?) of this path in the wilderness. Black flies and midges seem to make their head-quarters in this vicinity, and assail you at every point. Woe betide you, if you have not some preparation, with which to anoint your face and hands, and protect yourself in a measure from the attacks of these merciless freebooters! Tar and oil in generous quantities is the right thing in the right place while crossing the Mud Pond carry. Reaching the pond you paddle across it, and enter the stream that connects it with Chamberlain Lake. Running the rapids, you soon float out upon this attractive sheet of water, similar in character and appearance to Chesuncook. Chamberlain Lake proper is about twelve miles long, but including Telos Lake and the dead water between, it is over twenty. The Chamberlain Farm, furnishing a resting-place for weary voyagers, is a large clearing on the northern side of the lake belonging to E. S. Coe, of Bangor, and the Pingree heirs of Salem, Mass., who own large tracts of land in this section of the State. A log-house and several barns comprise the settlement, if it may be called such.

Continuing on in a south-east direction, you leave **Chamberlain Lake**, and pass over the dead water between that and **Telos**. A few miles of Telos, and you reach the canal. Thoreau, in his "Maine Woods," says: "Telos Lake, the head of the St. John on this side, and Webster Lake, the head of the East Branch of the Penobscot, are only about a mile apart, and they are connected by a ravine, in which but little digging is required to make the water of the former, which is the highest, flow into the latter. This canal, which is something less than a mile long, and about four rods wide, was made a few years before my first visit to Maine. Since then the lumber of the Upper Allaguash and its lakes has been run down the Penobscot, that is, up the Allaguash which here consists principally of a chain of large and stagnant lakes, whose thoroughfares, or river-links, have been made nearly equally stagnant by damming, and then down the Penobscot. The rush of the water has produced such changes in the canal, that it has now the appearance of a very rapid mountain stream flowing through a ravine, and you would not suspect that any digging had been required to persuade the waters of the St. John to flow into the Penobscot here. It was so winding that one could see but little way down."

You can run through the canal with your birch, and carry your load around. At least, this is the safest way to do, and there is an easy carry on the right-hand side of the stream. Embarking at the head of Webster Lake, which is only two or three miles long, you quickly cross it, and reach the dam. There is good fishing and hunting in this vicinity. Nearly all of the lakes in the wilderness region of Maine have been dammed, in the interests of the lumbering business.

For the next ten miles you have considerable carrying to do, as Webster Stream, although about sixty feet wide, is difficult to navigate. It is very shallow, except immediately after heavy rains, also rapid and rocky. In fact it is almost a succession of heavy rapids and perpendicular falls, from three to five feet in height, culminating in Grand Falls, fifty feet high, within two miles of its mouth.

Between the rocks and the shallows you find yourself in hot water most of the time if you attempt to run this stream, and if you don't stave your canoe you may consider yourself lucky. Occasionally there is a mile or two that can be run without danger, and these places give you a rest from the carries. Reaching the deep and narrow cañon at the head of Grand Falls, you run your canoe into an eddy on the left, under the shadows of a rock that towers five hundred feet heavenwards, and make a landing. A walk of three-quarters of a mile across Indian Carry will bring you to the East Branch proper, running at right angles with Webster Stream. But before leaving, take a look at Grand Falls, as they will more than repay you for the time and trouble.

Launching your boat on the East Branch you find the river narrow, swift, and deep, the banks fringed with tall meadow-grass. The mile and a half from the end of the Carry to Matagamonsis Lake is swiftly run, and you paddle out on that lovely body of water, dotted by small islands, and broken up into numerous bays by the many symmetrical points that make out from either shore. This lake is about one mile wide and nearly four long, and is surrounded by a beautiful forest of Norway pine. Some miles distant to the south-west are seen the tops of the Traveller Mountains. From Matagamonsis you have three miles of dead water before reaching Matagamon, or Grand Lake, containing a number of islands. A mile above Matagamon you pass Steele Lake, situated on the left of the stream, about two miles in extent, and shortly after you reach a bridge, from which a road leads to a farm located on Trout Brook stream. You can run your canoe under the bridge, but will have to climb over it yourself.

Trout Brook Farm consists of four hundred acres of cleared land, four houses, and eight or ten barns. It belongs to E. S. Coe, Esq., of Bangor, and is a good place to stop at, if you want to rest, or get short of provisions. Continuing on, you soon reach Matagamon Lake, six miles long, and, crossing it, take out your canoe at the dam at the outlet. This lake furnishes excellent trout fishing, and salmon are often taken from its waters. The eastern shore of the lake is low and meadowy, but the western is romantic and picturesque, the land beyond rising sharply to hills and mountains, the highest being Matagamon Mountain, a rocky and precipitous peak, attaining an elevation of six hundred feet. From Grand Lake to the junction of the East and West Branches of the Penobscot is about sixty-five miles. Some eight miles south-east of Matagamon Lake is a small pond on the head of Bowlin Brook, and tributary to the East Branch, whose waters are colored white from the presence of lime. A cave in the rock, and partially submerged, was explored several years ago by the State Geological Survey.

Leaving the dam, you have two miles of heavy rapids necessitating at some seasons of the year short carries, and then reach Grand Falls, higher than their namesake on Webster Stream. A carry of three-quarters of a mile through the woods, and you launch your canoe on the river again below the falls, doing but little paddling, as the current is very swift. You have successive reaches for a number of miles, of dead water, rapids, and falls, sandwiched in with several carries. After passing Spring Brook and Gravel Bed Falls, you find a mile or more of heavy rips, and then have several miles of dead water. Passing the mouth of big and little Seboois Rivers, you soon reach a clearing known as Hunt's Farm, the buildings on which were erected more than forty years ago. A Mr. Dunn has charge of the place, and will board you a while, or furnish you with supplies if you desire.

The ascension of Mount Katahdin can be readily made from Hunt's Farm, an easy ride on horseback, landing you within two miles of the summit. In fact it is much easier to ascend the mountain from here than from the West Branch. Hunt Mountain, in this vicinity, twelve hundred feet high, affords a magnificent view of the surrounding country, and will well repay a clamber up its rocky sides.

Two miles below the farm you reach Whetstone Falls, a series of beautiful cascades. You will have to carry by here as the water is strong, and the rapids bad. At the foot of the falls you make a fresh start, and after having a reach of good water, pass Grindstone, and shortly after Crowfoot Falls, each from ten to twenty feet high. You carry by both of these falls. As you near Medway, you reach Ledge Falls, and the last of the carries. Beyond here the stream grows wider, and it sweeps towards the sea with swift but silent flow; you leave the mountains rapidly behind, and in front glimpses of civilization meet you with every new turn of the river. You soon reach the junction of the East and West Branches at Medway, a small town on the left bank of the Penobscot River. The route from here having been described in a previous chapter, it is unnecessary to repeat it. This trip is one of the most romantic that can be made in Maine, and leads one through the very heart of the wilderness. Try it, by all means, when you have time.

NOTE.— A man by the name of Smith now keeps a team on the Mud Pond carry, and will haul canoes and baggage across for a consideration.

UP THE WEST BRANCH OF THE PENOBSCOT.

There being but few lakes and much shoal-water here, this is not a favorite line of travel with many. It is not, however, without its points of interest, and leads one through lonely by-ways. Canada Falls heads the list of its attractions, and the fishing at the mouth of the Nulhedus and other streams is excellent.

Parties who start up the West Branch, after reaching the Northwest Carry, paddle up this stream for about a mile, and make a landing on the left side. Carry Brook empties into the northwest arm of the lake, to the left of Lane's Clearing. A few yards from the landing runs the Old Canada Road, leading from Lane's to Canada Falls, and beyond to Canada.

From Carry Brook landing to Seeboomook Meadows is about two miles, the road being good in dry weather. Ferd. Lane will haul canoes and supplies across the Carry for two dollars per load. He will also furnish canoes and supplies, and act as guide, if parties desire.

Launching your canoe on the pond you cross it, and leaving the pond on the east side you run into a small stream, and through this you make your way to the Penobscot, about a quarter of a mile distant, entering the river opposite of Seeboomook Island, where you will find a good camping-place. From here to Swan's farm, seven miles above, the river is black and deep, and in some places the scenery is very fine. Passing the head of the island you find the river widens, and a mile and a half beyond you pass Nulhedus Stream, navigable for several miles. Just below Nulhedus, on the opposite side of the river, a good tote-road leads into the Old Canada Road. From the river to Lane's is about five miles.

A five-mile paddle from Nulhedus, during which you pass Logan Brook on the right, brings you to Swan's Farm, on the left of the river, and here you can camp if you wish. Gulliver Stream empties into the Penobscot on the right-hand side, about a mile above Swan's. In consequence of the shallowness of the river and the falls you will have to drag your canoe nearly the entire distance from Swan's Farm to the head of Gulliver Falls, unless the water should be unusually high, when you may be able to pole up.

Above Gulliver Falls you paddle easily along over two miles and a half of dead water, and then reach the Big Island which you can pass on either side, the right hand being the shortest. A short distance above the island, on the left of the river, is a logan, where small trout are plenty. Above Big Island the river is shallow and the current strong, and a two-mile paddle brings you to the Forks, where the North and South Branches unite. A mile below the Forks, at King's High Landing, there is good fishing on the left side of the river near some ledges.

Canada Falls, a very attractive piece of water scenery, are a mile and a half from the Forks, up the South Branch, and will amply repay you for a visit. As the water is bad between the Forks and the falls, leave your traps at Knight's, and make your trip overland *via* the Old Canada Road, that leads to the foot of the falls.

Leaving Knight's Farm at the Forks you commence the ascent of the

NORTH BRANCH OF THE PENOBSCOT.

Canoeing up this stream is attended with difficulties, and you will make slow progress. A mile and a half from the Forks you pass Lane Brook on the left; three-quarters of a mile more brings you to Leadbetter Brook on the same side, flowing from four small ponds, the first of which is about four miles from the river. A mile and a half farther on you reach Leadbetter Falls, passing on your way Little Lane Brook, which empties into the river on the right, and one of Spencer's old camps, also on the right. You will have to carry around Leadbetter Falls. The path is only a few rods long, and lies on the right side of the river.

Above the falls navigation is easier, there being more dead water, and six miles of fair canoeing brings you to the mouth of Dole Brook, a short distance below which, in a deep pool, you will find good fishing. Three miles above Dole Brook, you pass the North-west Branch, and from the Forks to Abacotnetic Lake it is about fifteen miles. Between Dole Brook and Abacotnetic Lake navigation is very bad, with the exception of the last four or five miles, where the stream is sluggish. The Carry from Abacotnetic Lake to Baker Brook is about a mile, and from the

North-east Branch of the Penobscot to St. John Pond is about two miles. The last Carry is preferable to the former, although longer, because there is more water in the Woboostoock than in the other branch, and parties going down the St. John River can make better time this way.

Those who can spare several days for hunting will find caribou and deer quite plenty in the vicinity of Dole Brook, and caribou are also to be found around Abacotnetic Bog.

CHAPTER XVI.

Tours beyond Moosehead — Down the St. John.

ONE of the finest trips that can be made in Northern Maine is a tour down the St. John River to New Brunswick. The route lies through the wildest part of Maine; but the trip can be made with safety and comfort during the summer or early fall. September is the best month for it, if you have the leisure at that time. It will take from two to four weeks. From Mt. Kineo to the mouth of the Allaguash, lakes and rivers succeed each other, without any large settlement.

Leaving Moosehead Lake, your way lies down the Penobscot to Chesuncook, across that lake, and then over the Umbazooksus and Mud Pond to Chamberlain Lake. This part of the route we have already been over in our tour down the East Branch. You pursue a northerly course across Chamberlain Lake, and, reaching the dam and locks, carry by them on the right. Afloat on the stream again, — the Allaguash River this time, — you follow it about three miles, where it empties into Eagle Lake. This is also known as Heron Lake, on account, we suppose, of the large number of birds of that species who make it their home. There are a number of islands in it, and the shore around it presents the same wild appearance as the other lakes, belted with dead trees, caused from the rising of water by the dam below. It is ten miles across the lake, and six more to Thoroughfare Brook. A short run from here and you reach Churchill Lake, about two-thirds the size of Eagle Lake. Your course lies over the whole length of the Churchill, through a country that grows wilder with every mile of your advance. At the foot of the lake you find the remains of a dam, and, taking out your canoe, cross Chase's Carry, by some dangerous rapids, about half a mile long. Beyond the quick water you launch your canoe, and continue on for five or six miles, when you enter Umsaskis Lake, containing a few islands. Umsaskis is about five miles long. Between this and Long Lake you have another carry. At Depot Farm, on Long Lake, you can rest, and obtain provisions if you need them. Chemquasabanticook Lake and River empty into the upper end of Long Lake from the south-west. Continuing on from Long Lake you paddle down the Allaguash, passing numerous streams that empty into the river on either hand. One of the largest is the Musquacook, that enters from the east. As you near the St. John you meet with some quick water, and a few miles from the mouth of the Allaguash you are brought to bay by a sharp pitch some twenty feet high, necessitating a portage. Between these falls and the St. John there is nothing dangerous, and, reaching the mouth of the Allaguash, bid it farewell, and turn easterly toward New Brunswick.

There are not many bad places on the main St. John, the worst being Great Falls, about seventy miles below the Allaguash. Here is the main feature of the river, the whole descent of the water being seventy-five or eighty feet. There is one perpendicular fall of forty feet, and such is the fury of the water that all sawed lumber and square timber, to escape destruction, must be hauled by. A light suspension-bridge, for foot-passengers, spans the river below, and from this one can obtain a fine view of the fall. We use up the better part of two days in going the next sixty miles. During high water in the spring the river is navigable this distance for a light-draft steamer; but in summer the boat runs only to Woodstock, where you can take passage for Fredericton, sixty miles, and the following day by another steamer to St. John, ninety miles. A day may be saved in going by rail. Sometimes the steamers do not run above Fredericton. If parties do not wish to visit the city of St. John, they can take the cars at Woodstock or Fredericton for Bangor direct, leaving the former place at 8 A.M., and arriving at 7 P.M.; distance, one hundred and seventy miles.

There are settlements all the way on the main St. John, and, instead of going as far as Great Falls, parties sometimes turn off some forty miles or more below the mouth of the Allaguash and strike north-west across the country to the St. Lawrence. For the first twenty miles they ascend the Madawaska River, a pretty stream, and one of the finest in the country for a canoe, being smooth and clear, with gravelly bottom and a moderate current. Then, crossing Temiscouate Lake, sixteen miles in length, take stage for Rivière du Loup, a settlement on the St. Lawrence thirty miles distant. From there, Quebec is reached in a day by rail or by steamer.

Another way of making the St. John tour is, upon leaving Chesuncook Lake, to follow up the Caucomgomoc, across Black Pond, then keep on up the river until you reach Caucomgomoc Lake. Entering this, we skirt along its northern shore until we reach the mouth of Avery Brook. From here you have a long carry to the Woboostoock Stream, striking the river not far from Baker Lake. Crossing the lake, and ascending the Woolastaqueguam, or South Branch, you enter the main St. John, about twenty miles beyond, and pursue your way as before.

Or, you may follow the first described route as far as Chamberlain Lake, then coast along this until you reach the Allaguash River. Turning into this you follow it up till you come to the falls. Carrying around these, you pursue your way across Allaguash Pond, a small bulge in the river; then two or three miles farther brings you to the lake. The Allaguash is a large lake, and contains a number of islands. You paddle the entire length of the lake, and at the south-western corner find the portage. This carry is between two and three miles long; beyond it lies Round Pond, into which you launch your birch, and, crossing the pond, find at its south-eastern end a small stream that you follow down to Caucomgomoc Lake. From here you proceed as in the second route.

This whole region of country is a complete net-work of lakes, ponds, and rivers, and, with a compass and a good guide, no doubt there are many other ways, at least for part of the distance, by which one could reach the St. John River. In leaving the old beaten paths of travel one is also more likely to meet with game, or to find waters where the trout have not yet learned to fight shy of artificial flies. And although the whole State has been pretty well covered, in their different trips by hunters, lumbermen, and surveyors, still we have no doubt of there being parts of the wilderness of Maine whereon yet the foot of man has never trod. If any of my readers are ambitious to go to such places, I am positive they are yet to be found around the head waters of the St. John River. If you can scorn the attack of flies, mosquitoes, and, worst of all, midges (no-see ums the Indians call them), live on fried pork, hard-tack, and the products of your rod and rifle, such an out-of-the-way trip will be a real benefit to you. As an old farmer remarked to me one time when I was tramping up to the Richardson Lakes, "It'll do yer good, if't don't make yer feet sore."

CHAPTER XVII.

Game Laws of Maine.

CHAPTER L.

AN ACT for the protection of Game and Birds: Moose, Deer, and Caribou.

Be it enacted, etc., as follows: —

SECTION 1. No person shall, before the first day of October, in the year of our Lord eighteen hundred and eighty, take, kill, or destroy any moose in this State. All persons who in any way aid or assist in so doing shall be deemed principals. Any person violating the provisions of this section shall forfeit the sum of one hundred dollars for every moose so taken, killed, or destroyed.

SECT. 2. Any person who shall, before the first day of October, in the year of our Lord eighteen hundred and eighty, have in his possession, keep, or sell, any moose-meat or moose-hide, shall be liable to the penalty provided in section 1.

SECT. 3. No person shall, after the first day of October, in the year of our Lord eighteen hundred and eighty, hunt, kill, or destroy, with dogs, any moose within this State, under a penalty of one hundred dollars for every moose so killed or destroyed; and no person shall, after the first day of October aforesaid, between the first day of January and the first day of October, in each year, in any manner hunt, kill, or destroy any moose under the same penalty as above provided.

SECT. 4. No person shall hunt, kill, or destroy with dogs, any deer or caribou within this State, under a penalty of forty dollars for every such deer or caribou so killed or destroyed; and no person shall, between the first day of January and the first day of October, in any manner hunt, kill, or destroy, any deer or caribou, under the same penalty as above provided. Any person may lawfully kill any dog found hunting moose, deer, or caribou.

SECT. 5. If any person has in his possession the carcass or hide, or any part thereof, of any such animal, between the first day of January and the first day of October, he shall be deemed to have hunted and killed the same contrary to law, and be liable to the penalties aforesaid; but he shall not be precluded from producing proof in defence.

SECT. 6. No person shall carry or transport from place to place in this State the carcass or hide, or any part thereof, of any such animal, during the period of time in which the killing of such animals is prohibited, under a penalty of forty dollars.

SECT. 7. The governor, with the advice of council, shall appoint one county moose and game warden for each county in the state, to hold his office for the term of four years, unless sooner removed, each of whom may appoint in writing one or more deputies under him, and require of them suitable bonds for the faithful performance of their duties, and the payment to him of his fees; and said wardens and their deputies in their several counties, shall faithfully enforce the provisions of this act. Each of the deputies shall annually, on or before the first day of December, render to his principal an account under oath of all the penalties by him enforced for the preceding year, and shall pay to him one-tenth part of the net proceeds thereof. Each county warden shall annually, in January, render to the secretary of state an account on oath of all the penalties enforced by himself, or returned to him by his deputies, for the year ending on the first day of December. The penalty for neglecting to do so shall be for a warden fifty dollars, and a deputy twenty-five dollars; and the warden shall immediately give notice to the county attorney of every county of such neglect of his deputy, and the secretary of state shall notify such county attorney of every such neglect of the warden; and the county attorney shall prosecute for every such neglect of which he has notice; and the penalties so recovered shall be for the use of the county. In such prosecutions the certificate of the secretary of state shall be sufficient evidence of the fact of such neglect to make return to him.

SECT. 8. The municipal officers of any town may insert in the warrant for their annual meeting an article for the choice of a town moose and game warden, who, in his town and anywhere within the distance of twelve miles from the exterior bounds thereof, shall have concurrent jurisdiction with, and the same powers and rights, as the county moose warden and his deputies; and he shall make a like return to the secretary of state, under a penalty of twenty-five dollars, to be proved, recovered, and appropriated in the same way. Each of said officers shall have the same authority to require aid in the execution of his office as sheriffs and their deputies have.

SECT. 9. The county wardens, their deputies or town wardens, may recover the penalties for unlawfully hunting and killing moose, deer, and caribou, in an action on the case in their own names, or by complaint or indictment in the name of the state; and such officers may be competent witnesses, and the sums recovered shall be paid, one-half to the warden or deputy warden, and the other to the county or town, as the case may be. Any person may prosecute by action, complaint or indictment for any of the acts herein forbidden, provided no such warden or deputy, within fourteen days after the offence is committed, prosecutes therefor, and the sums recovered shall be paid, one-half to the prosecutor, and the other to the county, and such action, complaint or indictment may be commenced in any county in which such animal is killed or hunted, or into which its carcass or hide, or any portion thereof, may be carried.

SECT. 10. The secretary of state is to communicate to the legislature, in each month of January, what has been done in execution of the preceding sections of this chapter as appears by the returns received.

FUR-BEARING ANIMALS.

SECT. 11. No person shall in any way destroy, between the first day of May and the fifteenth day of October of each year, any mink, beaver, sable, otter, or fisher, under penalty of ten dollars for each animal so destroyed, to be recovered on complaint, one-half thereof to the use of the county where the offence is committed, and one-half to the prosecutor.

BIRDS.

SECT. 12. No person shall kill, or have in his possession, except alive, or expose for sale, any wood duck, dusky duck, commonly called black duck, or other sea duck, between the first day of May and the first day of September; or kill, sell or have in possession except alive, any ruffed grouse, commonly called partridge, or woodcock, between the first day of December and the first day of September following; or kill, sell, or have in possession, except alive, any quail or pinnated grouse, commonly called prairie chicken, between the first day of January and the first day of September following, under a penalty of not less than five nor more than ten dollars for each bird so killed, or had in possession, or exposed for sale.

SECT. 13. No person shall at any time, or in any place within this State with any trap, net, snare, device, or contrivance, other than the usual method of sporting with firearms, take any wild duck of any variety, quail, grouse, partridge, or woodcock, under a penalty of five dollars for each bird so taken.

SECT. 14. No person shall at any time kill, or have in his possession, except alive, any of the birds commonly known as larks, robins, swallows, sparrows, or orioles, or other insectivorous birds, crows and hawks excepted.

SECT. 15. No person shall at any time wantonly take or destroy the nest, eggs, or unfledged young of any wild bird of any kind, except crows, hawks, and owls, or take any eggs or young from such nests, except for preserving the same as specimens, or of rearing said young alive, under a penalty of not less than one nor more than ten dollars for each nest, egg, or young so taken or destroyed.

SECT. 16. No person shall carry or transport from place to place, in this state, any of the birds named herein, during the period in which the killing of such birds is prohibited, under a penalty of five dollars for each bird so carried or transported.

SECT. 17. The provisions of this act shall not apply to taxidermists, commissioned by the governor, with the advice of the council, to take and kill birds for scientific purposes, provided they kill the birds for such purposes only.

SECT. 18. All penalties imposed by the seven preceding sections may be recovered by an action of debt, or by complaint or indictment in the name of the state, by any warden or his deputies, or any other person, before any court having jurisdiction thereof, in any county in which such offence may be committed or the accused resides; and in all actions therefor in the supreme judicial court, or any superior court for the county of Cumberland, if the plaintiff recovers, he shall recover full costs without regard to the amount of such recovery. Such penalties, when collected, shall be paid, one-half to the prosecutor, and the other to the overseers of the poor, for the use of the poor of the city or town where such prosecutor resides.

SECT. 19. This act shall not apply to the shooting of ducks on the seacoast.

SECT. 20. Chapter one hundred and six, and section two of chapter ninety-eight of the public laws of eighteen hundred and seventy-two, together with all acts and parts of acts inconsistent with this act, are hereby repealed; saving all actions, complaints, and indictments now pending, or which may hereafter be commenced for the violation of any such act before this act takes effect.— [Approved Feb. 19, 1878.]

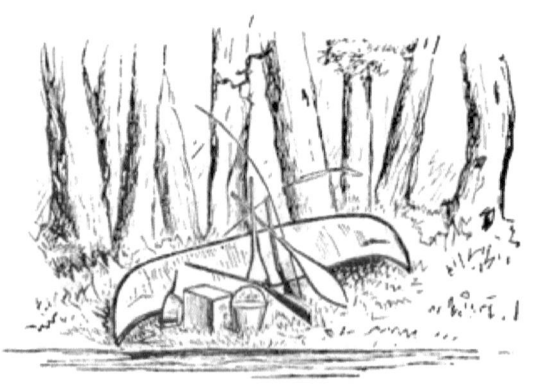

CHAPTER XVIII.

Game-Fish Laws of Maine.

CHAPTER LXXIV.

AN ACT to regulate and protect Fisheries and the Propagation of Fish.

Be it enacted, etc., as follows: —

SECTION 1. The governor, with the advice of the council, shall appoint one or two persons, as they may think best, to be commissioners of fisheries, who shall hold office for three years unless sooner removed, and have a general supervision of the fisheries, regulated by the following sections. He or they shall examine dams and all other obstructions existing in all rivers and streams in the state, and determine the necessity of fish-ways and the location, form, and capacity thereof; shall visit those sections where fisheries regulated by this act are carried on, and examine into the working of the laws; shall introduce and disseminate valuable species of fish into the waters of this state where they do not exist, and perform all other duties prescribed by law. He or they shall report annually on or before the thirty-first day of December, to the governor, who shall cause three thousand copies to be printed. He or they shall receive one thousand dollars and traveling and other expenses necessarily incurred in connection with his or their duties, which shall be audited by the governor and council, and it shall be his or their duty to see that all violations of the fish laws of the state are duly prosecuted.

SECT. 2. Every dam or other artificial obstruction in any river or stream naturally frequented by salmon, shad, or alewives, shall be provided by the owner or occupant thereof with a durable and efficient fish-way, of such form and capacity, and in such location as may be determined by the commissioners of fisheries. It shall also be incumbent on the owner or occupant of the dam to keep the fish-ways in repair, and open and free from obstruction for the passage of fish, during such times as may be prescribed by law; provided, that in case of disagreement between the commissioners of fisheries and the owner of any dam, as to the propriety and safety of the plan submitted to the owners or occupant of such dam for the location and construction of the fish-way, such owners or occupant may appeal to the county commissioners of the county where the dam is located, within twenty days after notice of the determination of the commissioners, by giving to the commissioners notice in writing of such appeal within that time, stating therein the reasons therefor, and at the request of the appellant or the commissioners, the senior commissioners in office of any two adjoining counties shall be associated with them, who shall appoint a time to view the premises and hear the parties, and shall give due notice thereof, and after such hearing they shall decide the question submitted, and cause record to be made thereof, and their decision shall be final as to the place and location appealed from. If the requirements of the commissioners are affirmed, the appellant shall be liable for the costs arising after the appeal, otherwise the costs shall be paid by the county.

SECT. 3. If a fish-way thus required to be built is not completed to the satisfaction of the commissioners within the time specified, any owner or occupant shall forfeit not more than one hundred nor less than twenty dollars for every day between the first day of May and the first day of November, during which such neglect continues.

SECT. 4. On the completion of any fish-way to the satisfaction of the commissioners, or at any subsequent time, they shall prescribe in writing the time during which the same shall be kept open and free from obstruction to the passage of fish each year, and a copy thereof shall be served on the owner or occupant of the dam. The commissioners may change the time as they see fit. Unless otherwise provided, a fish-way shall be kept open and unobstructed from the first day of May to the fifteenth day of July of each year. The penalty for neglecting to comply with the provisions of this section, or any regulations made in accordance herewith, shall be not less than twenty nor more than one hundred dollars for every day such neglect continues.

SECT. 5. In case the commissioners find any fish-way out of repair or needing alterations, they may, as in case of new fish-ways, require the owner or occupant to make such repairs or alterations; and all the proceedings in such cases, and the penalty for neglect, shall be as provided in the second, third, and fourth sections, without right of appeal.

SECT. 6. In case the dam is owned or occupied by more than one person, each shall be liable for the cost of erecting and maintaining such fish-way, in proportion to his interest in the dam, and if any owner or occupant shall neglect or refuse to join with the others in erecting or maintaining such fishway, the other owner or owners or occupants shall erect or repair the same, and shall have an action of case against such delinquent owner or occupant for his share of the expenses thereof.

SECT. 7. If the owner or occupant of such dam resides out of the state, said penalties may be recovered by a libel against the dam and land on which it stands, to be filed in the supreme judicial court in the county where the same is located, in the name of the commissioners of fisheries or any fish warden, who shall give to the owner or occupant of the dam, and all persons interested therein, such notice as the court, or any justice thereof in vacation, shall order, and the court may render judgment therein against said dam and lands for said penalties and costs, and order a sale thereof to satisfy such judgment and costs of sale, subject, however, to all said requirements for the erection, maintenance, or repair of said fish-way.

SECT. 8. The governor, with the advice of the council, shall appoint fish wardens where the same may be necessary, who shall enforce the provisions of all public laws relating to fisheries, prosecute all offences that come to their knowledge, and shall have the same power as sheriffs and deputy sheriffs to serve all criminal process for the violation of any of the provisions of this act; and they shall have a right, at all times, to visit any dam or any weir or other apparatus for taking fish, and in the exercise of their duties shall have the same right to require aid that sheriffs and their deputies have in executing the duties of their office, and any person neglecting to render it when required shall forfeit ten dollars. Each person so appointed shall hold office three years, unless sooner removed, and his pay shall be fixed by the governor and council, who shall audit his accounts and cause the same to be paid from the state treasury, provided that the whole amount paid to all wardens shall not exceed fifteen hundred dollars annually.

SECT. 9. No salmon, shad, or other migratory fish shall be taken or fished for within five hundred yards of any fish-way, dam, or mill-race, nor between the Bangor and Brewer bridge over the Penobscot river and the water works dam at Treat's Falls on said river; nor between the Augusta highway bridge over the Kennebec river and the Augusta dam on said river, between the first day of April and the first day of November in each year, except by the ordinary mode of angling with single hook and line or artificial flies; nor shall hook and line or artificial flies be used at any time within one hundred yards of any fish-way, dam, or mill-race. The penalty for violation of this section shall be a fine of not more than fifty nor less than ten dollars for each offence, and a further fine of ten dollars for each salmon, one dollar for each shad, so taken.

SECT. 10. There shall be a close time for salmon from the fifteenth day of July of each year to the first day of April following, during which no salmon shall be fished for, taken, or killed in any manner, under a penalty of not more than fifty nor less than ten dollars, and a further penalty of ten dollars for each salmon so taken or killed.

SECT. 11. No smelts shall be taken or fished for in any of the tidal waters of this state, in any other manner than by hook and line, between the first day of April and the first day of November, in each year, under a penalty of not less than ten dollars nor more than thirty dollars for each offence, and a further penalty of twenty cents for each smelt so taken; and all weirs for the capture of smelts shall be opened, and so remain, and all nets of any kind used in the smelt and tom-cod fishery shall be taken from the water on or before the said first day of April in each year, under a penalty of not less than twenty nor more than fifty dollars, and a further fine of five dollars per day for each day that any such weir or net remains in violation of law; but weirs which have catch-pounds covered with net, the meshes of which are one inch square in the clear, or greater, shall not be subject to the provisions of this section; provided, however, that dip-nets may be used from the first day of April to the twentieth day of May.

SECT. 12. Any inhabitant of this state, by obtaining the consent of the adjacent riparian proprietors, may plant oysters below low-water mark in any of the navigable waters of the state, in places where there is no natural oyster-bed, enclose such grounds with stakes, set at suitable distances, and extending at least two feet above high-water mark, but so as not to obstruct the free navigation of such waters, and have the exclusive right of taking such oysters; and if any person trespasses on such enclosure, or in any way injures such oyster-beds, he shall be liable in an action of trespass for all the damage; or if he takes any oysters therein without the consent of the owner, he shall forfeit not less than twenty nor more than fifty dollars, or be confined in jail not exceeding three months.

SECT. 13. There shall be an annual close time for land-locked salmon, commonly so called, trout, togue, black bass, Oswego bass, and white perch, in the waters of this state, as follows, viz.: For land-locked salmon, trout, and togue, from the first day of October to the first day of May following, excepting on the St. Croix river and its tributaries, and all the waters in Kennebec county, in which the close time shall be from the fifteenth day of September to the first day of May following; and for black bass, Oswego bass, and white perch, from the first day of April to the first day of July following.

SECT. 14. No person shall at any time catch, take, kill, or fish for any land-locked salmon, trout, togue, black bass, Oswego bass, or white perch, by means of any grapnel, spear, trawl, weir, net, seine, trap, spoon, set-line, or with any device or in any other way than by the ordinary way of angling with a single baited hook and line, or with artificial flies, under a penalty of not less than ten dollars nor more than thirty dollars for each offence, and a further fine of one dollar for each fish so caught, taken, or killed. And all set-lines, grapnels, spears, trawls, weirs, nets, seines, traps, spoons, and devices other than fair angling as aforesaid, are hereby prohibited on the fresh-water lakes, ponds, and streams of this state; and when found in use or operation on said lakes, ponds, or streams, they are hereby declared forfeit and contraband; and any person finding them in use in said waters is hereby authorized to destroy the same.

SECT. 15. No person shall take, catch, kill, or fish for, in any manner, any land-locked salmon, trout or togue, in any of the waters aforesaid, between the said first day of October and the first day of May following, nor in the St. Croix river and its tributaries, between the fifteenth day of September and the first day of May following; or black bass, Oswego bass, or white perch, between the first day of April and the first day of July following, under a penalty of not less than ten dollars nor more than thirty dollars, and a further fine of one dollar for each fish thus caught, taken, or killed as aforesaid. Provided, however, that during the months of February, March, and April, in each year, it shall be lawful for citizens of this state to fish for and take land-locked salmon, trout and togue, and convey the same to their own homes, but not otherwise.

SECT. 16. No person shall sell, expose for sale, or have in possession with intent to sell, or transport from place to place in this state, any land-locked salmon, trout, or togue, between the first day of October and the first day of May following, or any black bass, Oswego bass, or white perch, between the first day of April and the first day of July following, under a penalty of not less than ten dollars nor more than fifty dollars for each offence.

SECT. 17. Any person, or persons having in possession, except alive, any land-locked salmon, trout, or togue, between the first day of October and the first day of May following, or any black bass, Oswego bass, or white perch, between the first day of April and the first day of July following, or who shall transport from place to place within this state, any land-locked salmon, trout, or togue, between the first day of October and the first day of May following, or black bass, Oswego bass, or white perch, between the first day of April and the first day of July following, shall be deemed to have killed, caught, or transported the same contrary to law, and be liable to the penalties aforesaid.

SECT. 18. The provisions of this act shall not apply to white perch taken in any of the tide waters of this state.

SECT. 19. No person shall introduce fish of any kind, except trout, fresh and salt water salmon, fresh-water smelts, blue-back trout, and minnows, by means of the live fish or otherwise, to any waters now frequented by trout or salmon, except as hereinafter provided, under a penalty of not less than fifty dollars nor more than five hundred dollars.

SECT. 20. The commissioners of fisheries may take fish of any kind at such time and place as they may choose, and in such manner, for the purposes of science, and of cultivation and dissemination, and they may grant written permits to other persons to take fish for the same purposes, and they may introduce or permit to be introduced, any kind of fish to any waters they may see fit.

SECT. 21. The commissioners of fisheries may set apart any waters for the purpose of cultivation of fish, and after notice published three weeks successively in some newspaper published in the county where such waters are located, no person shall take, kill, or fish for any fish therein, under a penalty of not less than ten, nor more than one hundred dollars, and a further penalty of one dollar for each fish so taken or killed.

SECT. 22. Any person legally engaged in the artificial culture and maintenance of fishes, may take them in his own enclosed waters wherein the same are so cultivated and maintained, as and when he pleases, and may at all times sell them for the purpose of cultivation and propagation, but shall not sell them for food at seasons when the taking of such fish is prohibited by law, under a penalty of not less than ten nor more than one hundred dollars, and a futher penalty of not less than one dollar for each fish so sold.

SECT. 23. Any person engaged in the artificial propagation of fish known as trout, fresh and salt water salmon, on any water in this state, when the parent fish are taken from public waters in this state, shall retain not less than twenty-five per cent. of all eggs taken from said parent fish and cause the same to be properly cared for and hatched, and when hatched and in proper condition, to be returned to a suitable place for such young fish in the original waters from which the parent fish were taken, and to cause said parent fish to be returned to safe locations in the waters from which they were taken, under a penalty of not less than fifty nor more than five hundred dollars for each offence. But the provisions of this section shall not apply to cases in which the parent fish are taken in the manner and at the time and place permitted by law for the capture of such fish for food; nor shall it apply to any operations in fish-culture conducted for public purposes by permission of the commissioners of fisheries of this state, who may affix such conditions to their permits as they may see fit, but requiring in no case less than twenty-five per cent. of the young fish to be returned, as provided in this section.

SECT. 24. No person shall fish in that portion of a pond or other water in which fish are artificially cultivated or maintained, by the written permission of the fish commissioners, without the permission of the proprietor, under a penalty of not less than ten nor more than one hundred dollars, and an additional penalty of two dollars for each fish so taken or killed.

SECT. 25. It shall be the duty of all sheriffs, deputy-sheriffs, constables, and police-officers, as well as fish-wardens and their deputies, to cause any person or persons violating any of the provisions of this chapter to be promptly prosecuted for said offence, either by making complaint before some trial justice, municipal or police judge, or by given information to the county attorney of the county in which the offence is committed. Said sheriffs, deputy-sheriffs, constables, fish-wardens, deputy fish-wardens, and police-officers, shall be allowed for said services the same fees as are now prescribed by law for sheriffs and their deputies.

SECT. 26. All fines and penalties provided for in this act, unless otherwise provided, may be recovered before any competent tribunal by complaint, indictment, or action of debt; and in all actions of debt commenced in the supreme judicial court, or in the superior court for the county of Cumberland, the plaintiff recovering shall recover full cost, without regard to amount recovered. Judges of municipal and police courts, and trial justices, shall have concurrent jurisdiction of all offences described in this act, when the penalty for the offence complained of does not exceed thirty dollars. In cases where the offence described in this act is alleged to have been committed in any river, stream, pond, or lake forming a boundary between two counties, or where the fish are caught in one county and carried to another county, the action, complaint, or indictment may be commenced and prosecuted in either county. One-half of all fines and penalties recovered or imposed, when not otherwise provided, shall be for the benefit of the party prosecuting or making complaint, and the other half to the county in which the proceedings are commenced and prosecuted.

SECT. 27. The provisions of this act shall not apply to the taking of blue-back trout.

SECT. 28. All acts and parts of acts inconsistent with this act are hereby repealed; provided, however, that nothing in this section shall repeal the laws relating to the St. Croix. Denny, Pemmaquam, Cobscook, East Machias, and Narraguagus rivers. And this act shall not apply to fish taken in the weirs on St. Croix river.

SECT. 29. This act shall take effect when approved. — [Approved Feb. 21, 1879.]

ESTABLISHED HACK-FARES IN BOSTON.

For one or more adult passengers within the City Proper, or from one place to another within the limits of South Boston or of East Boston, Fifty Cents each.

Between the hours of 11 P.M. and 7 A.M., the fare for one adult passenger shall be One Dollar.

For two or more such passengers, Fifty Cents each.

For one adult passenger, from any part of the City Proper, to either South Boston or East Boston, or from East Boston or South Boston to the City Proper, One Dollar.

For two or more such passengers, between such points, Seventy-Five cents each.

For children, between four and twelve years of age, when accompanied by one adult, one-half of the above sums; and for children under four years of age, when accompanied by an adult, no charge is to be made.

By order of the Board of Aldermen,

S. F. McCLEARY,

City Clerk.

BAGGAGE. — One Trunk, a Valise, Box, Bundle, Carpet-Bag, Basket, or other article used in traveling, shall be free of charge; but for each additional Trunk, or other articles, Five Cents shall be paid.

HORSE-CAR CONVEYANCE. — Persons who travel light, *i.e.*, with little baggage, can save Hack-Fare in Boston by taking the Horse-Cars, which now run to all the depots, and to the wharf of the Portland steamers.

Additional Game and Game-Fish Laws passed during the winter of 1880.

CHAPTER 189. AN ACT to protect Quails.

Be it enacted, &c., as follows : —

No quail shall be killed, nor had in possession except alive, at any time previous to September first, eighteen hundred and eighty-three, under penalty of twenty-five dollars for every offence, and one dollar additional for each quail killed or had in possession except alive. [Approved February 28, 1880.]

CHAPTER 180. AN ACT for the protection of Blue-Back Trout.

Be it enacted, &c., as follows : —

SECTION 1. No person shall fish for, catch, take, kill or destroy any blue-back trout in any of the waters of this state, with any net, seine, weir or trap.

SECT. 2. Any person who shall violate the provisions of this act shall forfeit and pay the sum of five dollars for the attempt, and one dollar for each and every blue-back trout so taken, caught, killed or destroyed, to be recovered by complaint before any trial justice, one-half to the complainant and the other half to the town where the complaint is made.

SECT. 3. This act shall take effect when approved. [Approved February 23, 1880.]

CHAPTER 187. AN ACT to amend section ten, chapter seventy-five of the laws of eighteen hundred and seventy-eight, relating to fisheries.

Be it enacted, &c., as follows : —

SECT. 10. There shall be a close-time for salmon from the fifteenth day of July of each year to the first day of April following, during which no salmon shall be taken or killed in any manner, under a penalty of not more than fifty nor less than ten dollars, and a further penalty of ten dollars for each salmon so taken or killed. Provided, however, that from the said fifteenth day of July until the fifteenth day of September following, it shall be lawful to fish for and take salmon by the ordinary mode, with rod and single line, but not otherwise. [Approved February 28, 1880.]

CHAPTER 208. AN ACT to enlarge the powers and duties of the Commissioners of Fisheries and Wardens.

Be it enacted, &c., as follows : —

SECTION 1 The powers and duties of the commissioners of fisheries, and wardens, shall extend to all matters pertaining to game, and they shall have the same powers to enforce all laws pertaining to game as they now have in enforcing the laws relating to the fisheries.

SECT. 2. The governor is hereby authorized, with the advice and consent of the council, to appoint wardens, whose duty it shall be to enforce the provisions of all laws relating to game and the fisheries, arrest any person violating such laws, and prosecute for all offences against the same that may come to their knowledge; and shall have the same power as sheriffs and deputy sheriffs, to serve all criminal processes for violations of the provisions of any law pertaining to game and the fisheries, and shall be allowed for said services the same fees as are prescribed by law for sheriffs and their deputies for like services; and in the execution of their duties they shall have the same right to require aid that sheriffs and their deputies have in executing the duties of their office; and any person refusing or neglecting to render such aid when required, shall forfeit ten dollars, to be recovered upon complaint before any trial justice or municipal court.

SECT. 3. This act shall take effect when approved. [Approved March 9, 1880.]

NEW LAWS OF 1882-83.

An Act for the protection of moose, caribou, and deer.

Be it enacted, etc., as follows: —

SECTION 1. No person shall kill, destroy, or have in possession from the first day of October to the first day of January in each year, more than one moose, two caribou, or three deer, under a penalty of one hundred dollars for every moose and forty dollars for every caribou or deer killed, destroyed, or in possession in excess of the said number, and in case of conviction all such moose, caribou, or deer, or the carcasses or parts thereof, shall be decreed by the court forfeited to the use of the party prosecuting. Any person having in possession more than the aforesaid number of moose, caribou, or deer, or the carcasses or parts thereof, shall be deemed to have killed or destroyed them in violation of this act.

SECT. 2. Any person owning or having in possession dogs for the purpose of hunting moose, caribou, or deer, or that are used for such hunting, shall be liable to a penalty of not less than twenty nor more than one hundred dollars.

SECT. 3. The penalties prescribed in this act may be recovered in the manner provided by section twenty-five of chapter forty of the public laws of eighteen hundred and seventy-eight.

An Act making Sunday a close time for game and birds of all kinds.

Be it enacted, etc., as follows: —

SECTION 1. Sunday is hereby made a close time, on which day it shall not be lawful for any person to hunt, kill, or destroy game or birds of any kind, under the penalties imposed for the hunting, killing, or destroying the same, during any close time now established by law.

SECT. 2. This act shall not be construed to repeal or diminish the penalties already imposed for any violation of the Sunday laws.

An Act to repeal chapter one hundred and ninety-two of the laws of eighteen hundred and seventy-four and section seventeen of chapter fifty of the laws of eighteen hundred and seventy-eight, relating to taxidermists and all acts authorizing their appointment.

Be it enacted, etc., as follows: —

SECTION 1. Chapter one hundred and ninety-two of the laws of eighteen hundred and seventy-four and section seventeen of chapter fifty of the laws of eighteen hundred and seventy-eight are hereby repealed.

SECT. 2. All acts and parts of acts authorizing the appointment of taxidermists are hereby repealed.

An Act relating to seizure of fish and game under the fish and game laws.

Be it enacted, etc., as fol'ws. —

Any person whose fish or game has been seized for violation of any fish or game law, shall have such fish or game, so seized, returned to him on giving to the officer a bond with sufficient sureties, residents of this state, in double the amount of the fine for such violation; conditioned, that if the final judgment for such alleged violation shall be guilty, he will within thirty days thereafter pay such fine and costs. If such person neglects or refuses to give such bond and take the fish or game, so seized, he shall have no action against the officer for such seizure or loss thereof.

An Act to amend section fourteen of chapter fifty of the public laws of eighteen hundred and seventy-eight, relating to insectivorous birds.

Be it enacted, etc., as follows: —

Section fourteen of chapter fifty of the public laws of eighteen hundred and seventy-eight is hereby amended by adding thereto the following words, viz.: —

"Under a penalty of not less than one dollar nor more than five dollars for each of said birds killed, or in possession except alive," so that as amended said section will read as follows, viz.: —

SECT. 14. No person shall kill or have in his possession, except alive, any of the birds commonly known as larks, robins, swallows, sparrows, or orioles, or other insectivorous birds, crows and hawks excepted, under a penalty of not less than one dollar nor more than five dollars for each of said birds killed, and the possession by any person of such dead bird shall be *prima facie* evidence that such person killed such bird.

AN ACT for the protection of game-fish.

Be it enacted, etc., as follows: —

SECTION 1. No person shall fish for, take, catch, kill, or destroy any fish in any waters, except tide waters, with any net, seine, weir, or trap, under a penalty of fifty dollars for the offence and ten dollars for each salmon or landlocked salmon, so taken, caught, killed or destroyed.

SECT. 2. No person shall kill or destroy any landlocked salmon less than nine inches in length, or any trout less than five inches in length, under a penalty of five dollars for the offence and fifty cents for each and every landlocked salmon or trout so killed or destroyed. Any person having in possession any landlocked salmon or trout of less than the above dimensions shall be deemed to have killed or destroyed them in violation of the provisions of this section.

SECT. 3. No person shall take, catch, kill, or have in possession at any one time for the purpose of transportation more than fifty pounds in weigh of landlocked salmon or trout, or of both together, nor shall any such be transported except in the possession of the owner thereof, under a penalty of fifty dollars for the offence, and five dollars for each and every pound of landlocked salmon or trout, or both together, so taken, caught, killed, in possession or being transported in excess of fifty pounds in weight; and all such fish transported in violation of the provisions of this section shall be liable to seizure, on complaint, and shall be decreed by the court forfeited to the use of the party prosecuting. Any person having in possession more than fifty pounds in weight of the fish aforesaid, shall be deemed to have taken them in violation of this section.

SECT. 4. All penalties imposed by any of the sections of this act may be recovered in the manner provided by section **twenty-six**, chapter **seventy-five** of the public laws of 1878.

AN ACT relating to the disposition of fines and penalties recovered for the violation of the fish laws.

Be it enacted, etc., as follows: —

SECTION 1. All fines and penalties hereafter recovered for the violation of chapters fifty and seventy-five of the public laws of eighteen hundred and seventy-eight and all acts amendatory thereof and of all laws now in force in this state for the protection of fish and game, shall be paid one-half to the complainant and one-half to any game and fish protective society or other sportsmen's association which shall have been organized under the laws of Maine, and which may be located in the county where the said fines and penalties are recovered; *provided*, the said society or association shall expend the same in the propagation and cultivation of trout and salmon for the fresh-water lakes and ponds of Maine, to be done under the direction and supervision of the fish commissioners. In case there may be more than one such society or association located in the county where said fines and penalties are recovered, the fish commissioners shall designate which society the money shall be paid to, or they may cause the same to be divided between them. If there is no such society or association in the county where such fines and penalties are recovered, then such fines and penalties shall be paid to the state fish commissioners, who shall appropriate the same as they may deem proper.

SECT. 2. All acts or parts of acts inconsistent with this act are hereby repealed.

SECT. 3. This act shall take effect when approved.

AN ACT to amend sections three and four of chapter fifty of the laws of 1878.

Be it enacted, etc., as follows: —

SECTION 1. Section three of chapter fifty of the public laws of eighteen hundred and seventy-eight is hereby amended by inserting the word "hunted" before word "killed," so that as amended said section shall read as follows: —

SECT. 3. No person shall hunt, kill, or destroy with dogs any moose within this state, under a penalty of one hundred dollars for every moose so hunted, killed, or destroyed; and no person shall between the first day of January and the first day of October in each year, in any manner hunt, kill, or destroy any moose under the same penalty.

SECT. 2. Section four of said chapter fifty is hereby amended by inserting the word "hunted" before the word "killed," so that as amended said section shall read as follows: —

SECT. 4. No person shall hunt, kill, or destroy with dogs any deer or caribou within this state, under a penalty of forty dollars for every such deer or caribou so hunted, killed, or destroyed; and no person shall between the first day of January and the first day of October in any manner hunt, kill, or destroy any deer or caribou, under the same penalty as above provided. Any person may lawfully kill any dog found hunting moose, deer, or caribou.

Sheriffs, deputy sheriffs, police officers, and constables are hereby vested with all the powers conferred by law upon game wardens and their deputies, and shall be allowed for their services the same fees as are now prescribed for sheriffs and their deputies.

Lake Hebron, Looking West.

CHAPTER XIX.

List of Principal Hotels, Proprietors, Rates, and Accommodations.

BANGOR HOUSE, Bangor, Maine. F. O. Beal, Proprietor. Terms, $2.00 to $2.50 per day. Accommodates 200 guests.

CHAMBERLAIN FARM HOUSE, Chamberlain Lake. A. T. Nutter, Superintendent. Good accommodations. Reasonable prices.

CHESUNCOOK FARM HOUSE, Lake Chesuncook. Mr. Hatheway, Manager. Terms, $1.00 per day. Good accommodations.

COLBY HOUSE, Moose River, Maine. Mrs. Nancy Colby, Proprietor. Terms, $1.50 per day, $5.00 to $7.00 per week. Accommodates 12 guests.

EVELETH HOUSE, Greenville, Maine. Amos H. Walker, Proprietor. Terms, $2.00 per day, transient; $7.00 to $10.00 per week. Accommodates 50 guests.

FORKS HOTEL, Forks of the Kennebec, Maine. Mrs. Joseph Clark, Proprietor. $2.00 per day, $7.00 per week. Accommodates 100 guests.

HOTEL HESELTON, Skowhegan, Maine. Frank B. Heselton, Proprietor. Terms, $2.00 per day, $7.00 to $14.00 per week. Accommodates 100 guests.

LAKE HEBRON HOTEL, Monson, Maine. Elisha Taft, Proprietor. Terms, $2.00 to $2.50 per day. Accommodates 75 guests.

LAKE HOUSE, Greenville, Maine. Littlefield & Sawyer, Proprietors. Terms, $2.00 per day, transient; $7.00 to $10.00 per week. Accommodates 75 guests.

MORRIS FARM HOUSE, West Branch. Joseph Morris, Proprietor. Terms, $1.50 per day. Good accommodations.

MT. KINEO HOUSE, Moosehead Lake, Maine. O. A. Dennen, Superintendent. Terms for June, $2.00 per day; for July, $2.00 to $3.00 per day. Ten per cent. discount by the week. For August and September, $2.50 to $3.50 per day, transient; from $28.00 to $45.00 per week, two persons in one room. Ten per cent. discount for rooms taken by the month. Accommodates 500 guests.

NORTH-WEST CARRY HOUSE, Moosehead Lake, Maine. C. F. Lane, Proprietor. Terms, $1.50 per day; reduction by the week. Accommodates 20 guests.

OUTLET HOUSE, Kennebec Dam, Moosehead Lake, Maine. Henry I. Wilson, Proprietor. Terms, $2.00 per day, transient; $10.00 to $14.00 per week. Accommodates 40 guests.

PARLIN POND HOUSE, Parlin Pond, Maine. Geo. W. Savage, Proprietor. Terms, $1.00 to $1.50 per day. Reduction by the week. Accommodates 30 guests.

PARSONS HOTEL, Dead River, Maine. S. A. Parsons, Proprietor. Terms, $2.00 per day. Reduction by the week. Accommodates 75 guests.

PENOBSCOT EXCHANGE, Bangor, Maine. F. O. Beal, Proprietor. Terms, $2.00 to $2.50 per day. Accommodates 150 guests.

PREBLE HOUSE, Portland, Maine. M. S. Gibson, Proprietor. Terms, $2.00 to $2.50 per day. Reduction by the week. Accommodates 200 guests.

SILVER LAKE HOTEL, Katahdin Iron Works, Maine. Henry E. Capen, Manager. Terms, $2.00 per day, $7.00 to $10.00 per week. Accommodates 50 guests.

STAGE HOUSE, Bingham, Maine. John Frain, Proprietor. Terms, $1.00 per day, $5.00 per week. Accommodates 60 guests.

WINNEGARNOCK HOUSE, NORTH-EAST CARRY, HEAD OF MOOSEHEAD LAKE, MAINE. Simeon Savage, Proprietor. Terms, $2.00 per day, transient; $7.00 to $10.00 per week. Accommodates 30 guests.

Besides the above houses, there are farm-houses and camps scattered through the Wilderness, in different places, where the sportsman will always find a hearty welcome.

Parties visiting Lily Bay or Roach River will find good accommodations at Lily Bay Farm House or Roach River Farm House, at reasonable prices.

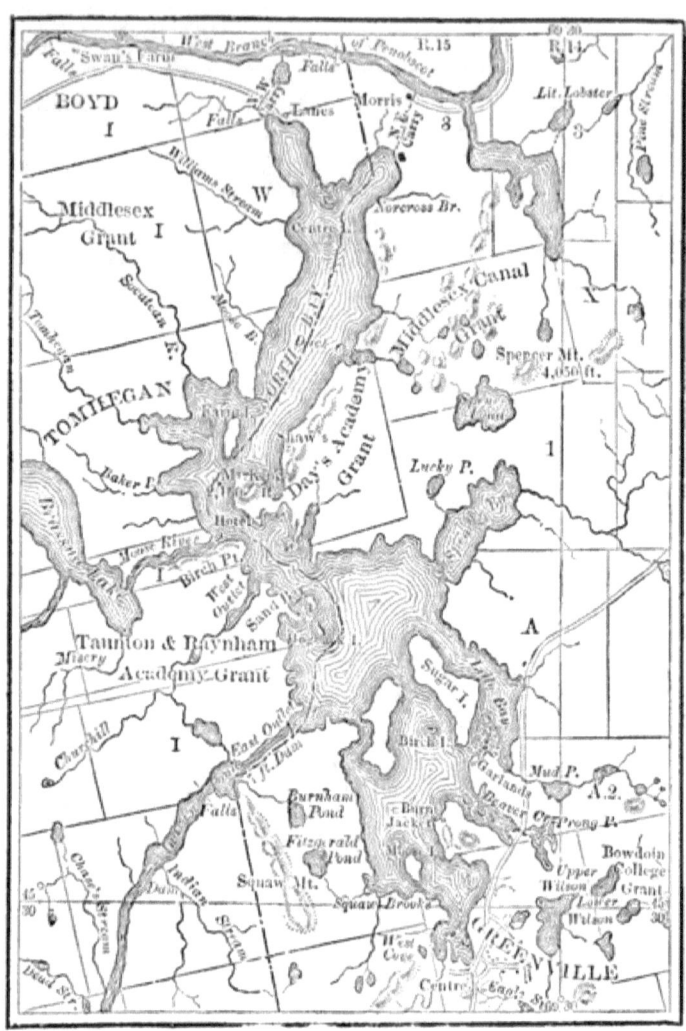

MAP OF MOOSEHEAD LAKE.

CHAPTER XX.

Table of Fares.

Philadelphia to New York, rail	$2 50
Philadelphia to Boston, N.Y. & Phil. new line, and Sound Steamers	4 00
Philadelphia to Boston, steamer, state-room and meals included	8 00
New York to Boston, Sound Steamers	4 00
" " " all rail, Shore line	5 00
" " Portland, M. S. Co.'s Steamers	3 00
" " " Norwich Steamers, and Portland and Worcester line	6 00
Boston to Portland, steamer	1 00
" " " rail (limited)	2 50
" " Bangor, rail (limited)	6 00
" " " Boston & Bangor Steamship Co.	3 50
" " Katahdin Iron Works	7 50
" " " " " steamer and rail	
" " South Sebec, rail	6 70
" " " steamer and rail	
" " Dover and Foxcroft, rail	6 75
" " Monson, rail	7 75
" " " steamer and rail	
" " Greenville, M. H. Lake, rail (limited)	8 00
" " Greenville, Moosehead Lake, rail (unlimited),	8 75
" " " " " steamer and rail,	
" " Kennebec Dam, Moosehead Lake, rail and steamer	8 75
" " Mt. Kineo, Moosehead Lake, rail and steamer,	8 75
" " " " " steamer and rail,	
Portland to Bangor, steamer	2 50
" " " rail	4 25
" " Katahdin Iron Works, rail	6 15
" " South Sebec, rail	5 20
" " Dover and Foxcroft, rail	5 25
Portland to Monson, rail	6 25
" " Greenville, rail	6 50
Bangor to Katahdin Iron Works, rail	2 50
" " South Sebec, rail	1 75
" " Dover and Foxcroft, rail	1 85
" " Monson, rail	2 85
" " Greenville, rail	3 00

Oldtown to Greenville, rail	$2 75
Greenville to Mt. Kineo, steamer	1 00
Mt. Kineo to North-east or North-west Carries	1 00
Oakland to North Anson, rail	1 00
North Anson to Solon, stage	50
Solon to Forks of the Kennebec, stage	1 75
Skowhegan to Forks of the Kennebec, stage	2 50
Forks of the Kennebec to Adams', stage	1 25
" " " " Moose River, stage	2 00
" " " " Sandy Bay, stage	2 50
Sandy Bay to St. Joseph, stage	2 50
St. Joseph to Quebec, rail	1 25
Boston to Mattawamkeag, rail (limited)	7 60
" " Woodstock, rail (limited)	9 00
North Anson to Dead River, stage	2 00
Dead River to Eustis, stage	1 25

ROUND TRIP EXCURSION TICKETS.

Boston to Forks of the Kennebec, and return, rail and stage, *via* Portland, Waterville, and Skowhegan	13 00
Rate from Portland	10 00
Boston to Dead River, and return, rail and stage, *via* Portland, Oakland, and North Anson	13 00
Rate from Portland	10 00
Boston to Smith's Farm and return, rail and stage, *via* Portland, Oakland, North Anson, and New Portland	13 50
Boston to Smith's Farm and return, rail and stage, *via* Portland, Farmington, Strong, and Kingfield	13 50
Rate from Portland, either route	10 50
Philadelphia to Mt. Kineo, and return, rail and steamer, *via* Boston, Portland, Bangor, and Greenville	25 00
New York to Mt. Kineo, and return, rail and steamer, *via* Boston, Bangor, and Greenville	21 00
Boston to Mt. Kineo, and return, rail and steamer, *via* Portland, Bangor, and Greenville	15 00
Rate from Portland	12 00
" " Bangor	7 00
Boston to Mt. Kineo, and return, steamer, rail and steamer, *via* Bangor and Greenville	13 00

The fares given in this table are liable to change, but are correct at the time the book is published.

SPECIAL NOTICES.

BANGOR HOUSE,

BANGOR, MAINE,

M. J. ROACH, - - - Manager.

TERMS, $2.00 to $2.50 PER DAY.

This is the largest and best located Hotel in Bangor, and has lately been newly furnished and repaired throughout. It stands in a square by itself, thus avoiding the danger of fire from other buildings, and making every room a front one. It has a brick partition between nearly every room, making it fire-proof.

PENOBSCOT EXCHANGE

(NOT THE LITTLE BANGOR EXCHANGE)

Is one of the reliable Hotels of Bangor. It is always first class in all its appointments. Carriages at all depots and steamboats. We guarantee satisfaction to our guests. Thankful to the travelling public for their liberal patronage, we hope to merit a continuance in the future.

J. E. HARRIMAN, Manager.

These are the only good-sized and first-class houses in Bangor.

THE OLD PINE-TREE STATE.

with "Dirigo" for its motto, still "leads" all others as a place for summer resort.

Its long stretch of sea-coast, its mountains, its unbroken forests, its innumerable lakes and rivers, offer attractions unsurpassed.

THE MAINE CENTRAL RAILROAD,

operating a system of over 500 miles, extends from Portland to and beyond Bangor to the boundary line between the State of Maine and the Province of New Brunswick, and unites the railroads of the United States and Maritime Provinces. It has just completed a branch from Bangor to Bar Harbor, so that it forms, with its own lines, branches and connections, the only rail route to and from Mt. Desert, and all parts of Maine east of Portland, and the provinces of New Brunswick and Nova Scotia, Cape Breton, and Prince Edward Island, and is also the best route to Moosehead and the Rangeley Lakes and all of the noted hunting and fishing resorts of northern Maine and New Brunswick.

It is the only route whereby Moosehead Lake can be surely reached the day following departure from Boston, and for the Rangeley Lakes is the only route connecting with the celebrated two-foot gauge Sandy River Railroad, running from Farmington to Phillips, only 18 miles from the lakes, and by which 15 miles of staging and 12 of steamer are saved to passengers for Indian Rock and Mooseluemaguntic House and Lake, over any other route.

Excursion tickets are on sale to Eustis (Smith's Farm), where a comparatively unexplored country for hunting and fishing is to be found.

Besides being the best route to the resorts mentioned, this line runs through or near numbers of picturesque cities and towns along the sea-coast and in the interior, which, with their attractive scenery and invigorating atmosphere, are rapidly and widely becoming known and appreciated, and drawing increased numbers of visitors each year.

Fares for round trip from Boston: Bar Harbor, $14.00; Bar Harbor, continuous passage in both directions, $11.50; Rangeley Lakes, $12.50; Indian Rock, $13.75; Eustis, $13.50; Forks of Kennebec, $13.00; Moosehead Lake, $15.00; Aroostook, $18.00. From Portland, $3.00 less.

Send for Time-Tables and Rates of Fare covering all Excursion points.

PAYSON TUCKER,
General Manager.

F. E. BOOTHBY,
General Pass. and Ticket Agent,
Portland, Me.

Lake Hebron Hotel, Monson, Maine.

MONSON RAILROAD.

The Monson Railroad will connect with all regular passenger trains on the Bangor and Piscataquis Railroad, at Monson Junction, during the season of summer travel.

Fare from Monson Junction to Monson, 50 cents.

This is a new two-foot narrow-gauge railroad, and is built and equipped in the best manner.

GEO. S. CUSHING,
General Manager.

LAKE HEBRON HOTEL,

MONSON, ME.

ELISHA TAFT, Proprietor.   CHAS. E. TAFT, Clerk.

Terms, $2.00 and $2.50 per day.

This new and spacious hotel is first-class in every respect, and offers the best of accommodations to the sportsmen, tourists, and pleasure-seekers who visit the Monson and Elliottsville lakes and ponds. It is beautifully located near the shore of Lake Hebron, and its broad piazzas command some of the finest landscape views in New England. Every floor in the house is supplied with pure water from the Sherman Hill Springs.

Teams will be found in waiting at the depot on the arrival of every train, to convey passengers to the hotel.

THE
BOSTON & MAINE
RAILROAD

IS THE

Great Pleasure Route

TO ALL THE

SUMMER RESORTS

OF

Maine, Northern New England and the Provinces.

IT IS THE

Only Line via Wells, Kennebunk and Old Orchard Beaches

AND

PORTLAND

TO

RANGELEY LAKES,
MOOSEHEAD LAKE, MOUNT DESERT

AND THE

WHITE MOUNTAINS.

Shortest Line to Lake Winnipisseogee.

For tickets and information apply at
280 Washington St., Boston, at the Station, Haymarket Sq.,
or at any principal Ticket Office in the country.

JAS. T. FURBER,   D. J. FLANDERS,
Gen. Supt.   *Gen. Pass. and Ticket Agt.*

SPECIAL NOTICES.

PORTLAND, BANGOR, MT. DESERT, AND MACHIAS STEAMBOAT CO.

Commencing about June 20, steamboat express trains leave Boston, *via* Boston & Maine R.R. and Eastern R.R., at 7.00 P.M., connecting in Portland with Steamer "Lewiston," 1,127 tons, Capt. Chas. Deering, which leaves Railroad Wharf every Tuesday and Friday evening, at 11.15 o'clock, or on arrival of Express trains from Boston, for Rockland, Castine, Deer Isle, Sedgwick (stage from Sedgwick to Blue Hill on arrival of each steamer), South-West and Bar Harbors, Millbridge, Jonesport, and Machiasport. Returning, will leave Machiasport every Monday and Thursday morning, at 4.30, and Mt. Desert at about 10.00, arriving in Portland the same evening, connecting with the Pullman train for Boston.

Above trains will also connect with Steamer "City of Richmond," 1,000 tons, Capt. W. E. Dennison, which will leave the same wharf every Monday, Wednesday, and Saturday evening, at 11.15 o'clock, or on arrival of Steamboat Express trains from Boston, for Mount Desert (South-west and Bar Harbors), touching at Rockland only, and arriving at Bar Harbor at about 10.00 A.M. next day. Connects with steamer for Sullivan from Bar Harbor. Returning, will leave Bar Harbor, 7.00 A.M., Monday, Wednesday, and Friday, touching at South-west Harbor and Rockland, arriving in Portland about 5.00 P.M., connecting with trains for Boston, arriving in Boston at 10.00 P.M. Will also connect at Rockland with noon train, *via* Knox & Lincoln R.R., for Portland and Boston. Ample time for supper in Portland.

☞ Until about June 20, Steamer "Lewiston" time-table will be in effect only.

GEO. L. DAY, *General Ticket Agent.*

WM. G. DAVIS, *General Manager.*

SPECIAL NOTICES.

SOMERSET RAILWAY.

The most comfortable and direct route to the fishing and hunting grounds of Northern Maine. Daily stage connections at North Anson for Flag-Staff, Eustis, Tim Pond, Dead River, New Portland, Forks of the Kennebec, Pleasant Ridge Ponds, Parlin Ponds, Solon, Bingham, and all points in the Upper Kennebec Valley.

Excursion tickets on sale at the principal offices of the Eastern, Boston & Maine, and Maine Central Railroads, for Eustis and Tim Ponds, the acknowledged Best-Stocked Trout Ponds in Maine.

ARRANGEMENT OF TRAINS.

Leave Boston (E. and B. & M. R.R.'s)	9.00 A.M.
Portland (M. C. R.R)	1.25 P.M.
Lewiston " "	2.58 "
Oakland (Somerset R.R.)	4.45 "
Arrive North Anson	6.05 "

Ask for Tickets *via* Somerset Railway, the most Pleasant and Direct Route to the Dead River Region, and take no other.

W. M. AYER, *Sup't.*

SPECIAL NOTICES.

Boston and Bangor Steamship Company Steamers.

PENOBSCOT, 1,500 TONS; CAMBRIDGE, 1,400 TONS; KATAHDIN, 1,240 TONS; MOUNT DESERT, 500 TONS; ROCKLAND, 220 TONS.

Daily Line, June 1 to October 15, 1884. BOSTON TO BANGOR AND BAR HARBOR (Mt. Desert). Commencing June 1, 1884, the palatial steamers of this line will leave Boston daily (except Sunday), at 5 o'clock P.M., for *Bangor* via *Rockland*, *Camden*, *Northport* (July and August) *Belfast*, *Searsport*, *Fort Point* (July and August) *Bucksport*, *Winterport*, and *Hampden*; making close connection at *Rockland* with steamer Mount Desert for So. W. HARBOR and BAR HARBOR (Mt. Desert), every morning (except Monday); with same steamer for No. Haven, Green's Landing, Swan's Island, and Bass Harbor, every Wednesday and Saturday morning; at Bar Harbor, with steamer *Rockland* to and from So. Gouldsboro', Lamoine, Hancock, and Sullivan, *daily*.

The steamers of this line also connect at *Rockland* with steamer *Lewiston* for Castine, Deer Isle, Sedgwick, Millbridge, Jonesport, and Machiasport, every Wednesday and Saturday morning; with steamer Henry Morrison for Deer Isle, Bluehill, Surry and Ellsworth, every Tuesday, Thursday, and Saturday morning.

At *Belfast*, with steamer for Castine, Islesboro', and Brooksville, *daily*.

At *Bucksport*, with stage for Ellsworth, *daily*.

At *Bangor*, with Maine Central R.R. for Oldtown, Milo Junction, Sebec, Dover and Foxcroft, Monson, Greenville, Moosehead Lake (Mt. Kineo House), and Katahdin Iron Works.

Returning (going West), steamers leave Bangor for Boston and intermediate landings on Penobscot River and Bay *daily* (Sundays excepted), at 11 o'clock A.M. Leave BAR HARBOR for *Rockland* via So. W. HARBOR *daily*, at 1 o'clock P.M. (Mondays 10 A.M.). Leave Bass Harbor for Rockland via Swan's Island, Green's Landing, and No. Haven, every Monday and Thursday. Leave Machiasport, etc., for *Rockland* same days. Leave Ellsworth, etc., for *Rockland* every Monday, Wednesday, and Friday, *connecting at Rockland* with steamers of this line for *Boston direct* same days.

Steamers leaving Portland Tuesday and Friday evenings connect at *Rockland*, on the mornings following, with steamers of the Boston and Bangor S. S. Co. for Bangor and intermediate landings on Penobscot Bay and River. Returning, connect at Rockland Monday and Thursday evenings for Portland.

FOUR TRIPS PER WEEK. — Prior to June 1, 1884, commencing April 15, the steamers of this line leave Boston for Bangor, via intervening points on Penobscot Bay and River, every Monday, Tuesday, Thursday, and Friday, at 5 o'clock P.M. Returning, leave Bangor every Monday, Wednesday, Thursday and Saturday, at 11 o'clock A.M. (which schedule will be resumed Oct. 15, and continue until Dec. 1, 1884.)

Tickets can be secured on the steamers for the *White Mountains*, *Moosehead Lake*, Lowell, Lawrence, New York, and all principal points South and West, and baggage checked through.

For further particulars see small folders.

WM. H. HILL, JR.,   JAMES LITTLEFIELD,
Treasurer.   *Superintendent.*
CALVIN AUSTIN,
General Freight Agent.

MAINE'S GREAT SUMMER RESORT
FOR
Sportsmen and Tourists

MOOSEHEAD LAKE AND VICINITY

Reached from Boston by Eastern, or Boston and Maine, and Maine Central Railroads,

And Boston and Bangor Steamship Co.'s Line of Steamers running direct to Bangor, where connection is made with the

Bangor and Piscataquis Railroad
For MOOSEHEAD LAKE.

The extension of this road from Blanchard to the foot of the Lake is to be opened for travel about the first of July, and opens up the most picturesque and attractive scenery to be found anywhere in Maine.

The New Mount Kineo House

is beautifully located on the Lake shore, and will accommodate 500 guests. The management of the house, under O. A. Dennen, its competent superintendent, is perfection.

The Lake House and the Eveleth House

at Greenville, at the foot of the Lake, are both good hotels, and possess superior accommodations.

EXCURSION TICKETS to go and return are for sale in **BOSTON**, at the Eastern and Boston & Maine Railroad Ticket offices, and on Bangor steamers, at Lincoln Wharf.

MOOSEHEAD LAKE,

With its beautiful scenery, delightful sailing, and excellent fishing and hunting, may surely be reached the day following departure from Boston.

THE ROUTE From Boston is *via* morning trains of Boston & Maine or Eastern Railroads, and from other points *via* any route to Portland; thence by noon train of Maine Central Railroad to Bangor, and stop over night; or take the night Express Train, with Pullman Sleeping Cars attached, leaving Eastern Railroad Depot at 7.00 P.M., and Portland soon after 11.00, arriving in Bangor about 6.00 the following morning, connecting with Bangor & Piscataquis Railroad for the Lake.

EXCURSION TICKETS From New York are sold by all of the Sound Lines, and from Providence, Worcester, and Nashua by the W. & N. R.R.

FARES.

From Boston to Mt. Kineo House and Return $15.00
Portland, Brunswick, Bath, and Lewiston 12.00
Gardiner . . . . . . $10.50   Augusta and Belfast . 10.00

M. GIDDINGS,	H. W. BLOOD,	ARTHUR BROWN,
President.	Treasurer.	Superintendent.

The Mount Kineo House, Moosehead Lake.

SPECIAL NOTICES.

THE TRAVELERS' OFFICIAL RAILWAY GUIDE

OF THE

RAILWAY AND STEAM NAVIGATION LINES OF THE UNITED STATES AND THE DOMINION OF CANADA.

The most complete Railway Guide in the world.

The time-tables are carefully corrected for each issue from information furnished by the officials of each road.

The afternoon trains are distinguished from morning trains by being printed in dark type.

All telegraph and coupon stations shown.

Full lists of railway officials in all principal departments. Notices of changes and appointments published monthly.

Also a large Sectional Railroad Map of the United States, with map of New England and the Middle States upon an enlarged scale and cut into pages for facility of reference.

Also a list of names by which various roads were formerly known, with their present titles.

Explanations of the manner of using the Guide printed in the French, Spanish, and German languages.

Published under the auspices of the General Ticket and Passenger Agents' Associations. Price, $4.00 per annum, 50 cents per copy.

Also,

THE KNICKERBOCKER READY REFERENCE GUIDE

To ONE THOUSAND Points around New York City, arranged alphabetically, showing Railroads, Time of Trains, Fares, Steamboats, Population, Post Offices, Times of closing of Mails, Stages, Express and Telegraph Companies, etc., etc. With large map of vicinity of New York for fifty miles in all directions, and latest Official Time-Tables of all Railroads within that territory. New York and Brooklyn Hotels, Theatres, and Street-car Lines.

Price, $2.50 per annum; 25 cents per copy.

National Railway Publication Company,

46 Bond Street, New York; 229 and 231 S. Fifth Street, Philadelphia, Penn.; 148 Monroe Street, Chicago, Ill.

SPECIAL NOTICES.

THE RAND-McNALLY GUIDE AND TRAVELER'S HANDBOOK.

A Pocket Railway Guide (size, 5 × 7 inches).

States population of the several cities and towns, shows distances, ticket fares, etc. Illustrated with numerous sectional maps, and contains a fine General Railway Map, handsomely colored.

A description of the prominent features of scenery, etc., on the principal routes, especially compiled for this work, has recently been added to its pages, and will be found both valuable and interesting to travelers and tourists.

The Handbook describes the principal business interests of the larger towns and cities, the location of the railroad depots, and the names of the principal hotels and public halls.

Issued monthly. Price, 40 cents per copy.

NATIONAL RAILWAY PUBLICATION COMPANY,

148 Monroe Street, Chicago, Ill.; 46 Bond Street, New York; 229 & 231 S. Fifth Street, Philadelphia, Penn.

SPECIAL NOTICES.

For Collations, Excursionists, Sportsmen, Yachting, etc., etc.,

HUCKINS' SOUPS

TOMATO, MOCK TURTLE,
OX TAIL, JULIENNE,
PEA, BEEF,
CHICKEN, MACARONI,
VERMICELLI, CONSOMMÉ
OKRA OR GUMBO, SOUP AND BOUILLI,
GREEN TURTLE, TERRAPIN,
MULLAGATAWNEY.

Rich and Perfectly Seasoned.

Require only to be heated, and are then ready to serve.

Put up in quart cans, which are soldered entirely on the outside.

HUCKINS' SANDWICH MEATS

SANDWICH HAM, SANDWICH CHICKEN,
SANDWICH TONGUE, SANDWICH TURKEY,

—AND—

LUNCH HAM, LUNCH TONGUE,

SLICED OX TONGUE,

Prepared with Great Care,

From only the best material, and the cans are soldered entirely on the outside.

J. H. W. HUCKINS & CO.,

BOSTON, MASS., U.S.A.

FOR CAMPERS AND EXCURSIONISTS.

HERMETICALLY SEALED PROVISIONS
of the best quality,

SEALED BY THE **PORTLAND PACKING CO.,**
Portland, Maine.

These goods have been favorably known for many years to miners, explorers, and excursionists the world over. They have been used by the government of the United States, Artic explorers, and miners on the Pacific coast, and always with the greatest satisfaction.

See that the canisters bear the signature of the Portland Packing Company, as there are many imitations of our labels.

Principal office, 305 Commercial st.

ENGRAVING ON WOOD.

JOHNSON & THOMPSON,

9 MILK STREET,

BOSTON.

G. E. JOHNSON, 28 SCHOOL STREET, ROOM 64.

SPECIAL NOTICES.

FOREST AND STREAM.

A weekly journal of twenty-four pages, devoted to field sports, practical natural history, fish culture, protection of game, preservation of forests, yachting and boating, rifle practice, and all out-door recreation and study.

It is the only journal in this country that fully supplies the wants and meets the necessities of the gentleman sportsman.

Terms, $4.00 a year.

☞ Send for a specimen copy.

FOREST AND STREAM PUBLISHING CO.,
39 & 40 Park Row, New York.

The Surveyor-General of Washington Territory, who sends a club of five subscribers, writes, saying: "I consider that your journal has done more to properly educate the sportsmen of this country than all the other publications put together. I shall induce every true sportsman to become a subscriber that I can."

Mr. Thomas A. Logan ("Gloan") says: "You are doing good work with the paper, and you have — more and probably greater than you dream of — the wishes and God-speed of the *gentlemen of the gun*."

Hundreds of similar indorsements from prominent gentlemen sportsmen might be added, showing the estimation in which "Forest and Stream" is held by its readers.

SPECIAL NOTICES.

If you are going to Moosehead Lake, Rangeley Lakes, Richardson Lakes, Bar Harbor, South West Harbor, Passamaquoddy Bay, Boothbay, Castine, Poland Springs, Bethel, Andover, or to any other place in the State of Maine or the Maritime Provinces, you will find it advantageous to take tickets and travel from Boston *via* Portland by the EASTERN RAILROAD, the Sea Shore Line.

THE EASTERN RAILROAD

Also forms the direct short route to all points in the White Mountains, its trains running to Fabyan's, without change, through Crawford Notch, saving forty miles over any other line.

Among its many points of interest not already named are Swampscott, Marblehead, Beverly Farms, Magnolia, Manchester-by-the-Sea, Gloucester, Rockport, Pigeon Cove, Salisbury, Boar's Head, Rye and Hampton Beaches, Newburyport, Portsmouth, York, Newcastle, The Isles of Shoals, Wolfboro', Lake Winnipiseogee, and the Islands in Casco Bay, at Portland.

Its equipment is unexcelled. Pullman Palace Cars and Observation Cars are used. Fast and frequent trains are supplied and every endeavor is made to maintain this as the *Tourist's Line.*

Through and Excursion tickets procurable at principal ticket offices.

Depot in Boston, on Causeway St., opposite Friend St. City Ticket Office, 306 Washington St., next door to Old South Church.

LUCIUS TUTTLE, *G. P. and T. A.*

D. W. SANBORN, *Mast. Trans.*, BOSTON.

FINE FISHING-TACKLE.

Hexagonal Split Bamboo Trout and Salmon Rods.

Superior all Lancewood Rods,
For Trout, Bass, etc.

JOINTED BAMBOO RODS
(over 30 different patterns), from 50 cents to $10.00 each.

REELS of leading English and American manufacturers. ARTIFICIAL FLIES and BAITS for all waters. LINES, HOOKS, LEADERS, FLY-BOOKS. etc.

A long experience in manufacturing and dealing in these goods enables us to offer unusual inducements.

J. S. TROWBRIDGE & CO.
88 Washington Street,
BOSTON.

☞ Repairing of all kinds promptly done.

www.ingramcontent.com/pod-product-compliance
Lightning Source LLC
Chambersburg PA
CBHW031750230426
43669CB00007B/564